D0123311

BETA TESTING THE APOCALYPSE

Also by Tom Kaczynski:

TRANS TERRA: TOWARDS A CARTOON PHILOSOPHY

BETA TESTING THE APOCALYPSE

By Tom Kaczynski

Editor and Associate Publisher: Eric Reynolds
Design by Tom Kaczynski
Additional Production by Paul Baresh
Published by Gary Groth and Kim Thompson

Fantagraphics Books, Inc.
7563 Lake City Way NE
Seattle WA 98115 USA
fantagraphics.com

Beta Testing the Apocalypse is copyright © 2012 Tom Kaczynski.
This edition © 2012 Fantagraphics Books, Inc. All rights reserved.
Permission to reproduce material from this book, except for
purposes of review and/or notice, must be obtained by the
publisher or author.

First printing: October 2012

ISBN 978-1-60699-541-9

Printed in Hong Kong

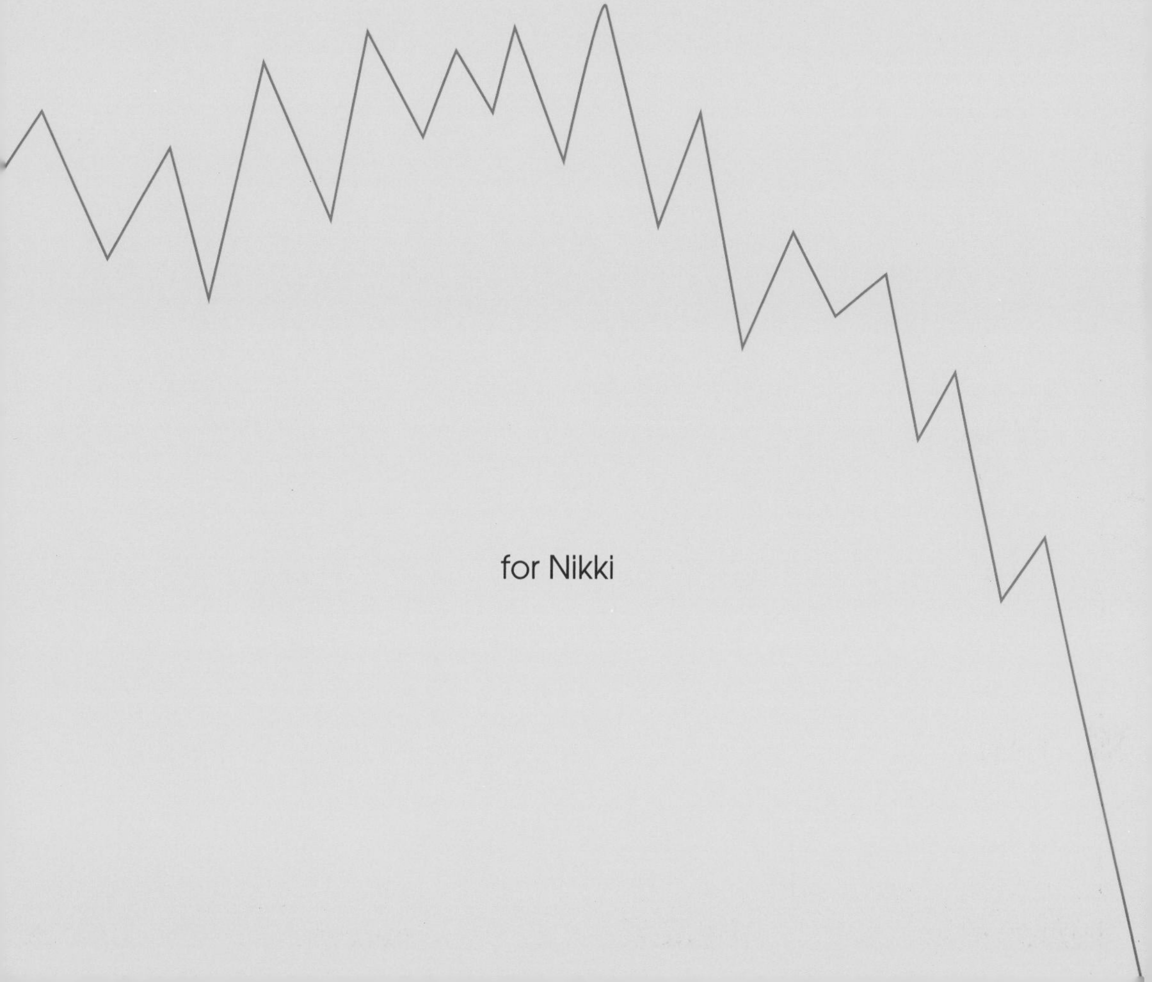

for Nikki

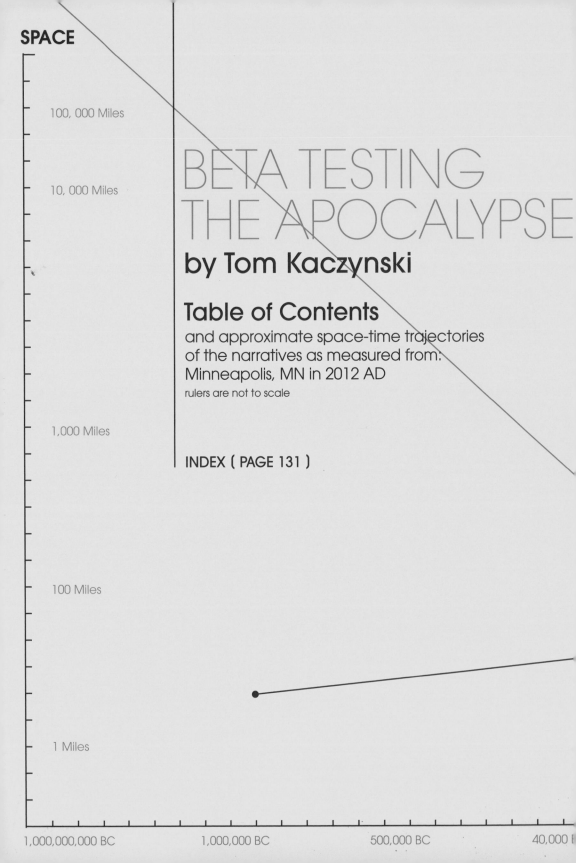

SPACE

100, 000 Miles

10, 000 Miles

BETA TESTING
THE APOCALYPSE

by Tom Kaczynski

Table of Contents
and approximate space-time trajectories
of the narratives as measured from:
Minneapolis, MN in 2012 AD
rulers are not to scale

1,000 Miles

INDEX (PAGE 131)

100 Miles

1 Miles

1,000,000,000 BC   1,000,000 BC   500,000 BC   40,000

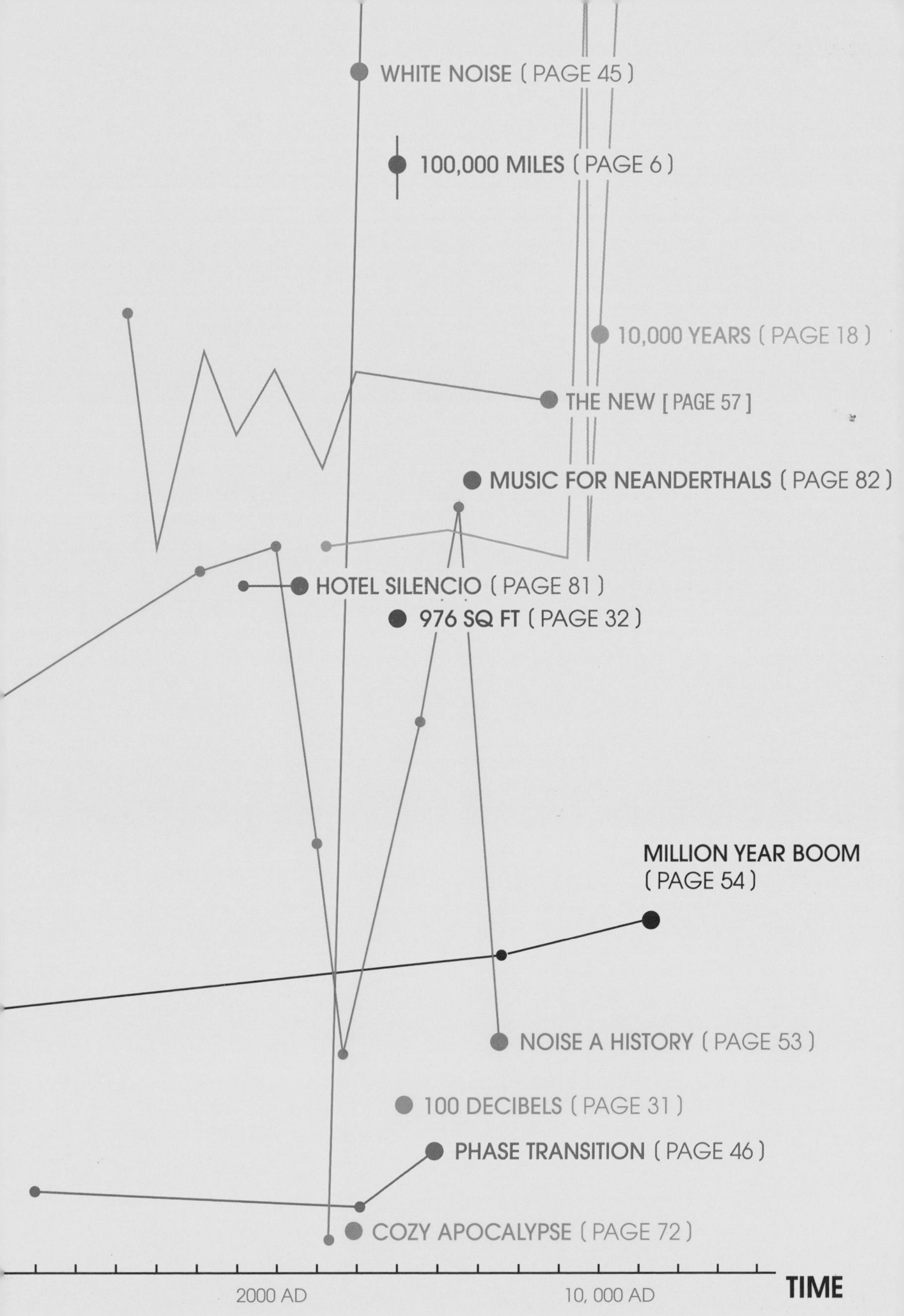
WHITE NOISE (PAGE 45)
100,000 MILES (PAGE 6)
10,000 YEARS (PAGE 18)
THE NEW [PAGE 57]
MUSIC FOR NEANDERTHALS (PAGE 82)
HOTEL SILENCIO (PAGE 81)
976 SQ FT (PAGE 32)
MILLION YEAR BOOM (PAGE 54)
NOISE A HISTORY (PAGE 53)
100 DECIBELS (PAGE 31)
PHASE TRANSITION (PAGE 46)
COZY APOCALYPSE (PAGE 72)
2000 AD
10, 000 AD
TIME

SPACE

100, 000 Miles

10, 000 Miles

100,000 MILES

Originally appeared in *Backwards City Review*, 2006
First appearance in color: *MOME 7*, 2007

1,000 Miles

100 Miles

1 Miles

1,000,000,000 BC   1,000,000 BC   500,000 BC   40,000 B

2000 AD
10, 000 AD
TIME

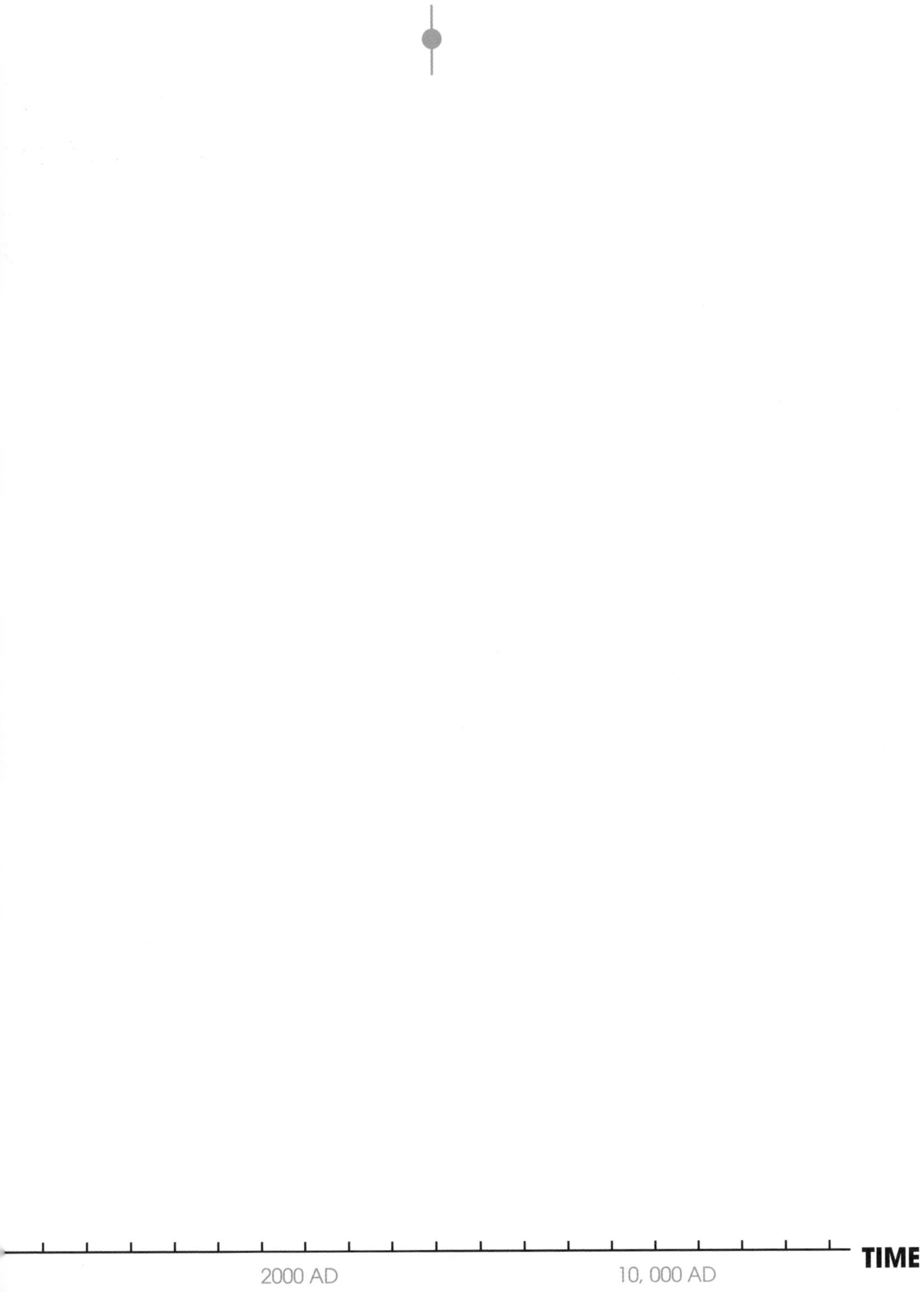

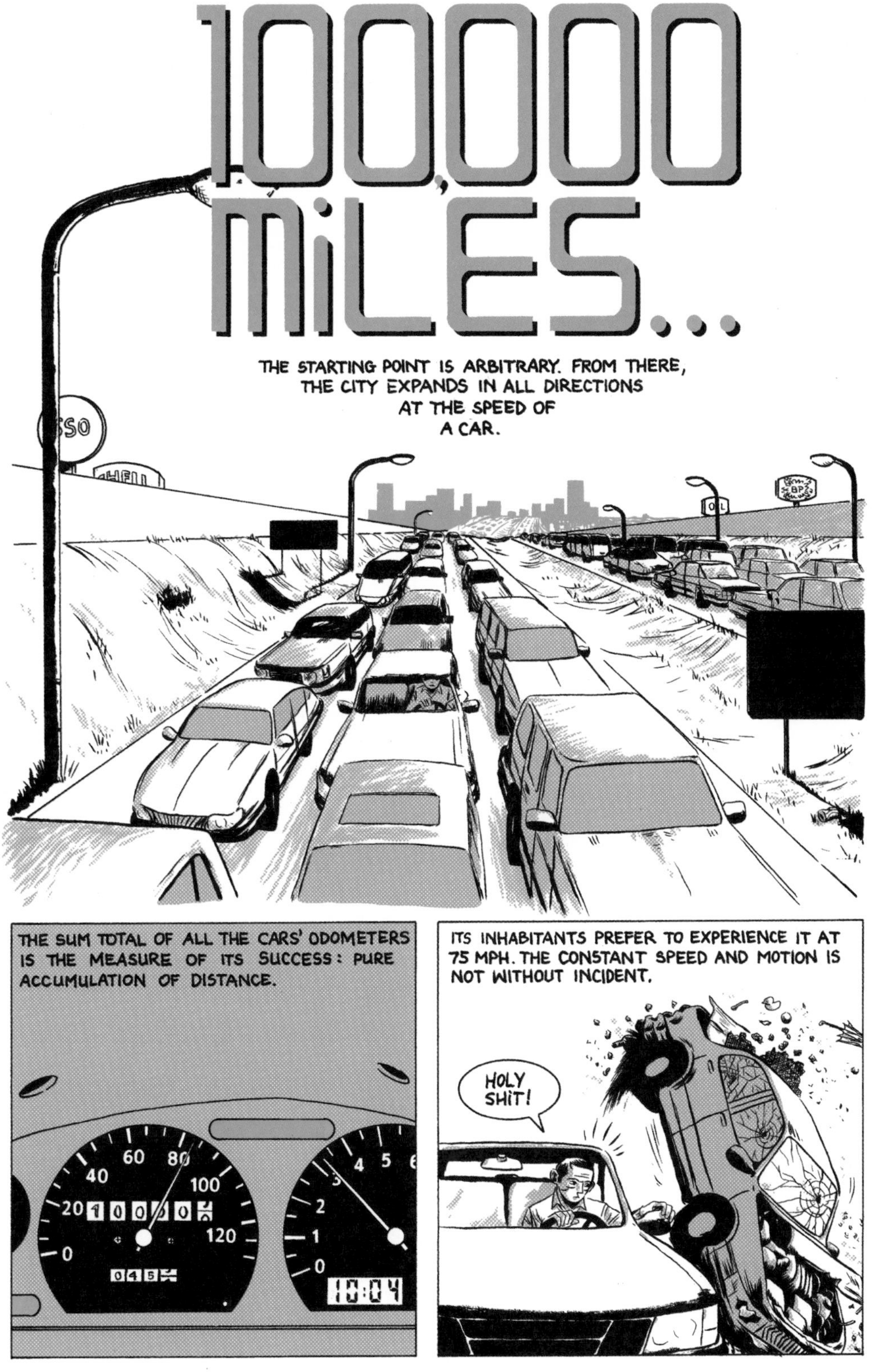
100,000 MILES...
THE STARTING POINT IS ARBITRARY. FROM THERE, THE CITY EXPANDS IN ALL DIRECTIONS AT THE SPEED OF A CAR.
BP
THE SUM TOTAL OF ALL THE CARS' ODOMETERS IS THE MEASURE OF ITS SUCCESS: PURE ACCUMULATION OF DISTANCE.
ITS INHABITANTS PREFER TO EXPERIENCE IT AT 75 MPH. THE CONSTANT SPEED AND MOTION IS NOT WITHOUT INCIDENT.
HOLY SHIT!

THE CRASH IS A VIOLENT CONTRACTION OF SPACE, A SUDDEN COLLAPSE OF THE CITY IN MINIATURE.

THE VEHICLE, LIKE A MECHANICAL PROCRUSTES, TRANSFORMS ITS PASSENGERS INTO ABSTRACT PORTRAITS OF THE CITY.

THE CRASH REVEALS THE HIDDEN LOGIC OF THE MORNING COMMUTE, THE TRIP TO THE MALL, THE PLEASURE DRIVE, THE TRAFFIC JAM.

GOTTA GET AN SUV...

R26COM

EVERY WEEKDAY THE PEOPLE ENDURE GREAT DISTANCES TO REACH THEIR PLACES OF WORK.

Versailles
Office Park

Next Exit

THE AMBITION TO ACCUMULATE CAPITAL IS DIRECTLY PROPORTIONAL TO THE DISTANCE FROM THE CITY CENTER. ALL INFRASTRUCTURE NO CIVITAS.

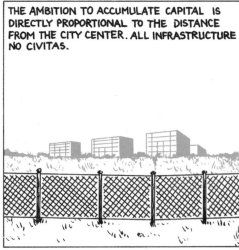

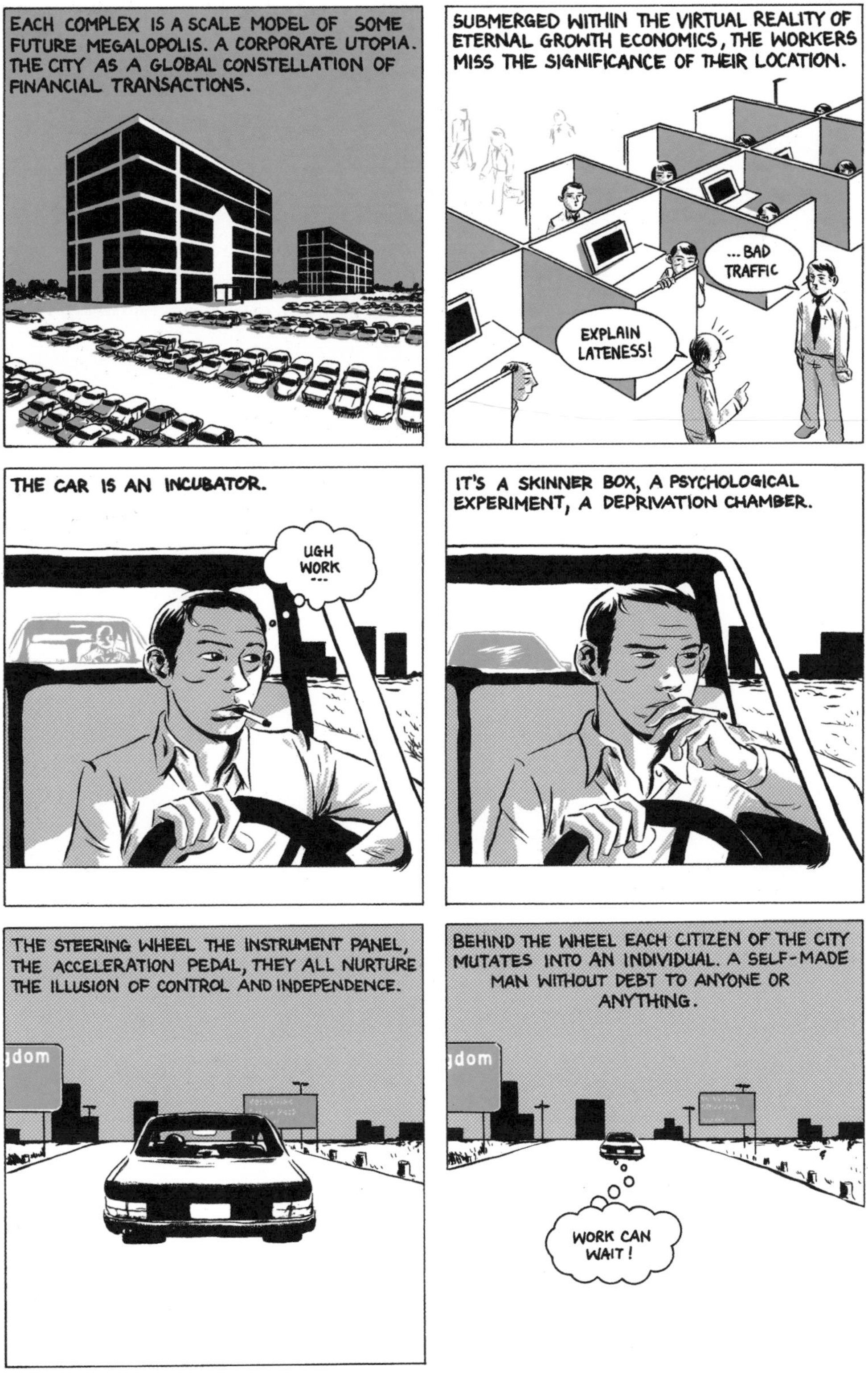
EACH COMPLEX IS A SCALE MODEL OF SOME FUTURE MEGALOPOLIS. A CORPORATE UTOPIA. THE CITY AS A GLOBAL CONSTELLATION OF FINANCIAL TRANSACTIONS.
SUBMERGED WITHIN THE VIRTUAL REALITY OF ETERNAL GROWTH ECONOMICS, THE WORKERS MISS THE SIGNIFICANCE OF THEIR LOCATION.
...BAD TRAFFIC
EXPLAIN LATENESS!
THE CAR IS AN INCUBATOR.
UGH WORK ...
IT'S A SKINNER BOX, A PSYCHOLOGICAL EXPERIMENT, A DEPRIVATION CHAMBER.
THE STEERING WHEEL THE INSTRUMENT PANEL, THE ACCELERATION PEDAL, THEY ALL NURTURE THE ILLUSION OF CONTROL AND INDEPENDENCE.
BEHIND THE WHEEL EACH CITIZEN OF THE CITY MUTATES INTO AN INDIVIDUAL. A SELF-MADE MAN WITHOUT DEBT TO ANYONE OR ANYTHING.
WORK CAN WAIT!

THE ROAD AS LIFE. EACH EXIT AN UNDISCOVERED POSSIBILITY.

Eighth Wonder Shopping Centre

Next 3 Exits

MAYBE I SHOULD CHECK OUT NEW GADGETS AT THE MALL?

THE CONDITIONING BEGINS EARLY. THE MEMORIES OF THE CITY ARE CAR MEMORIES.

MORE THAN MEETS THE EYE!

THE CAR AND DESIRE BECOME LOCKED IN A CARNAL EMBRACE BEHIND THE WINDOWS OF A SUBURBAN VAN.

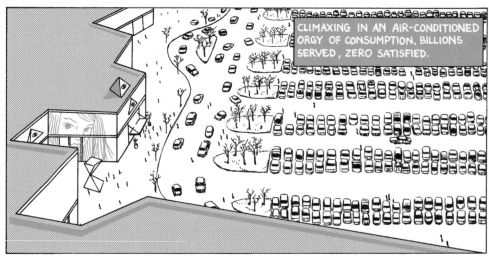

CLIMAXING IN AN AIR-CONDITIONED ORGY OF CONSUMPTION. BILLIONS SERVED, ZERO SATISFIED.

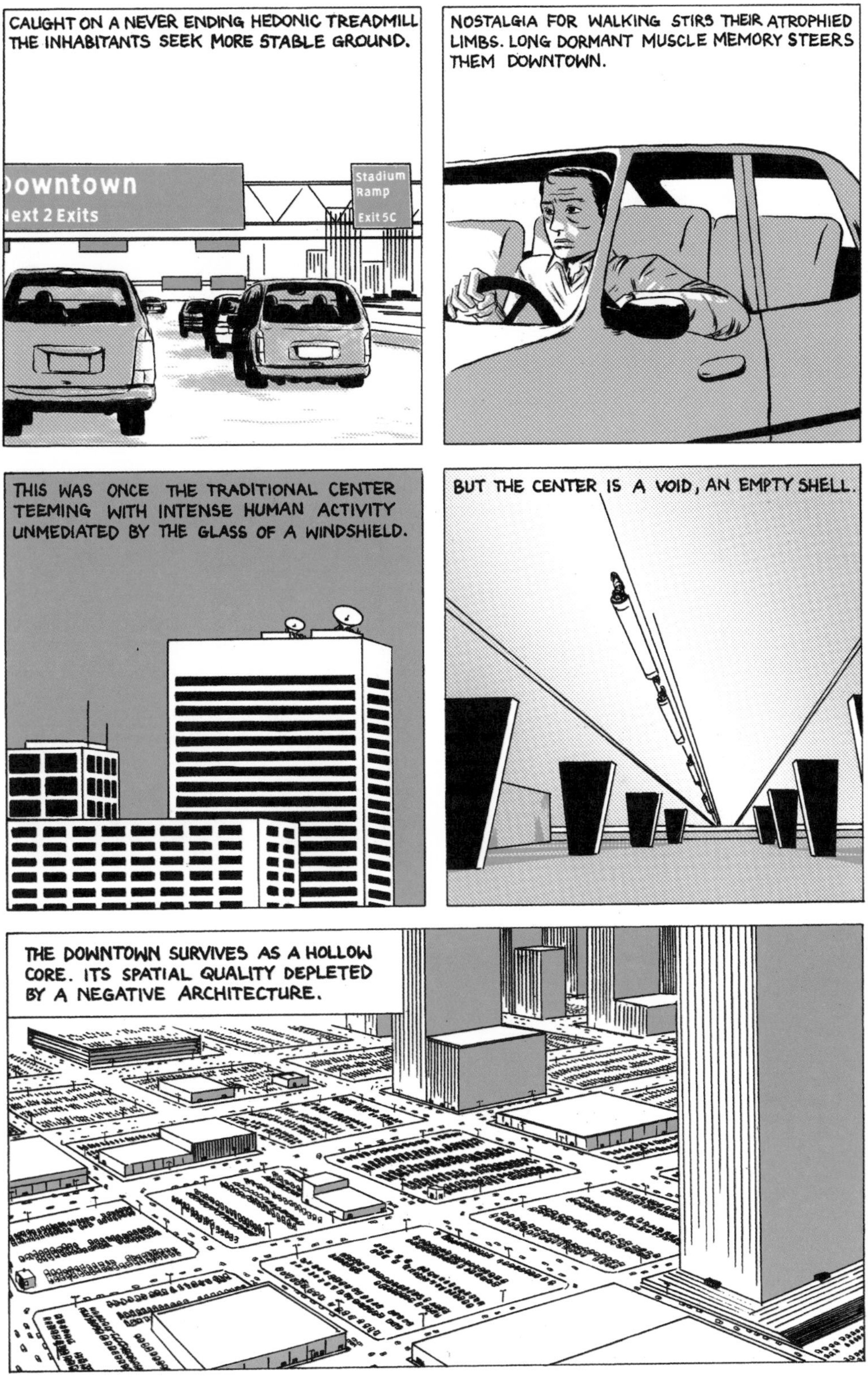
CAUGHT ON A NEVER ENDING HEDONIC TREADMILL THE INHABITANTS SEEK MORE STABLE GROUND.
owntown
lext 2 Exits
Stadium
Ramp
Exit 5C
NOSTALGIA FOR WALKING STIRS THEIR ATROPHIED LIMBS. LONG DORMANT MUSCLE MEMORY STEERS THEM DOWNTOWN.
THIS WAS ONCE THE TRADITIONAL CENTER TEEMING WITH INTENSE HUMAN ACTIVITY UNMEDIATED BY THE GLASS OF A WINDSHIELD.
BUT THE CENTER IS A VOID, AN EMPTY SHELL.
THE DOWNTOWN SURVIVES AS A HOLLOW CORE. ITS SPATIAL QUALITY DEPLETED BY A NEGATIVE ARCHITECTURE.

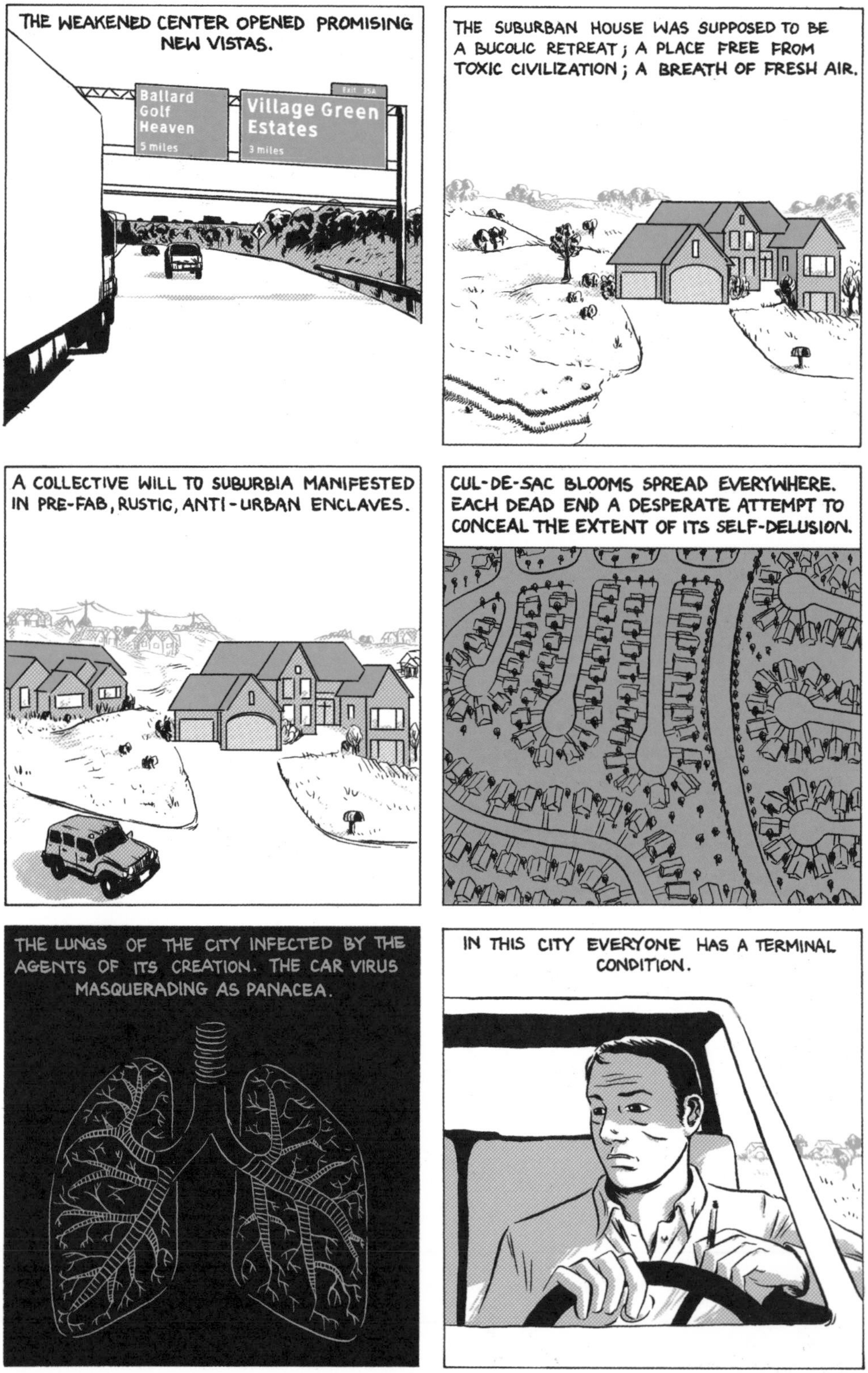
THE WEAKENED CENTER OPENED PROMISING NEW VISTAS.
Ballard Golf Heaven 5 miles
Exit 35A
Village Green Estates 3 miles
THE SUBURBAN HOUSE WAS SUPPOSED TO BE A BUCOLIC RETREAT; A PLACE FREE FROM TOXIC CIVILIZATION; A BREATH OF FRESH AIR.
A COLLECTIVE WILL TO SUBURBIA MANIFESTED IN PRE-FAB, RUSTIC, ANTI-URBAN ENCLAVES.
CUL-DE-SAC BLOOMS SPREAD EVERYWHERE. EACH DEAD END A DESPERATE ATTEMPT TO CONCEAL THE EXTENT OF ITS SELF-DELUSION.
THE LUNGS OF THE CITY INFECTED BY THE AGENTS OF ITS CREATION. THE CAR VIRUS MASQUERADING AS PANACEA.
IN THIS CITY EVERYONE HAS A TERMINAL CONDITION.

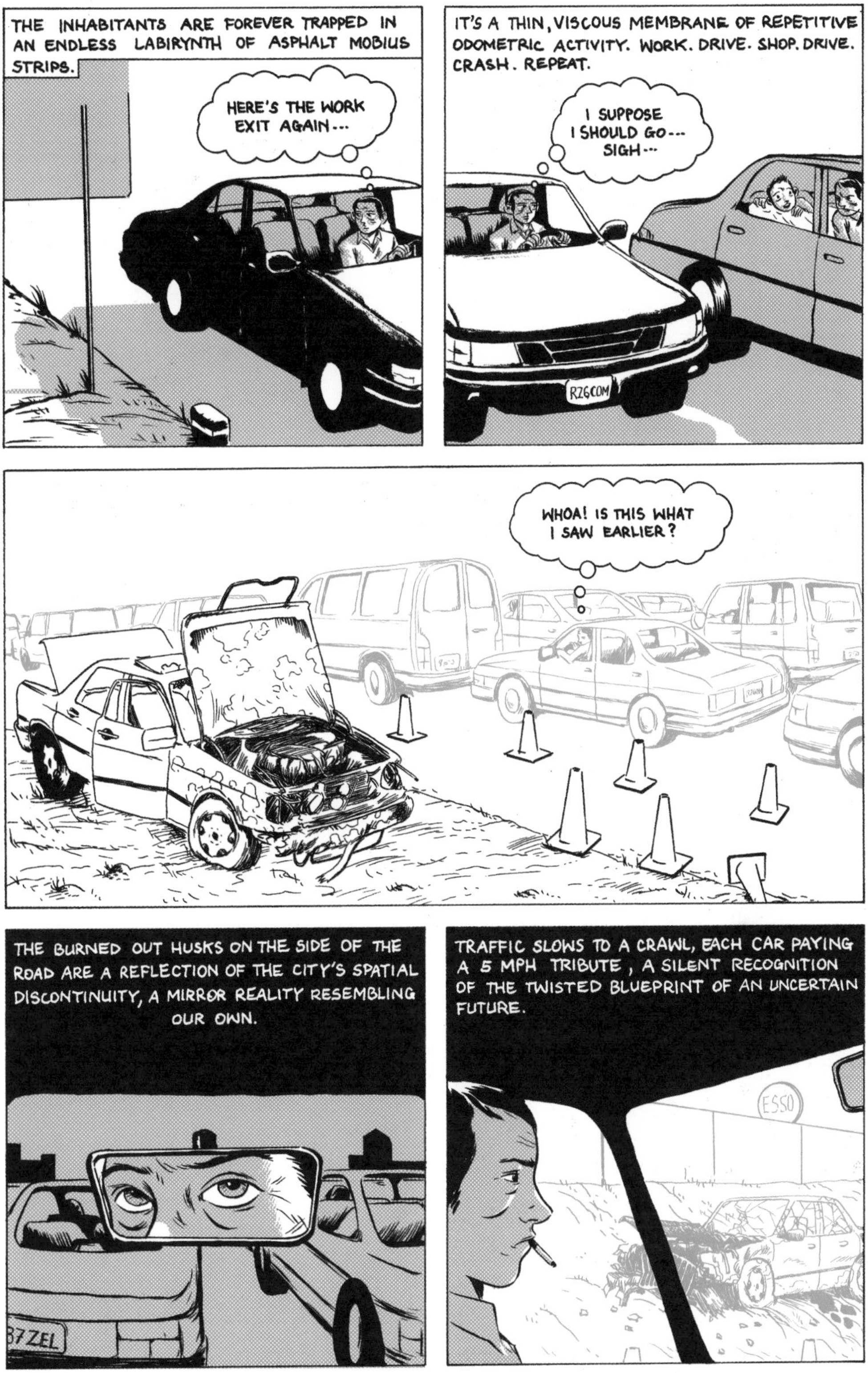
THE INHABITANTS ARE FOREVER TRAPPED IN AN ENDLESS LABIRYNTH OF ASPHALT MOBIUS STRIPS.
HERE'S THE WORK EXIT AGAIN---
IT'S A THIN, VISCOUS MEMBRANE OF REPETITIVE ODOMETRIC ACTIVITY. WORK. DRIVE. SHOP. DRIVE. CRASH. REPEAT.
I SUPPOSE I SHOULD GO--- SIGH---
WHOA! IS THIS WHAT I SAW EARLIER?
THE BURNED OUT HUSKS ON THE SIDE OF THE ROAD ARE A REFLECTION OF THE CITY'S SPATIAL DISCONTINUITY, A MIRROR REALITY RESEMBLING OUR OWN.
TRAFFIC SLOWS TO A CRAWL, EACH CAR PAYING A 5 MPH TRIBUTE, A SILENT RECOGNITION OF THE TWISTED BLUEPRINT OF AN UNCERTAIN FUTURE.
ESSO

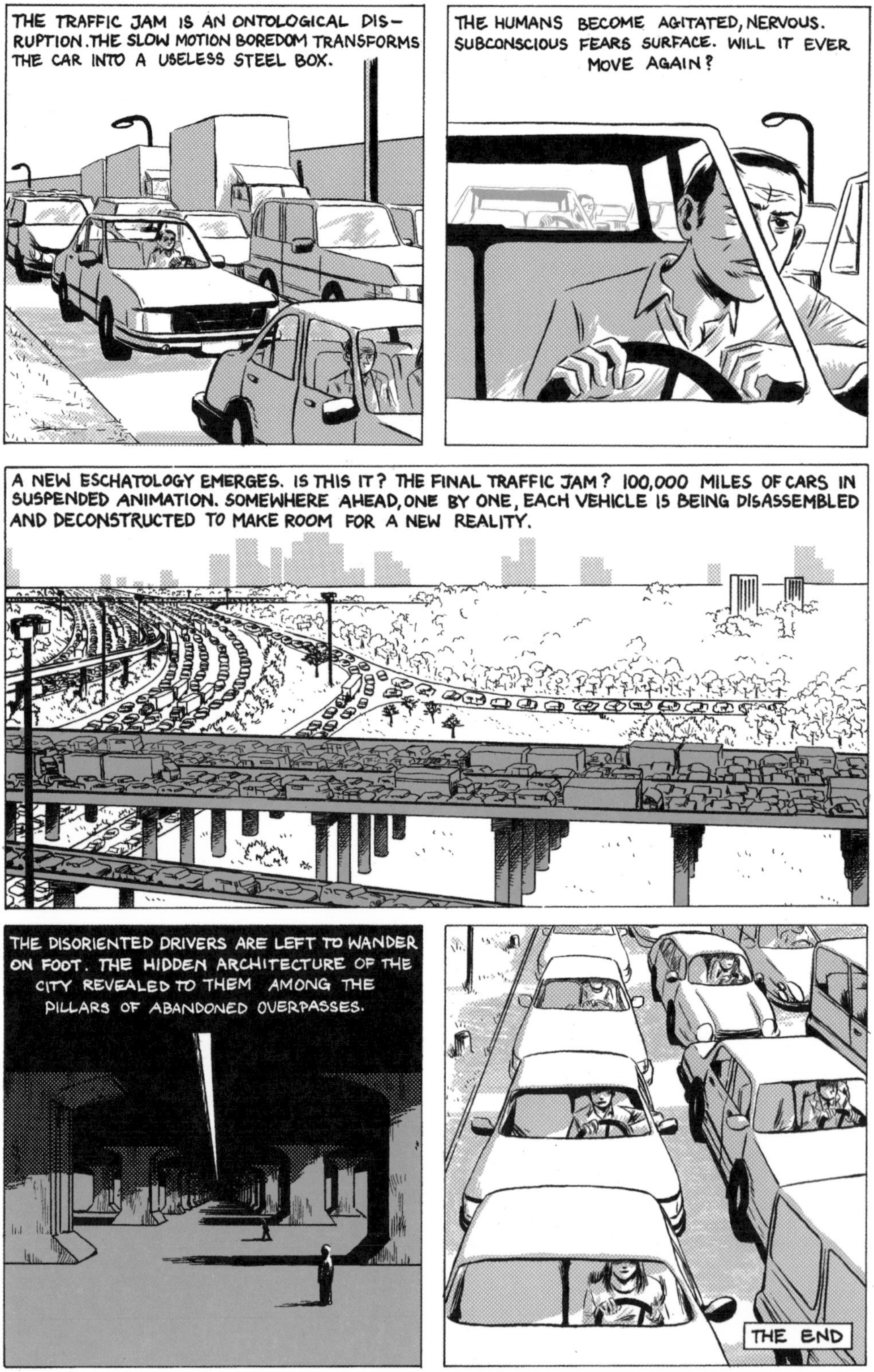
THE TRAFFIC JAM IS AN ONTOLOGICAL DISRUPTION. THE SLOW MOTION BOREDOM TRANSFORMS THE CAR INTO A USELESS STEEL BOX.
THE HUMANS BECOME AGITATED, NERVOUS. SUBCONSCIOUS FEARS SURFACE. WILL IT EVER MOVE AGAIN?
A NEW ESCHATOLOGY EMERGES. IS THIS IT? THE FINAL TRAFFIC JAM? 100,000 MILES OF CARS IN SUSPENDED ANIMATION. SOMEWHERE AHEAD, ONE BY ONE, EACH VEHICLE IS BEING DISASSEMBLED AND DECONSTRUCTED TO MAKE ROOM FOR A NEW REALITY.
THE DISORIENTED DRIVERS ARE LEFT TO WANDER ON FOOT. THE HIDDEN ARCHITECTURE OF THE CITY REVEALED TO THEM AMONG THE PILLARS OF ABANDONED OVERPASSES.
THE END

10,000 YEARS

First appearance: *MOME 8*, 2007

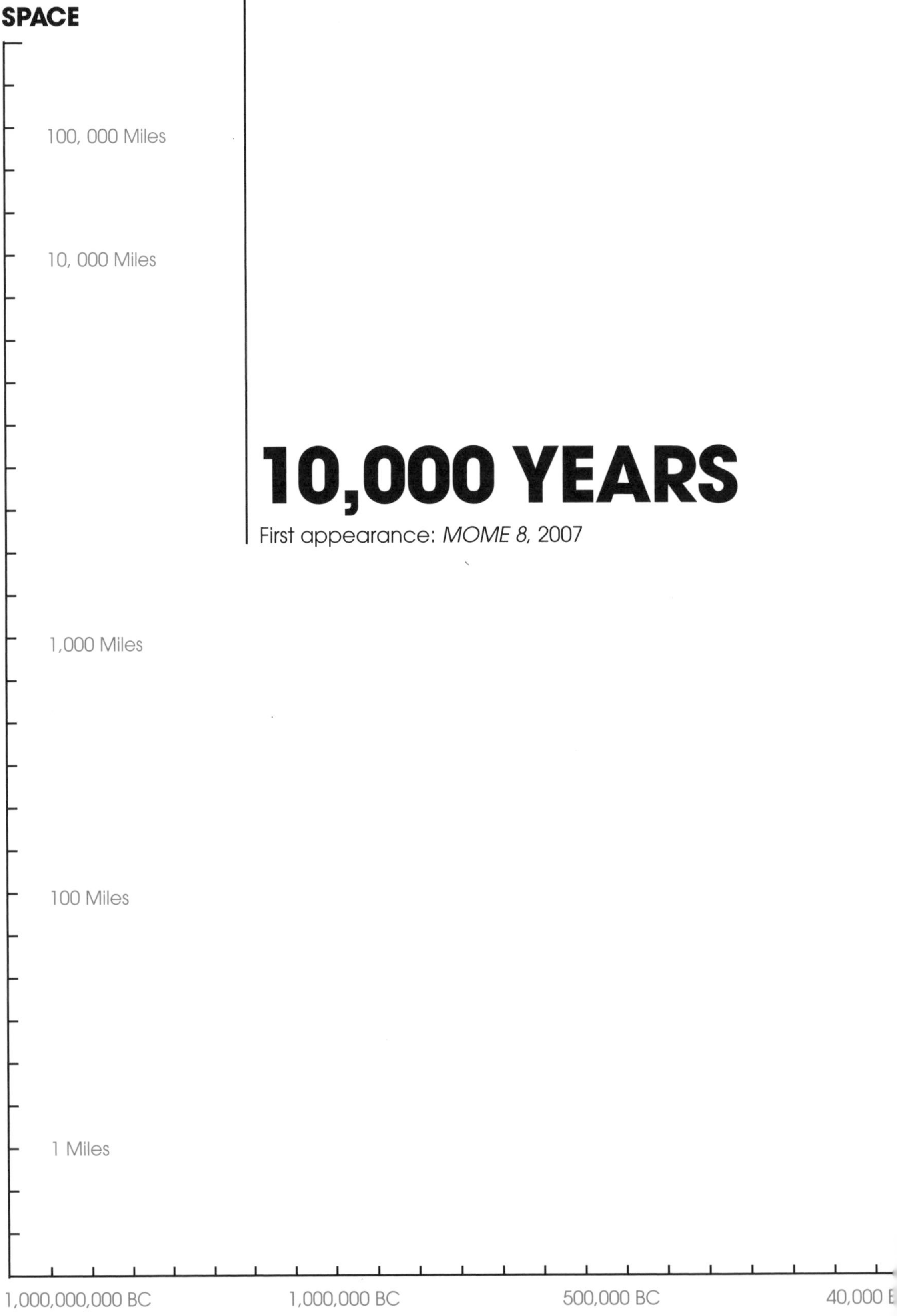
SPACE
100, 000 Miles
10, 000 Miles
1,000 Miles
100 Miles
1 Miles
1,000,000,000 BC
1,000,000 BC
500,000 BC
40,000

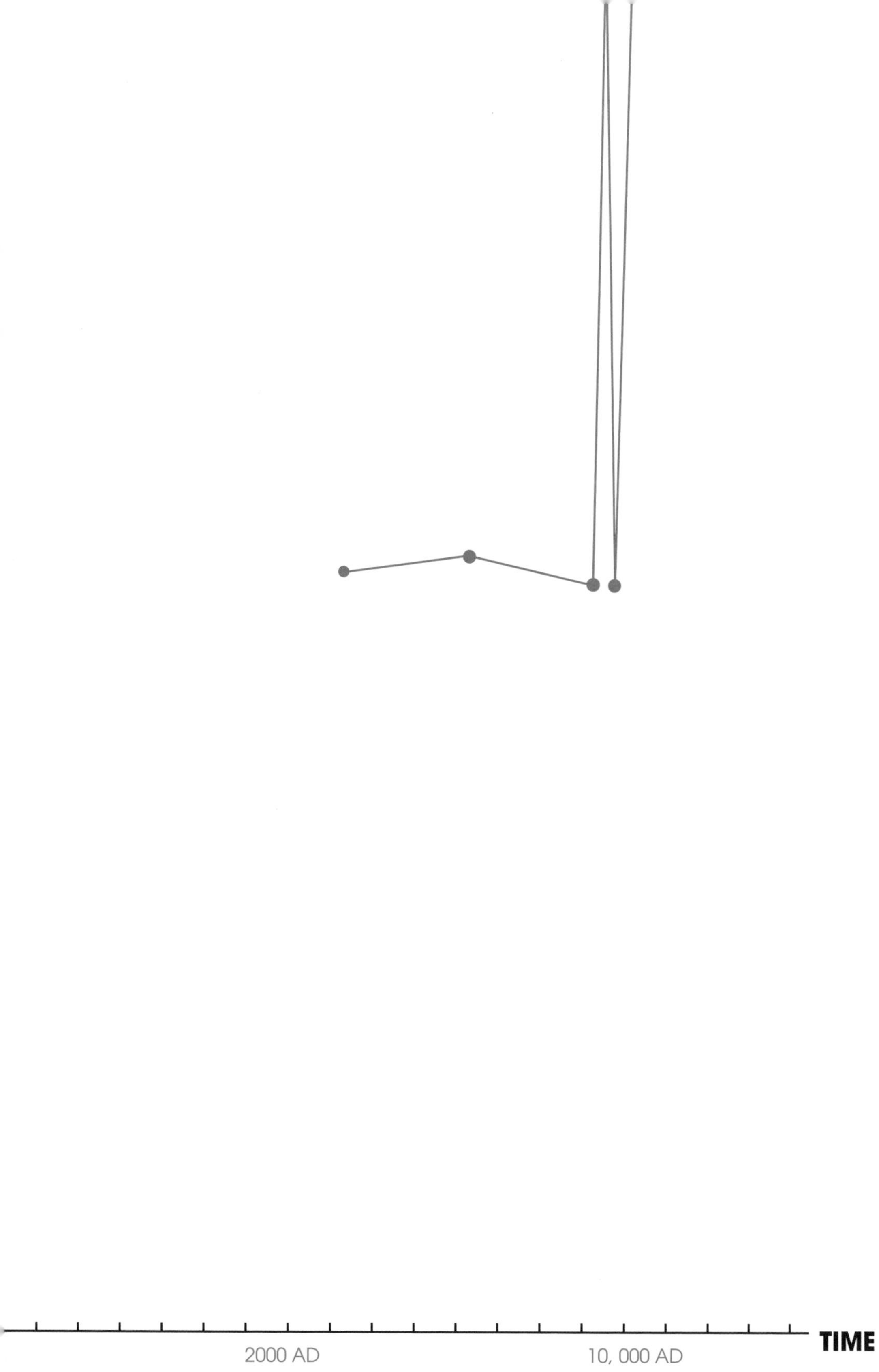

2000 AD
10, 000 AD
TIME

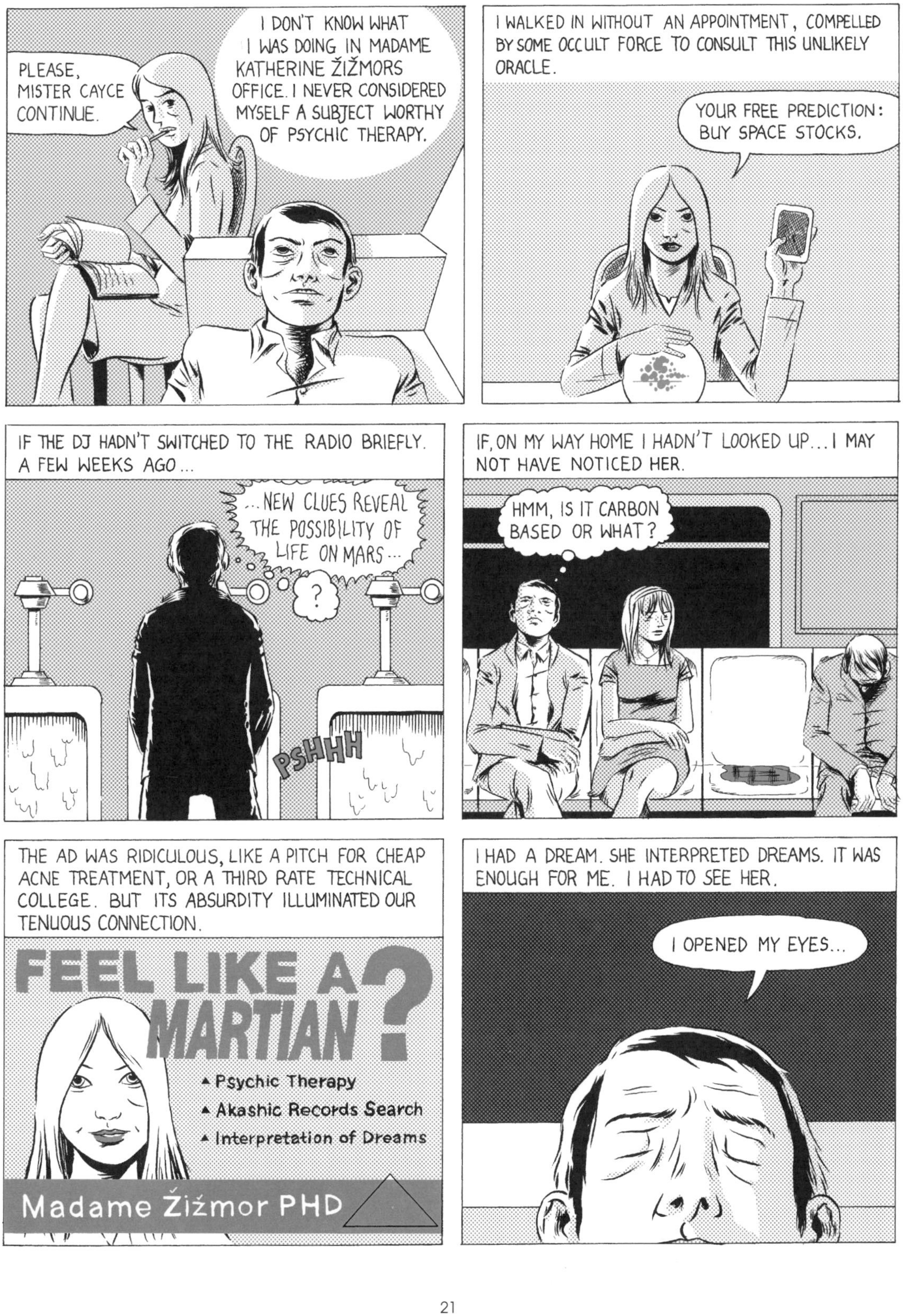

PLEASE, MISTER CAYCE CONTINUE.
I DON'T KNOW WHAT I WAS DOING IN MADAME KATHERINE ŽIŽMORS OFFICE. I NEVER CONSIDERED MYSELF A SUBJECT WORTHY OF PSYCHIC THERAPY.
I WALKED IN WITHOUT AN APPOINTMENT, COMPELLED BY SOME OCCULT FORCE TO CONSULT THIS UNLIKELY ORACLE.
YOUR FREE PREDICTION: BUY SPACE STOCKS.
IF THE DJ HADN'T SWITCHED TO THE RADIO BRIEFLY. A FEW WEEKS AGO...
...NEW CLUES REVEAL THE POSSIBILITY OF LIFE ON MARS...
?
PSHHH
IF, ON MY WAY HOME I HADN'T LOOKED UP... I MAY NOT HAVE NOTICED HER.
HMM, IS IT CARBON BASED OR WHAT?
THE AD WAS RIDICULOUS, LIKE A PITCH FOR CHEAP ACNE TREATMENT, OR A THIRD RATE TECHNICAL COLLEGE. BUT ITS ABSURDITY ILLUMINATED OUR TENUOUS CONNECTION.
FEEL LIKE A MARTIAN?
▲ Psychic Therapy
▲ Akashic Records Search
▲ Interpretation of Dreams
Madame Źiźmor PHD
I HAD A DREAM. SHE INTERPRETED DREAMS. IT WAS ENOUGH FOR ME. I HAD TO SEE HER.
I OPENED MY EYES...

I FELT REBORN... OR RATHER I FELT THE WORLD WAS REBORN AROUND ME...

I WAS WEAK AT FIRST. I COULD ONLY CONSUME LIQUIDS.

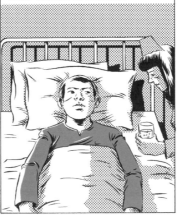

I REGAINED STRENGTH RAPIDLY. AND STARTED CRAVING SOLIDS.

THE HOSPITAL PSYCHOLOGIST TOLD ME THAT I HAD "SLEPT" FOR TEN THOUSAND YEARS.

IT WAS SOME KIND OF TRANCE?

YES.

THE FUTURE WAS A LITTLE DISAPPOINTING. I EXPECTED SOMETHING RADICALLY DIFFERENT, NOT A JOB IN AN ADVERTISING AGENCY.

MANY FAMILIAR PRODUCTS WERE STILL AROUND, BUT WITH EXOTIC NEW FLAVORS.

NEW TASTE

AS EXPECTED, TECHNOLOGY PRO-GRESSED. PORTABLE DEVICES WERE MORE POWERFUL AND THINNER THAN EVER BEFORE.

WHO IS THIS?

HOLD

SNAP WRIST

THWIP

READY

THE WORLD WAS FOR SALE AGAIN.

SHOE CITY

SHAPE+ blob

iPILL
INGEST SOUND

NOSTALGIA®

GHOST BEARD

NEW SHAVE

ORO SKY HOMES
AFFORDABLE LUXURY

STRETCH BEAST

ACID WASH

ACID DETER-GENT.

PURE CHOCOLATE LAXATIVE

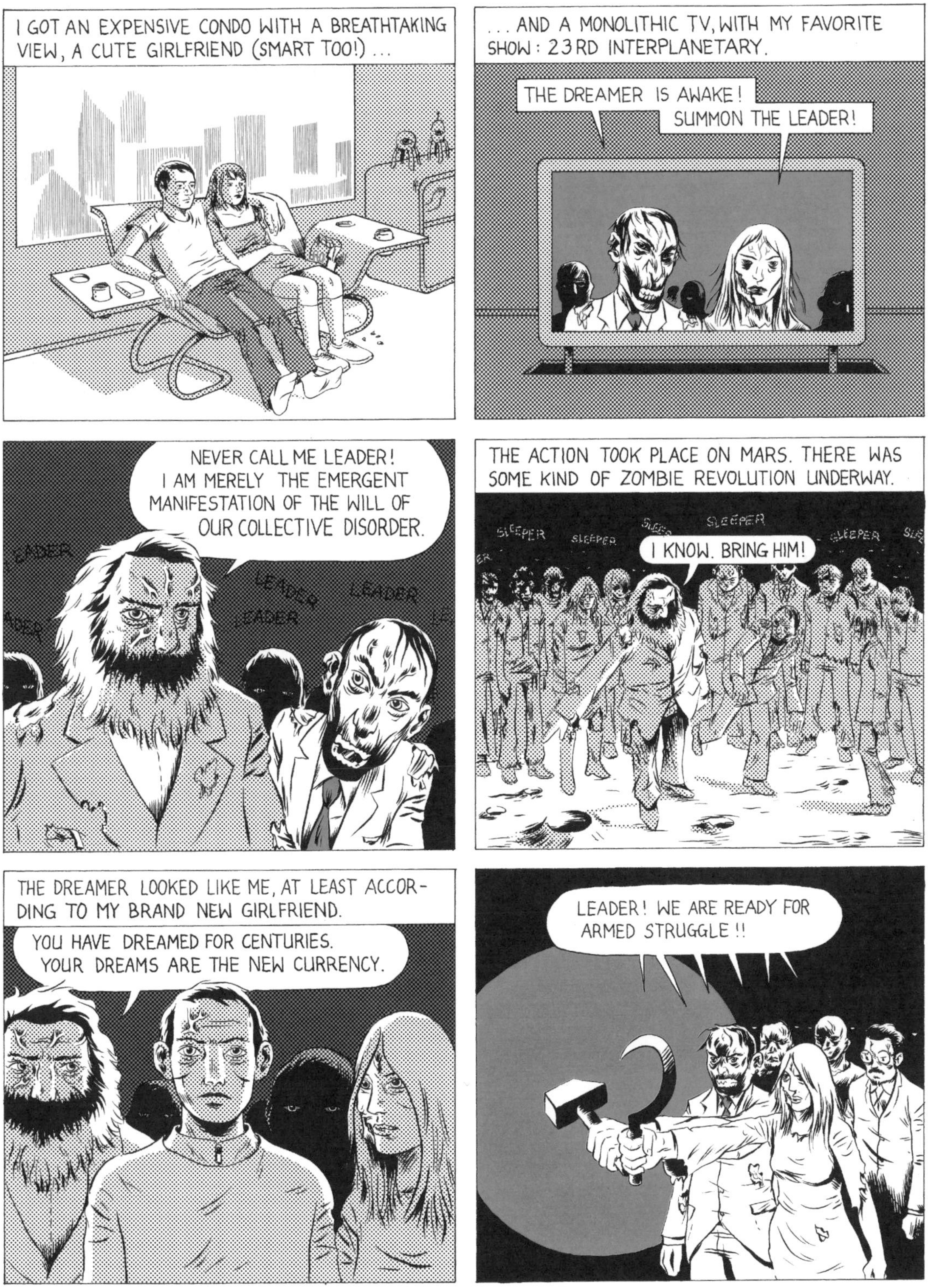

I GOT AN EXPENSIVE CONDO WITH A BREATHTAKING VIEW, A CUTE GIRLFRIEND (SMART TOO!) . . .
. . . AND A MONOLITHIC TV, WITH MY FAVORITE SHOW: 23RD INTERPLANETARY.
THE DREAMER IS AWAKE!
SUMMON THE LEADER!
NEVER CALL ME LEADER! I AM MERELY THE EMERGENT MANIFESTATION OF THE WILL OF OUR COLLECTIVE DISORDER.
LEADER
LEADER
LEADER
THE ACTION TOOK PLACE ON MARS. THERE WAS SOME KIND OF ZOMBIE REVOLUTION UNDERWAY.
SLEEPER
SLEEPER
SLEEPER
SLEEPER
I KNOW. BRING HIM!
THE DREAMER LOOKED LIKE ME, AT LEAST ACCORDING TO MY BRAND NEW GIRLFRIEND.
YOU HAVE DREAMED FOR CENTURIES. YOUR DREAMS ARE THE NEW CURRENCY.
LEADER! WE ARE READY FOR ARMED STRUGGLE!!

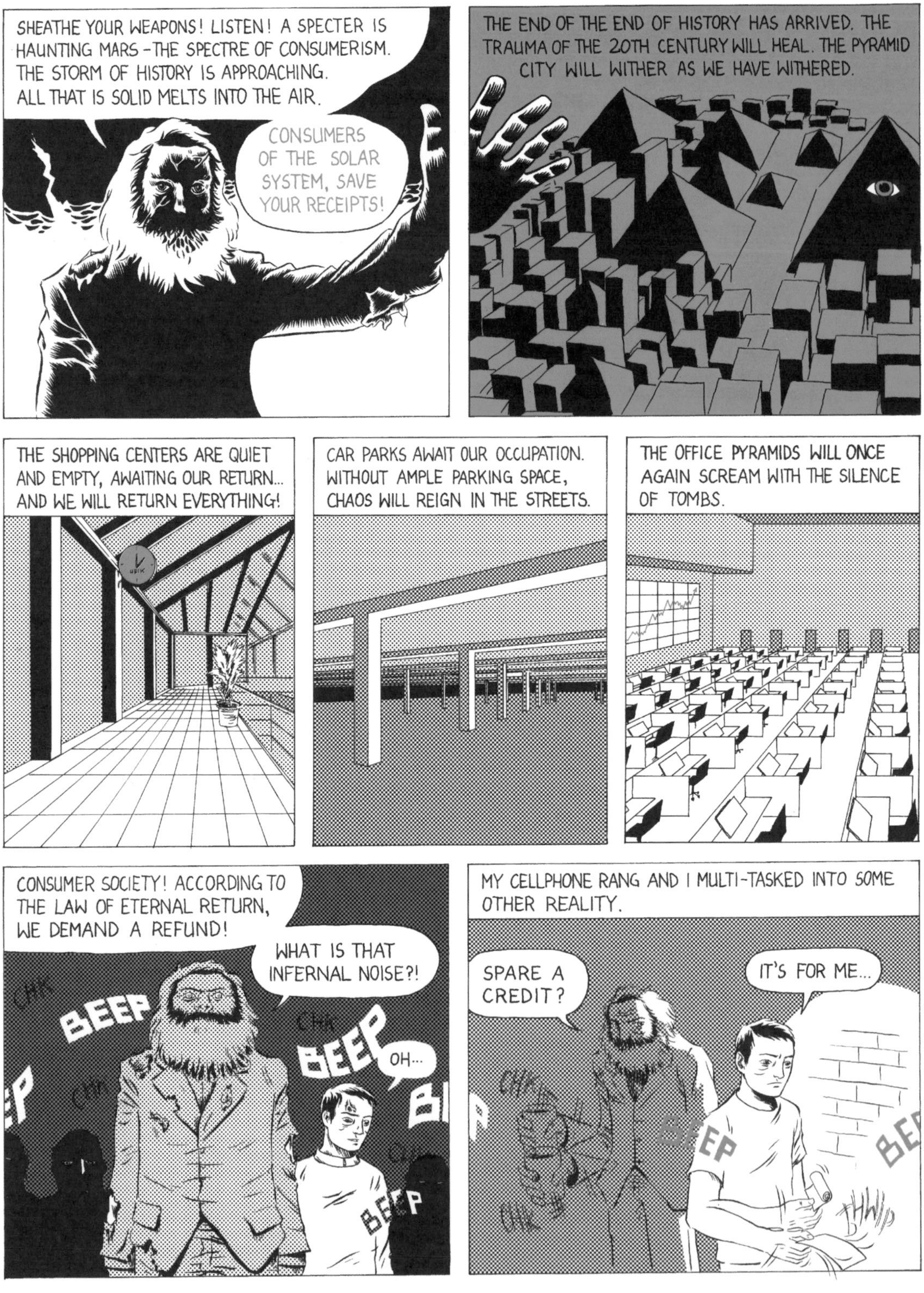
SHEATHE YOUR WEAPONS! LISTEN! A SPECTER IS HAUNTING MARS - THE SPECTRE OF CONSUMERISM. THE STORM OF HISTORY IS APPROACHING. ALL THAT IS SOLID MELTS INTO THE AIR.
CONSUMERS OF THE SOLAR SYSTEM, SAVE YOUR RECEIPTS!
THE END OF THE END OF HISTORY HAS ARRIVED. THE TRAUMA OF THE 20TH CENTURY WILL HEAL. THE PYRAMID CITY WILL WITHER AS WE HAVE WITHERED.
THE SHOPPING CENTERS ARE QUIET AND EMPTY, AWAITING OUR RETURN... AND WE WILL RETURN EVERYTHING!
CAR PARKS AWAIT OUR OCCUPATION. WITHOUT AMPLE PARKING SPACE, CHAOS WILL REIGN IN THE STREETS.
THE OFFICE PYRAMIDS WILL ONCE AGAIN SCREAM WITH THE SILENCE OF TOMBS.
CONSUMER SOCIETY! ACCORDING TO THE LAW OF ETERNAL RETURN, WE DEMAND A REFUND!
WHAT IS THAT INFERNAL NOISE?!
CHK
BEEP
CHK
BEEP
OH...
CHK
BEEP
MY CELLPHONE RANG AND I MULTI-TASKED INTO SOME OTHER REALITY.
SPARE A CREDIT?
IT'S FOR ME...
CHK
CHK
BEEP
THWIP

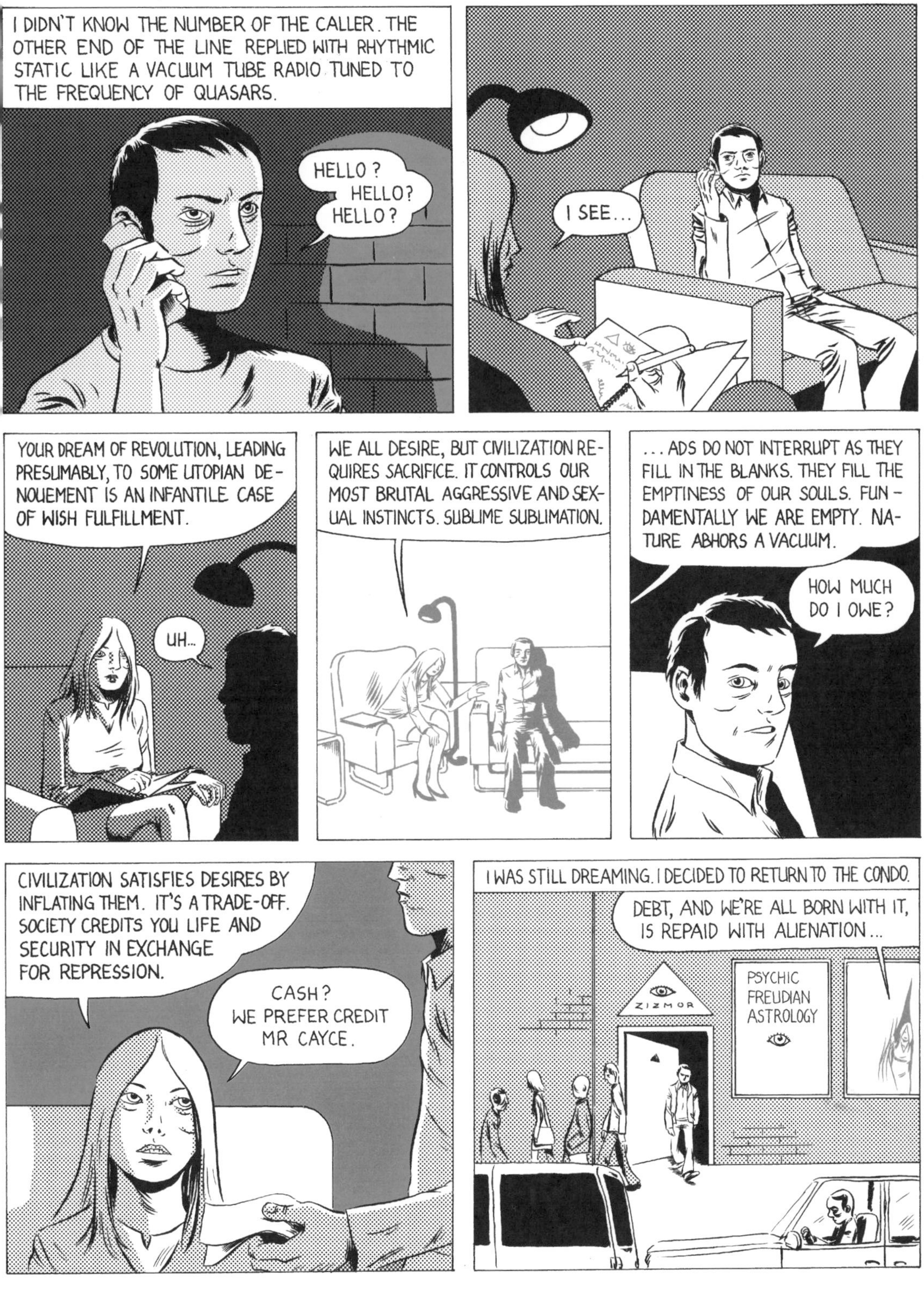
I DIDN'T KNOW THE NUMBER OF THE CALLER. THE OTHER END OF THE LINE REPLIED WITH RHYTHMIC STATIC LIKE A VACUUM TUBE RADIO TUNED TO THE FREQUENCY OF QUASARS.
HELLO? HELLO? HELLO?
I SEE...
YOUR DREAM OF REVOLUTION, LEADING PRESUMABLY, TO SOME UTOPIAN DENOUEMENT IS AN INFANTILE CASE OF WISH FULFILLMENT.
UH...
WE ALL DESIRE, BUT CIVILIZATION REQUIRES SACRIFICE. IT CONTROLS OUR MOST BRUTAL AGGRESSIVE AND SEXUAL INSTINCTS. SUBLIME SUBLIMATION.
...ADS DO NOT INTERRUPT AS THEY FILL IN THE BLANKS. THEY FILL THE EMPTINESS OF OUR SOULS. FUNDAMENTALLY WE ARE EMPTY. NATURE ABHORS A VACUUM.
HOW MUCH DO I OWE?
CIVILIZATION SATISFIES DESIRES BY INFLATING THEM. IT'S A TRADE-OFF. SOCIETY CREDITS YOU LIFE AND SECURITY IN EXCHANGE FOR REPRESSION.
CASH? WE PREFER CREDIT MR CAYCE.
I WAS STILL DREAMING. I DECIDED TO RETURN TO THE CONDO.
DEBT, AND WE'RE ALL BORN WITH IT, IS REPAID WITH ALIENATION...
ZIZMOR
PSYCHIC FREUDIAN ASTROLOGY

I LIVED IN THE CONDOMINIUM DISTRICT. THE ULTRA-MODERN HIGH RISES WERE ERECTED IN A SINGLE WEEK OF BUILDING ORGY. INSTANT NEIGHBORHOOD.

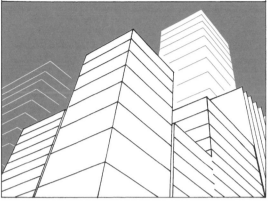

THE STATE OF THE HALLWAYS REFLECTED THE MOOD OF THE RESIDENTS. I WAS MOVING THROUGH THE CORRIDORS OF SOME KIND OF SLOW MOTION APOCALYPSE.

THE APARTMENT LOOKED MORE 21ST CENTURY THAN BEFORE. ETERNAL SAMENESS PERMEATED ALL OBJECTS. THE FUTURE WAS IN RETREAT.

MY GIRLFRIEND WAS DEAD ASLEEP... OR JUST DEAD... SICK... DEFECTIVE? I COULDN'T BE SURE. I WAS NO LONGER SURE WHAT CENTURY THIS WAS.

I DIDN'T KNOW WHAT TO DO SO I JUST SAT DOWN. TIME FLOWED IN NO PARTICULAR DIRECTION.

I'M NOT SURE AT WHICH MOMENT I NOTICED THAT EVERYTHING WAS AN ELABORATE SET CONSTRUCTED OUT OF PAPIER MÂCHÉ. I WAS SURROUNDED BY HOLLOW EFFIGIES.

"HI"

I TRIED TO RESIST THE BIOLOGICAL COMPULSION TO EX-CHANGE GENETIC INFORMATION. WE PERFORMED THE TASK MECHANICALLY AND DISPASSIONATELY, LIKE DAMAGED AUTOMATA MIMICKING PORNOGRAPHY.

THE BRIEF MOMENTS POST-ORGASM ARE A STATE OF COMMUNION WITH THE INANIMATE. THE CONSCIOUSNESS WANDERS, ROOTLESS AMONG THE CHEMICAL AND MI-NERAL COMPONENTS OF THE BODY SEEKING THE MYSTERY OF ITS EXISTENCE.

I TRAVELED IN TIME AGAIN, THIS TIME TO ONE BILLION B.C. IN THE OXYGEN-LESS SKY I SAW A MARTIAN METEOR PENETRATE THE EARTH. THE ORIGIN OF LIFE INFECTED.

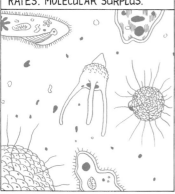

SUDDENLY EVOLUTION MAKES SENSE. PROTOPLASMIC CAPITALISM. PROTEIN CURRENCY. AMINO ACID EXCHANGE RATES. MOLECULAR SURPLUS.

FERAL COMPETITION. CARNIVOROUS CONFLICT. REPTILIAN EXPLOITATION. COLD-BLOODED SHOPPING.

PALEOLITHIC CORPORATIONS. CRO-MAG-NON CAPITAL. NEANDERTHAL PROFITS. VIRILE ENTERPRENEURS.

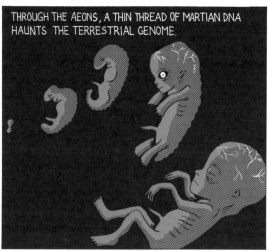

THROUGH THE AEONS, A THIN THREAD OF MARTIAN DNA HAUNTS THE TERRESTRIAL GENOME.

IT'S INSIDE ME. I'M MARTIAN. I DON'T HAVE THE RIGHT CONSTITUTION FOR THIS WORLD. I'M ON THE WRONG PLANET.

WHAT PLANET DO YOU THINK YOU'RE ON MISTER CAYCE?

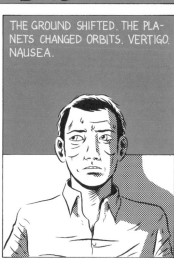

THE GROUND SHIFTED. THE PLANETS CHANGED ORBITS. VERTIGO. NAUSEA.

THE ENTIRE SPACE-TIME CONTINUUM BECAME SUSPECT. THE ZODIAC WAS AN ALIEN BESTIARY. CIVILIZATION WAS AN ANCIENT BURIAL GROUND WITH UNFAMILIAR FUNERARY RITES.

MISTER CAYCE

ASTRAL DISASTER.

WE DON'T HAVE A REFUND POLICY...

SURPLUS GRAVITY, THE COMPOSITION OF THE ATMO-
SPHERE, THE ELECTRO-MAGNETIC RADIATION MADE
EVERY STEP AN AGONY.

WITH EFFORT I MADE IT UP TO THE APARTMENT.

THE SOUND OF RUNNING WATER SLOWLY DISSOLVED
THE MEMORIES OF THE DREAM AND MADAME
ŽIŽMOR.

PSSSHH

THE BUOYANCY OF WATER RELIEVED THE PRESSURE
OF GRAVITY. THE WORLD DROWNED IN MY TUB.

BUT MARS REMAINS. I CAN FEEL
MY HUMANITY MELT AWAY.

THE ALIEN INSIDE ME GROWS
STRONGER.

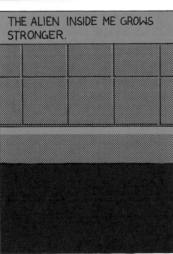

THE FACE ON MARS NODS IN
SILENT APPROVAL.

END

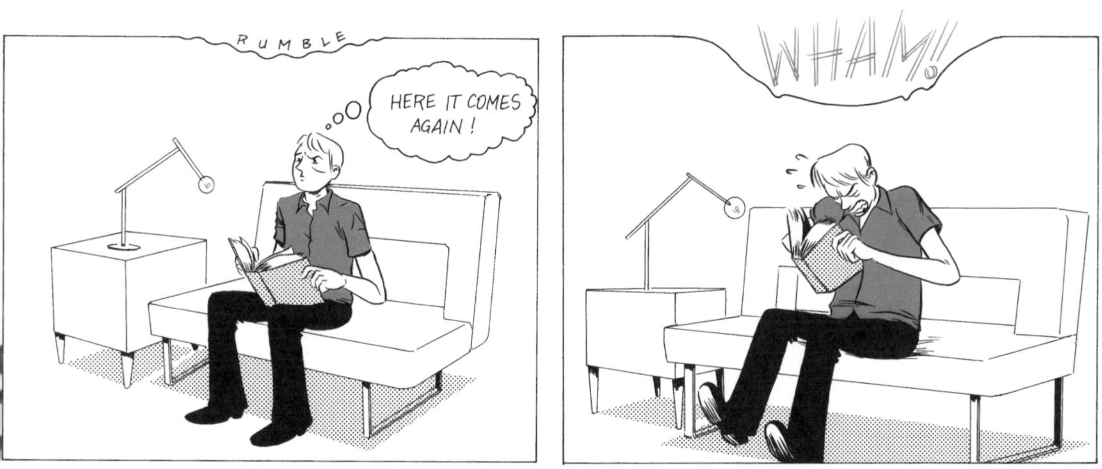
RUMBLE
HERE IT COMES AGAIN!
WHAM!!

100 DECIBELS

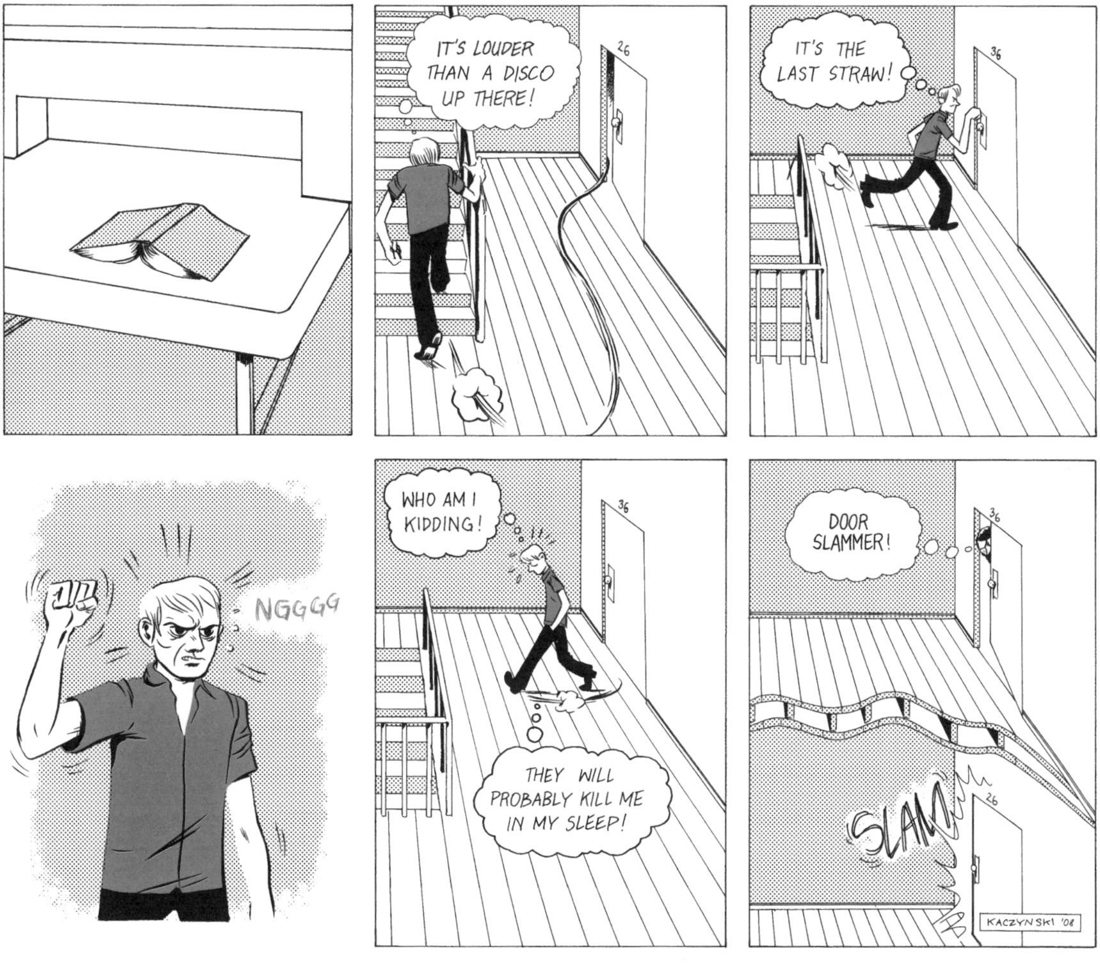
IT'S LOUDER THAN A DISCO UP THERE!
26
IT'S THE LAST STRAW!
36
NGGGG
WHO AM I KIDDING!
THEY WILL PROBABLY KILL ME IN MY SLEEP!
DOOR SLAMMER!
SLAM
KACZYNSKI '08

SPACE

100, 000 Miles

10, 000 Miles

976 SQ. FT.

First appearance: *MOME 9,* 2007

1,000 Miles

100 Miles

1 Miles

1,000,000,000 BC   1,000,000 BC   500,000 BC   40,000

TIME

2000 AD   10, 000 AD

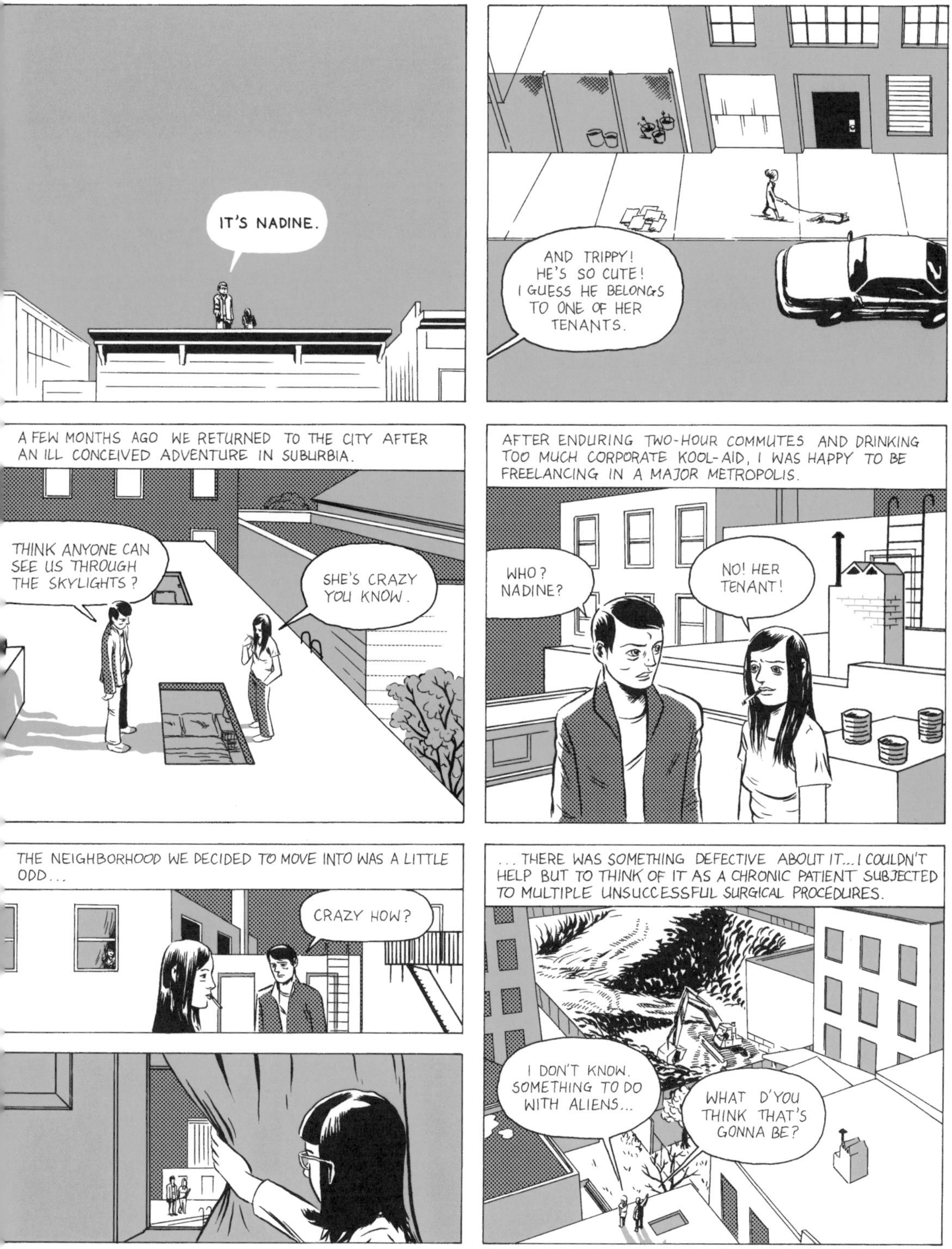
IT'S NADINE.
AND TRIPPY! HE'S SO CUTE! I GUESS HE BELONGS TO ONE OF HER TENANTS.
A FEW MONTHS AGO WE RETURNED TO THE CITY AFTER AN ILL CONCEIVED ADVENTURE IN SUBURBIA.
THINK ANYONE CAN SEE US THROUGH THE SKYLIGHTS?
SHE'S CRAZY YOU KNOW.
AFTER ENDURING TWO-HOUR COMMUTES AND DRINKING TOO MUCH CORPORATE KOOL-AID, I WAS HAPPY TO BE FREELANCING IN A MAJOR METROPOLIS.
WHO? NADINE?
NO! HER TENANT!
THE NEIGHBORHOOD WE DECIDED TO MOVE INTO WAS A LITTLE ODD...
CRAZY HOW?
... THERE WAS SOMETHING DEFECTIVE ABOUT IT... I COULDN'T HELP BUT TO THINK OF IT AS A CHRONIC PATIENT SUBJECTED TO MULTIPLE UNSUCCESSFUL SURGICAL PROCEDURES.
I DON'T KNOW. SOMETHING TO DO WITH ALIENS...
WHAT D'YOU THINK THAT'S GONNA BE?

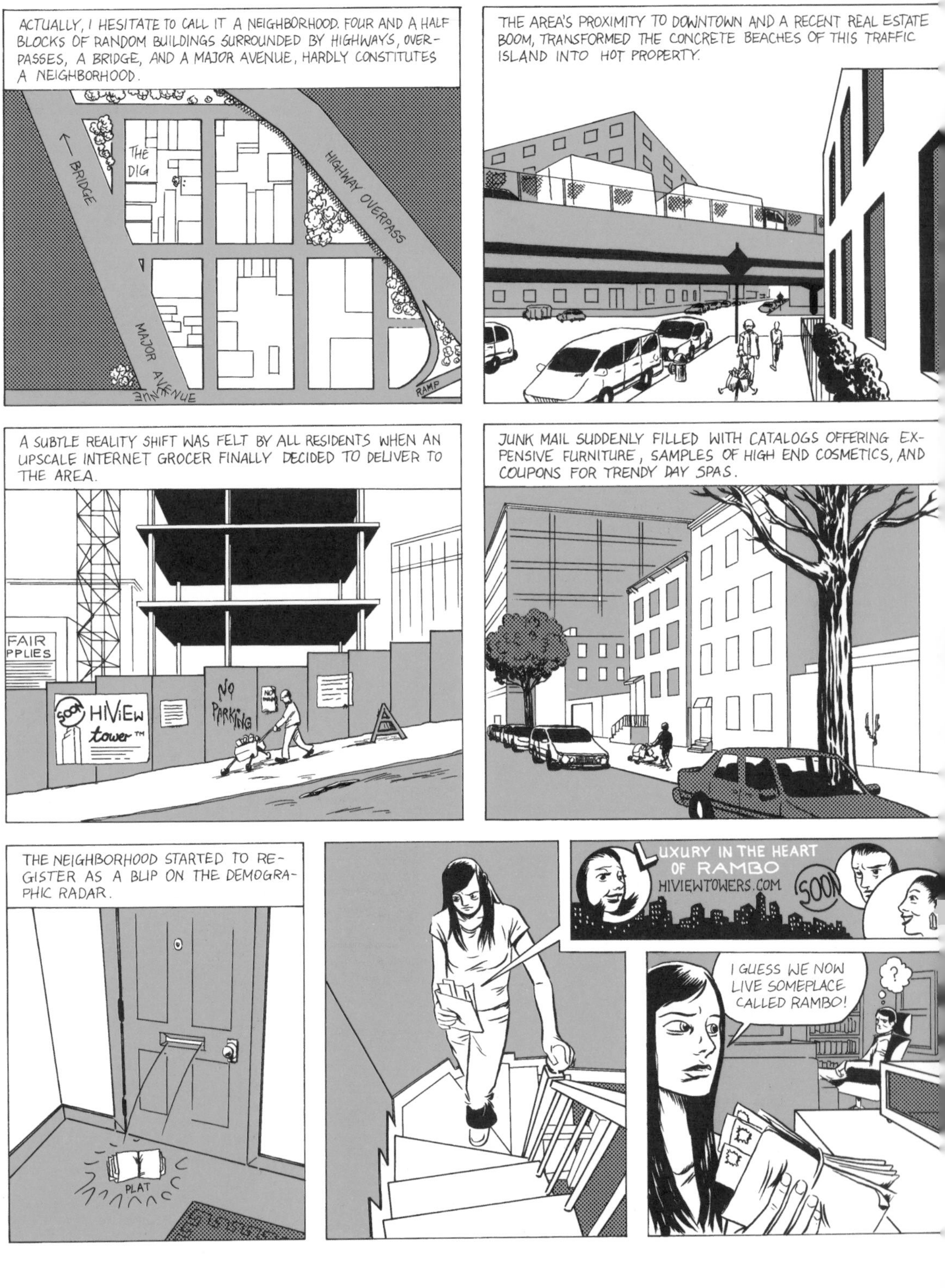
ACTUALLY, I HESITATE TO CALL IT A NEIGHBORHOOD. FOUR AND A HALF BLOCKS OF RANDOM BUILDINGS SURROUNDED BY HIGHWAYS, OVER-PASSES, A BRIDGE, AND A MAJOR AVENUE, HARDLY CONSTITUTES A NEIGHBORHOOD.
← BRIDGE
THE DIG
HIGHWAY OVERPASS
MAJOR AVENUE
RAMP
THE AREA'S PROXIMITY TO DOWNTOWN AND A RECENT REAL ESTATE BOOM, TRANSFORMED THE CONCRETE BEACHES OF THIS TRAFFIC ISLAND INTO HOT PROPERTY.
A SUBTLE REALITY SHIFT WAS FELT BY ALL RESIDENTS WHEN AN UPSCALE INTERNET GROCER FINALLY DECIDED TO DELIVER TO THE AREA.
FAIR
PPLIES
SOON
HIViEW tower ™
NO PARKING
JUNK MAIL SUDDENLY FILLED WITH CATALOGS OFFERING EX-PENSIVE FURNITURE, SAMPLES OF HIGH END COSMETICS, AND COUPONS FOR TRENDY DAY SPAS.
THE NEIGHBORHOOD STARTED TO RE-GISTER AS A BLIP ON THE DEMOGRA-PHIC RADAR.
PLAT
LUXURY IN THE HEART OF RAMBO
HIVIEWTOWERS.COM
SOON
I GUESS WE NOW LIVE SOMEPLACE CALLED RAMBO!
?

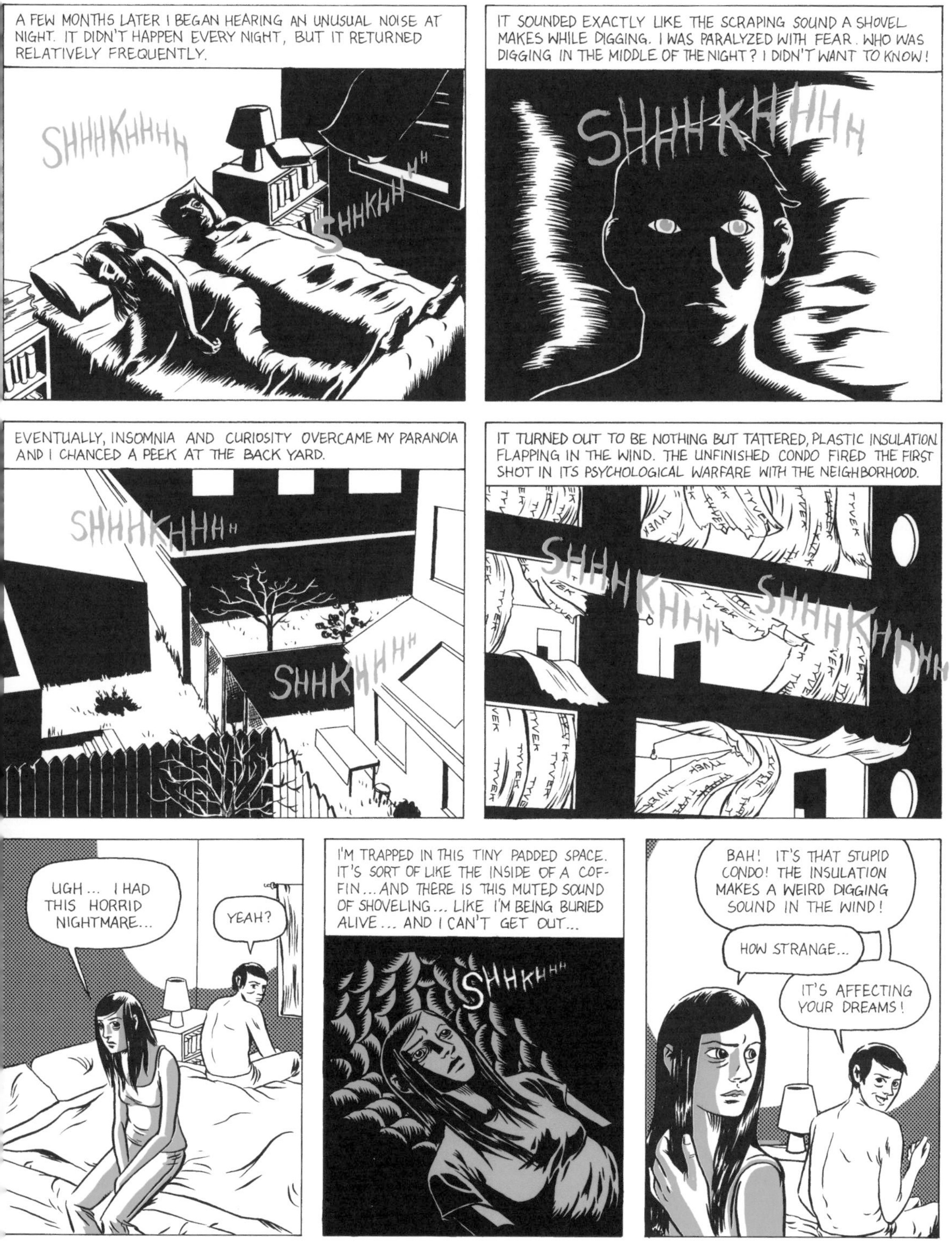
A FEW MONTHS LATER I BEGAN HEARING AN UNUSUAL NOISE AT NIGHT. IT DIDN'T HAPPEN EVERY NIGHT, BUT IT RETURNED RELATIVELY FREQUENTLY.
SHHHKHHHH
SHHKHHHH
IT SOUNDED EXACTLY LIKE THE SCRAPING SOUND A SHOVEL MAKES WHILE DIGGING. I WAS PARALYZED WITH FEAR. WHO WAS DIGGING IN THE MIDDLE OF THE NIGHT? I DIDN'T WANT TO KNOW!
SHHHKHHHHH
EVENTUALLY, INSOMNIA AND CURIOSITY OVERCAME MY PARANOIA AND I CHANCED A PEEK AT THE BACK YARD.
SHHHKHHHH
SHHKHHHH
IT TURNED OUT TO BE NOTHING BUT TATTERED, PLASTIC INSULATION FLAPPING IN THE WIND. THE UNFINISHED CONDO FIRED THE FIRST SHOT IN ITS PSYCHOLOGICAL WARFARE WITH THE NEIGHBORHOOD.
SHHHKHHH
SHHHKHHHH
UGH... I HAD THIS HORRID NIGHTMARE...
YEAH?
I'M TRAPPED IN THIS TINY PADDED SPACE. IT'S SORT OF LIKE THE INSIDE OF A COFFIN... AND THERE IS THIS MUTED SOUND OF SHOVELING... LIKE I'M BEING BURIED ALIVE... AND I CAN'T GET OUT...
SHHKHHH
BAH! IT'S THAT STUPID CONDO! THE INSULATION MAKES A WEIRD DIGGING SOUND IN THE WIND!
HOW STRANGE...
IT'S AFFECTING YOUR DREAMS!

AS THE CONDO GREW, SO DID ITS GRIP ON THE COLLECTIVE IMAGI-NATION OF THE NEIGHBORHOOD. A KIND OF FOLKLORE BEGAN TO ACCUMULATE AROUND IT. APPARENTLY IT WAS THE DREAM PROJECT OF A RECLUSIVE MULTIMILLIONAIRE.

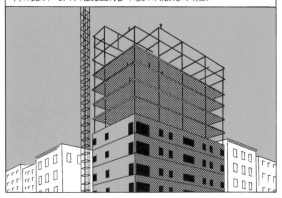

HIS PHANTOM PRESENCE WAS ANNOUNCED BY THE APPEARANCE OF AN ENORMOUS BLACK HUMMER. WE NEVER SAW THE VEHICLE IN MOTION. IT WAS EITHER THERE, OR NOT THERE, AS IF IT MATERIAL-IZED FROM ANOTHER DIMENSION.

CAREFUL! YOU'LL TRIGGER THE FORCE FIELD!

I JUST WANT SEE IF IT'S BIGGER ON THE INSIDE...

THE ORIGIN OF THE CONDO WAS SHROUDED IN MYSTERY. ACCORDING TO SOME LOCALS, THE MILLIONAIRE WAS IMPRESSED BY A SIMILAR STRUCTURE IN HIS NATIVE SHANGHAI.

HOW MUCH WOULD IT COST TO BUILD THAT IN THE US?

NADINE WAS CONVINCED THAT HE WAS INSPIRED BY THE BEACH CONDOMINIUMS OF MIAMI. HE WAS STRUCK BY THE ACOUSTIC SIMILARITY BETWEEN OCEAN WAVES AND TRAFFIC FLOWS.

LISTEN... IT'S LIKE A HIGHWAY...

THE REAL REASON WAS PROBABLY FAR MORE BANAL AND FRIGHTENING, LIKE AN IMPULSE PURCHASE AT AN ARCHI-TECTURAL WHOLESALER.

HMM... HOW MANY STORIES IS IT?

HIRISE CATALOG VOL 3

YOU CAN HAVE AS MANY AS LOCAL PERMITS ALLOW ...

NADINE'S PROPERTY WAS PROBABLY THE MOST AFFECTED BY THE CONSTRUCTION. AFTER LIVING IN THE NEIGHBORHOOD SINCE THE 1920'S, HER SOUTHERN SUN EXPOSURE WAS NOW ENTIRELY BLOCKED.

HI NADINE.

GOD FORBID!

I HOPE THAT STUPID CONDO DOESN'T FALL ON YOU!

THIS SEASON, HER ANNUAL TOMATO AND PICKLE CROP FAILED TO DEVELOP.

POOR NADINE!

WHAT'S THAT?

THE CONDO ON THE OTHER HAND KEPT SPROUTING NEW MUTANT FLORA.

WE TOTALLY HAVE TO GO SOMETIME!

HIViEW tower™ OPEN HOUSE SAT & SUN 1-4 FROM 976 SQ FT AFFORDABLE LUXURY

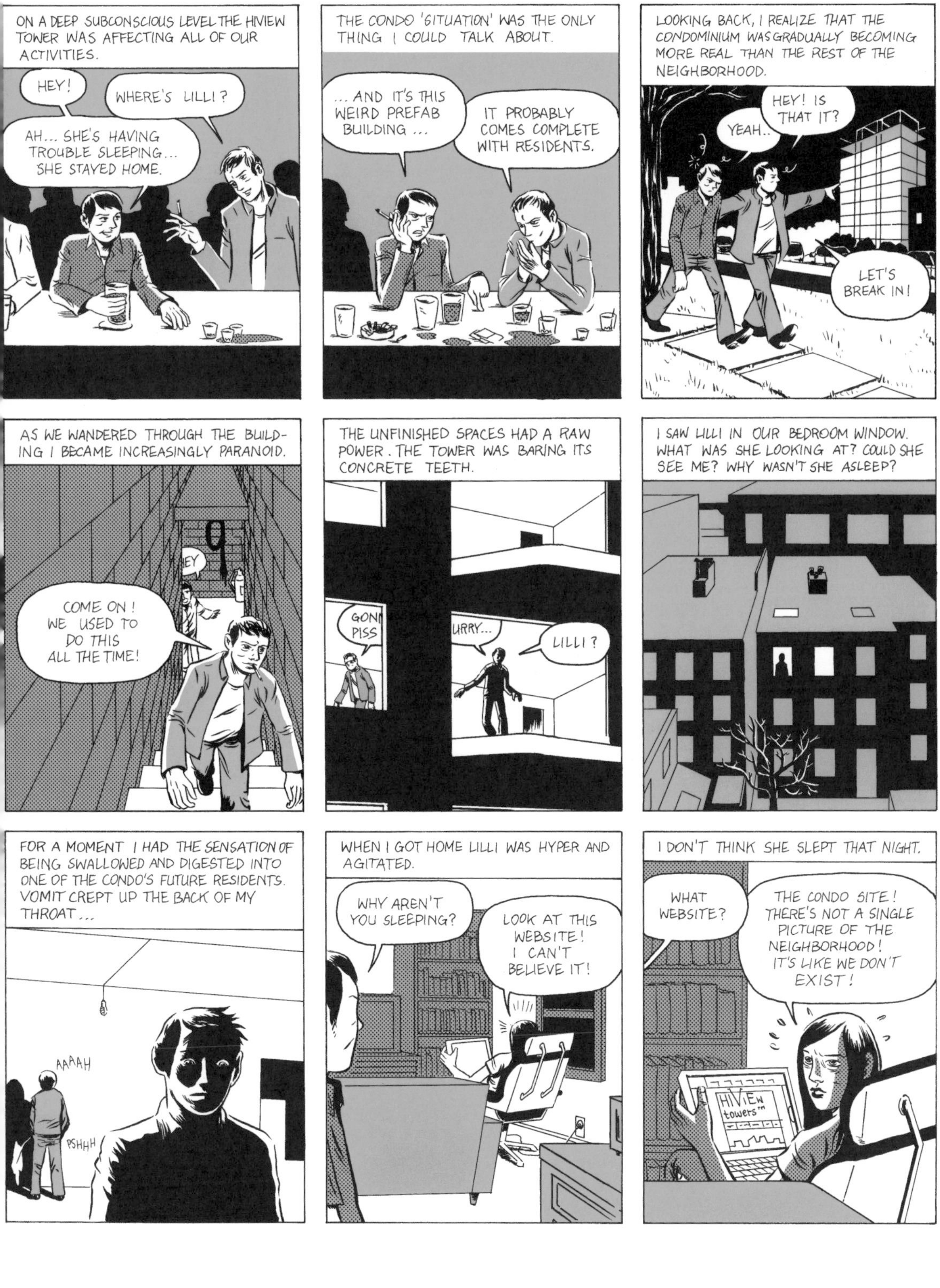

ON A DEEP SUBCONSCIOUS LEVEL THE HIVIEW TOWER WAS AFFECTING ALL OF OUR ACTIVITIES.
HEY!
WHERE'S LILLI?
AH... SHE'S HAVING TROUBLE SLEEPING... SHE STAYED HOME.
THE CONDO 'SITUATION' WAS THE ONLY THING I COULD TALK ABOUT.
...AND IT'S THIS WEIRD PREFAB BUILDING...
IT PROBABLY COMES COMPLETE WITH RESIDENTS.
LOOKING BACK, I REALIZE THAT THE CONDOMINIUM WAS GRADUALLY BECOMING MORE REAL THAN THE REST OF THE NEIGHBORHOOD.
YEAH..
HEY! IS THAT IT?
LET'S BREAK IN!
AS WE WANDERED THROUGH THE BUILDING I BECAME INCREASINGLY PARANOID.
COME ON! WE USED TO DO THIS ALL THE TIME!
THE UNFINISHED SPACES HAD A RAW POWER. THE TOWER WAS BARING ITS CONCRETE TEETH.
LILLI?
I SAW LILLI IN OUR BEDROOM WINDOW. WHAT WAS SHE LOOKING AT? COULD SHE SEE ME? WHY WASN'T SHE ASLEEP?
FOR A MOMENT I HAD THE SENSATION OF BEING SWALLOWED AND DIGESTED INTO ONE OF THE CONDO'S FUTURE RESIDENTS. VOMIT CREPT UP THE BACK OF MY THROAT...
AAAAH
PSHHH
WHEN I GOT HOME LILLI WAS HYPER AND AGITATED.
WHY AREN'T YOU SLEEPING?
LOOK AT THIS WEBSITE! I CAN'T BELIEVE IT!
I DON'T THINK SHE SLEPT THAT NIGHT.
WHAT WEBSITE?
THE CONDO SITE! THERE'S NOT A SINGLE PICTURE OF THE NEIGHBORHOOD! IT'S LIKE WE DON'T EXIST!
HIVIEW towers™

A FEW MONTHS LATER WE FINALLY GOT A CHANCE TO TAKE ADVANTAGE OF THE HIVIEW TOWER OPEN HOUSE.

...STYLE CABINETS WITH MATTE LACQUER FINISH. CUSTOM-QUARRIED IMHOTEP EGYPTIAN STONE COUNTERTOPS, COMPLEMENTED BY ICE-GLASS BACK...

THE POTENTIAL BUYERS WERE UNCOMFORTABLE. THEY SAW THEMSELVES AS SHOCK TROOPS OF GENTRIFICATION. ALL OF THEM WISHED THEY COULD AFFORD REAL ISLANDS INSTEAD OF BEING STRANDED ON THIS CONCRETE REEF.

...HIVIEW TOWER WILL BRING UNDERSTATED ELEGANCE TO THE RAMBO STREETSCAPE MERGING URBAN GRIT WITH GLAMOUR...

THE WORDS OF THE SALES GIRL SOUNDED LIKE SOME KIND OF OTHER DIMENSIONAL JARGON. IT WAS AMUSING FOR A WHILE...

...SPA-STYLE MASTER BATHS PROVIDE A TRANQUIL RETREAT WITH HIGH END FINISHES. DURANGO STONE, CUBO FIXTURES, KTULU FAUCETS...

Please do not urinate here!

Por favor no orine aqui!

SOON A KIND OF CREEPINESS SET IN. THE MONOTONOUS DELIVERY OF THE SALES PITCH TOOK ON THE QUALITY OF A TRANCE-INDUCING CHANT.

...24 HOUR FULL SER CONCIERGE, FITNESS FACILITY, ONSITE VA

SPACE BECAME CHARGED WITH LUMINOUS OTHERWORDLY ENERGY... GEOMETRY BEGAN TO FLUCTUATE... LILLI SEEMED MESMERIZED... DIAPHANOUS...

I KNEW THE ROOMS WERE EMPTY SHELLS OF CHEAP DRY WALL... BUT FOR AN INSTANT WE SAW SPECTERS OF DESIGNER FURNITURE...

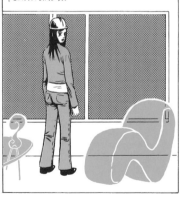

OUTSIDE AN UNFAMILIAR VISTA UNFOLDED.

WHAT HAPPENED TO THE NEIGHBORHOOD?

AFFORDABLE LUXURY IS A HERMETIC UTOPIA. A NEIGHBORHOOD IS UNNECESSARY.

...AND A COURTESY SHUTTLE TO THE SUBWAY!

AND DON'T FORGET THE COMPLIMENTARY HIVIEW MUGS!

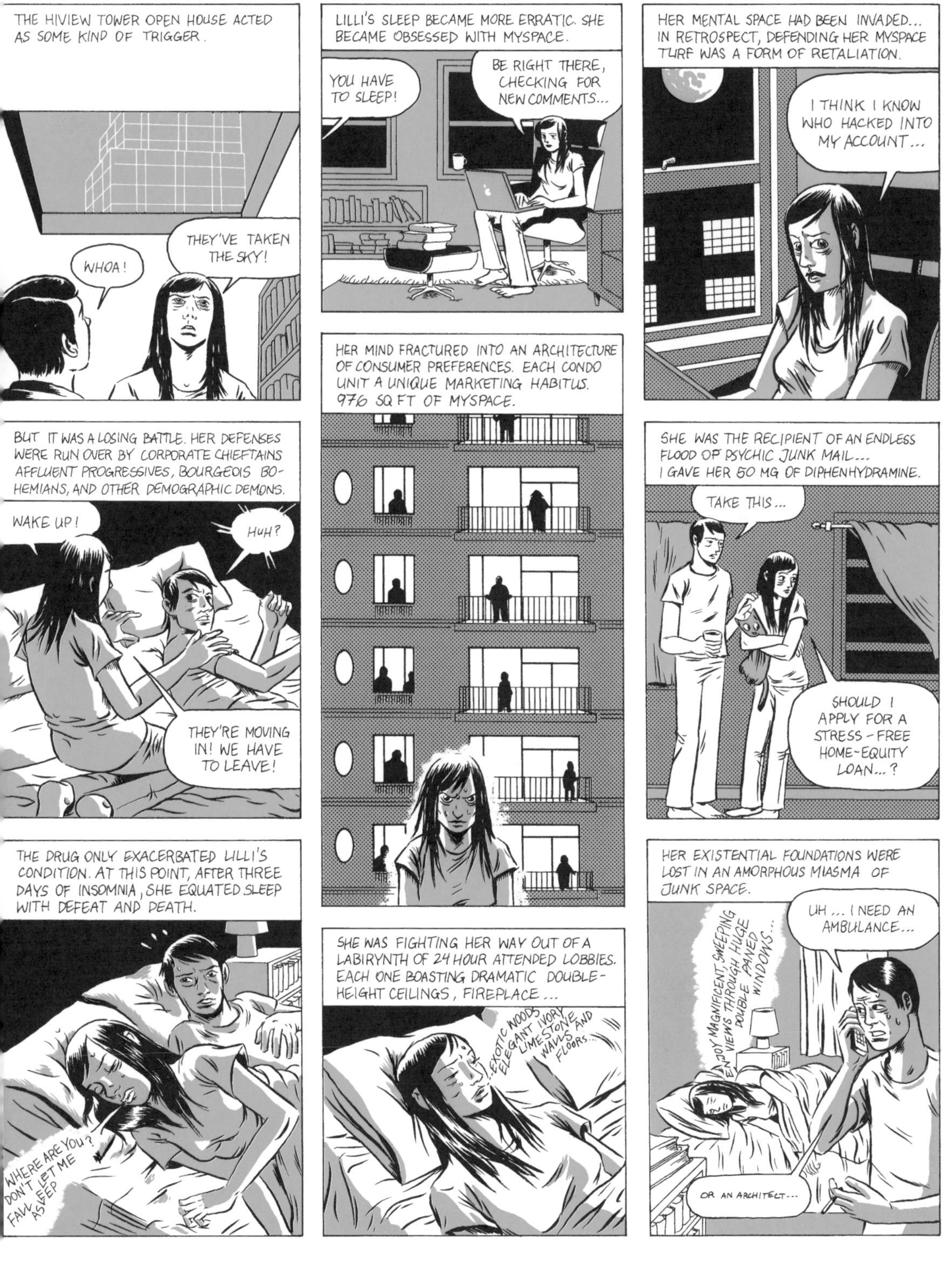

THE HIVIEW TOWER OPEN HOUSE ACTED AS SOME KIND OF TRIGGER.
WHOA!
THEY'VE TAKEN THE SKY!
LILLI'S SLEEP BECAME MORE ERRATIC. SHE BECAME OBSESSED WITH MYSPACE.
YOU HAVE TO SLEEP!
BE RIGHT THERE, CHECKING FOR NEW COMMENTS...
HER MENTAL SPACE HAD BEEN INVADED... IN RETROSPECT, DEFENDING HER MYSPACE TURF WAS A FORM OF RETALIATION.
I THINK I KNOW WHO HACKED INTO MY ACCOUNT...
BUT IT WAS A LOSING BATTLE. HER DEFENSES WERE RUN OVER BY CORPORATE CHIEFTAINS AFFLUENT PROGRESSIVES, BOURGEOIS BOHEMIANS, AND OTHER DEMOGRAPHIC DEMONS.
WAKE UP!
HUH?
THEY'RE MOVING IN! WE HAVE TO LEAVE!
HER MIND FRACTURED INTO AN ARCHITECTURE OF CONSUMER PREFERENCES. EACH CONDO UNIT A UNIQUE MARKETING HABITUS. 976 SQ FT OF MYSPACE.
SHE WAS THE RECIPIENT OF AN ENDLESS FLOOD OF PSYCHIC JUNK MAIL... I GAVE HER 50 MG OF DIPHENHYDRAMINE.
TAKE THIS...
SHOULD I APPLY FOR A STRESS-FREE HOME-EQUITY LOAN...?
THE DRUG ONLY EXACERBATED LILLI'S CONDITION. AT THIS POINT, AFTER THREE DAYS OF INSOMNIA, SHE EQUATED SLEEP WITH DEFEAT AND DEATH.
WHERE ARE YOU? DON'T LET ME FALL ASLEEP
SHE WAS FIGHTING HER WAY OUT OF A LABIRYNTH OF 24 HOUR ATTENDED LOBBIES. EACH ONE BOASTING DRAMATIC DOUBLE-HEIGHT CEILINGS, FIREPLACE...
EXOTIC WOODS ELEGANT IVORY LIMESTONE WALLS AND FLOORS...
HER EXISTENTIAL FOUNDATIONS WERE LOST IN AN AMORPHOUS MIASMA OF JUNK SPACE.
ENJOY MAGNIFICENT, SWEEPING VIEWS THROUGH HUGE DOUBLE PANED WINDOWS...
UH... I NEED AN AMBULANCE...
OR AN ARCHITECT...

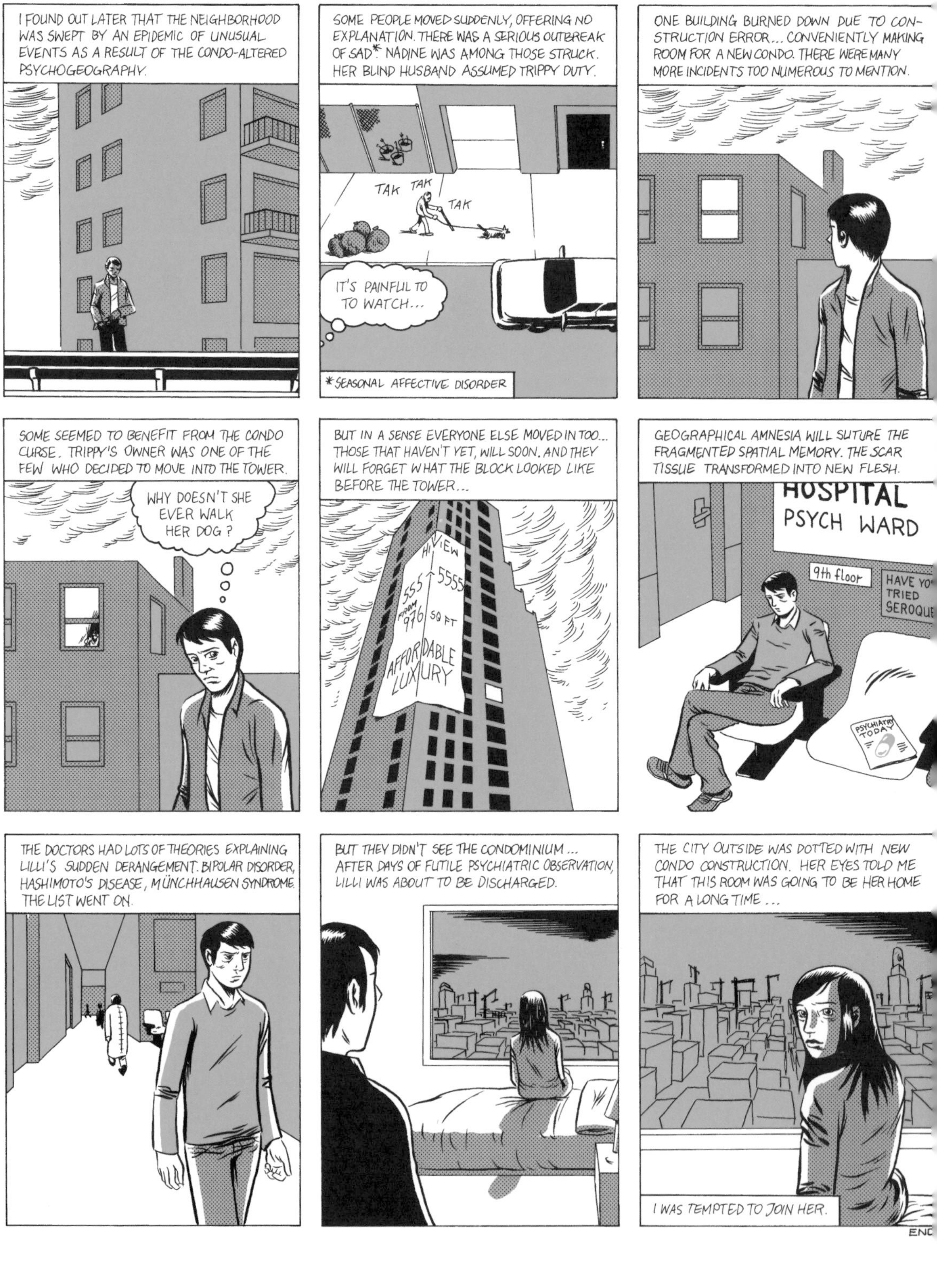

I FOUND OUT LATER THAT THE NEIGHBORHOOD WAS SWEPT BY AN EPIDEMIC OF UNUSUAL EVENTS AS A RESULT OF THE CONDO-ALTERED PSYCHOGEOGRAPHY.
SOME PEOPLE MOVED SUDDENLY, OFFERING NO EXPLANATION. THERE WAS A SERIOUS OUTBREAK OF SAD.* NADINE WAS AMONG THOSE STRUCK. HER BLIND HUSBAND ASSUMED TRIPPY DUTY.
TAK TAK
TAK
IT'S PAINFUL TO TO WATCH...
*SEASONAL AFFECTIVE DISORDER
ONE BUILDING BURNED DOWN DUE TO CONSTRUCTION ERROR... CONVENIENTLY MAKING ROOM FOR A NEW CONDO. THERE WERE MANY MORE INCIDENTS TOO NUMEROUS TO MENTION.
SOME SEEMED TO BENEFIT FROM THE CONDO CURSE. TRIPPY'S OWNER WAS ONE OF THE FEW WHO DECIDED TO MOVE INTO THE TOWER.
WHY DOESN'T SHE EVER WALK HER DOG?
BUT IN A SENSE EVERYONE ELSE MOVED IN TOO... THOSE THAT HAVEN'T YET, WILL SOON. AND THEY WILL FORGET WHAT THE BLOCK LOOKED LIKE BEFORE THE TOWER...
HI VIEW
FROM 555 ↑ 5555
976 SQ FT
AFFORDABLE LUXURY
GEOGRAPHICAL AMNESIA WILL SUTURE THE FRAGMENTED SPATIAL MEMORY. THE SCAR TISSUE TRANSFORMED INTO NEW FLESH.
HOSPITAL
PSYCH WARD
9th floor
PSYCHIATRY TODAY
THE DOCTORS HAD LOTS OF THEORIES EXPLAINING LILLI'S SUDDEN DERANGEMENT. BIPOLAR DISORDER, HASHIMOTO'S DISEASE, MÜNCHHAUSEN SYNDROME. THE LIST WENT ON.
BUT THEY DIDN'T SEE THE CONDOMINIUM... AFTER DAYS OF FUTILE PSYCHIATRIC OBSERVATION, LILLI WAS ABOUT TO BE DISCHARGED.
THE CITY OUTSIDE WAS DOTTED WITH NEW CONDO CONSTRUCTION. HER EYES TOLD ME THAT THIS ROOM WAS GOING TO BE HER HOME FOR A LONG TIME...
I WAS TEMPTED TO JOIN HER.

YOU CAN RECOGNIZE THE MOMENT ALMOST INSTANTLY. THOSE ALREADY ASLEEP ARE JARRED AWAKE.

WHAT YOU NOTICE IS THE LACK OF SOUND. THE CONSTANT DIN OF CIVILIZATION HAS GROUND TO A HALT. EVEN THE FRIDGE STOPPED PURRING REASSURINGLY. IS THIS JUST A NORMAL FLUCTUATION OF THE POWER GRID?

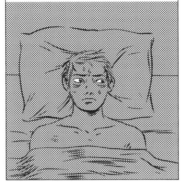

THEN YOU NOTICE THE INSECTS. SCREECHING SWARMS... OBLIVIOUS TO YOUR PRESENCE. HOW MANY ARE THERE? THEY WERE HERE BEFORE MANKIND. THEY WILL STILL BE HERE AFTER HUMANS GO EXTINCT.

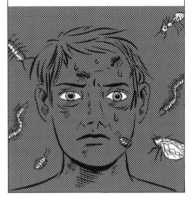

THE CARDIOVASCULAR SYSTEM RESPONDS. BLOOD RUSHES THROUGH THE VEINS WITH DEADENING VIOLENCE ACTIVATING OBSCURE GLANDS AND LONG FORGOTTEN SENSORY ORGANS.

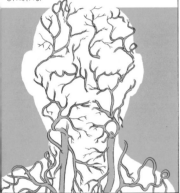

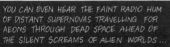

WHITE NOISE

THE IMPERCEPTIBLE TECTONIC DRIFT COMES INTO SHARP RELIEF... CONTINENTAL SHELVES CRASH INTO EACH OTHER... ANCIENT REMAINS SHIFT UNEASILY BENEATH EARTH'S CRUST...

GRIND

YOU CAN EVEN HEAR THE FAINT RADIO HUM OF DISTANT SUPERNOVAS TRAVELLING FOR AEONS THROUGH DEAD SPACE AHEAD OF THE SILENT SCREAMS OF ALIEN WORLDS...

ENGULFED IN COUNTLESS SOLAR HOLOCAUSTS...

CLACK

WHHHRRR

clyde

WHHHRRRRr

ZZZZz

100, 000 Miles

10, 000 Miles

PHASE TRANSITION

First appearance: *MOME 10,* 2008

1,000 Miles

100 Miles

1 Miles

1,000,000,000 BC   1,000,000 BC   500,000 BC   40,000 B

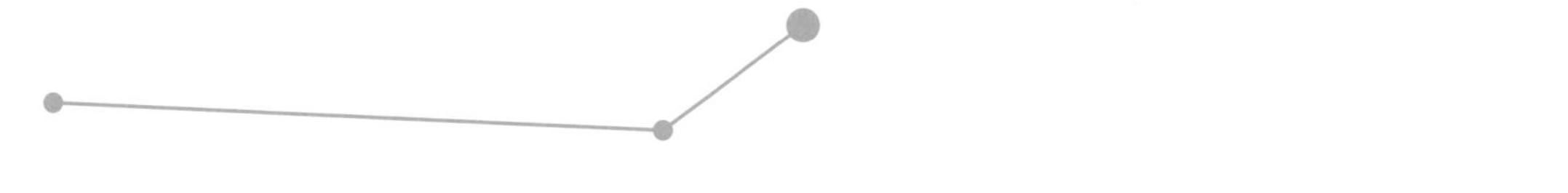

TIME
2000 AD
10, 000 AD

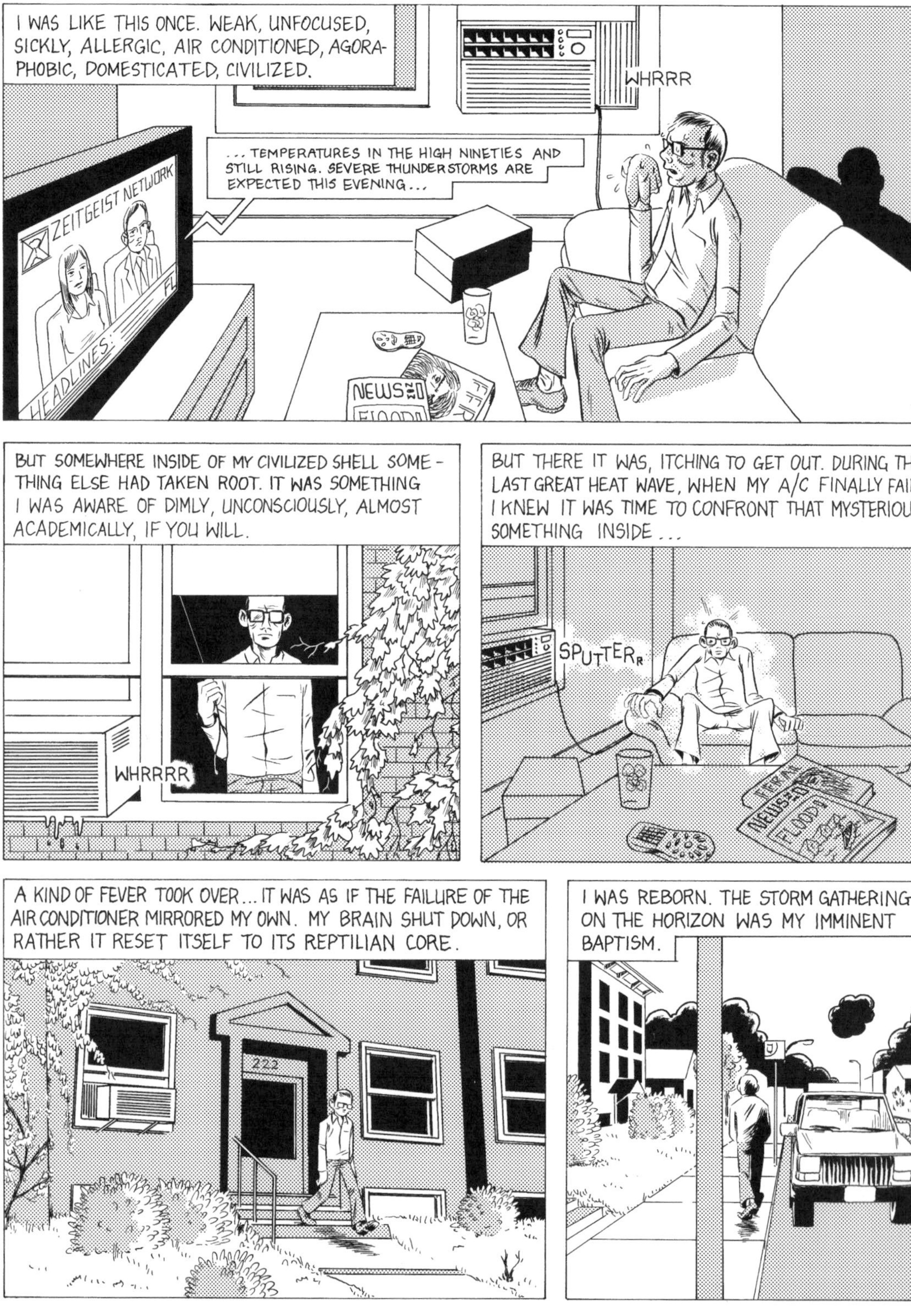
I WAS LIKE THIS ONCE. WEAK, UNFOCUSED, SICKLY, ALLERGIC, AIR CONDITIONED, AGORA-PHOBIC, DOMESTICATED, CIVILIZED.
WHRRR
ZEITGEIST NETWORK
HEADLINES:
...TEMPERATURES IN THE HIGH NINETIES AND STILL RISING. SEVERE THUNDERSTORMS ARE EXPECTED THIS EVENING...
NEWS
BUT SOMEWHERE INSIDE OF MY CIVILIZED SHELL SOME-THING ELSE HAD TAKEN ROOT. IT WAS SOMETHING I WAS AWARE OF DIMLY, UNCONSCIOUSLY, ALMOST ACADEMICALLY, IF YOU WILL.
WHRRRR
BUT THERE IT WAS, ITCHING TO GET OUT. DURING THE LAST GREAT HEAT WAVE, WHEN MY A/C FINALLY FAILED, I KNEW IT WAS TIME TO CONFRONT THAT MYSTERIOUS SOMETHING INSIDE...
SPUTTERR
FERAL
NEWS
FLOOD!
A KIND OF FEVER TOOK OVER... IT WAS AS IF THE FAILURE OF THE AIR CONDITIONER MIRRORED MY OWN. MY BRAIN SHUT DOWN, OR RATHER IT RESET ITSELF TO ITS REPTILIAN CORE.
222
I WAS REBORN. THE STORM GATHERING ON THE HORIZON WAS MY IMMINENT BAPTISM.

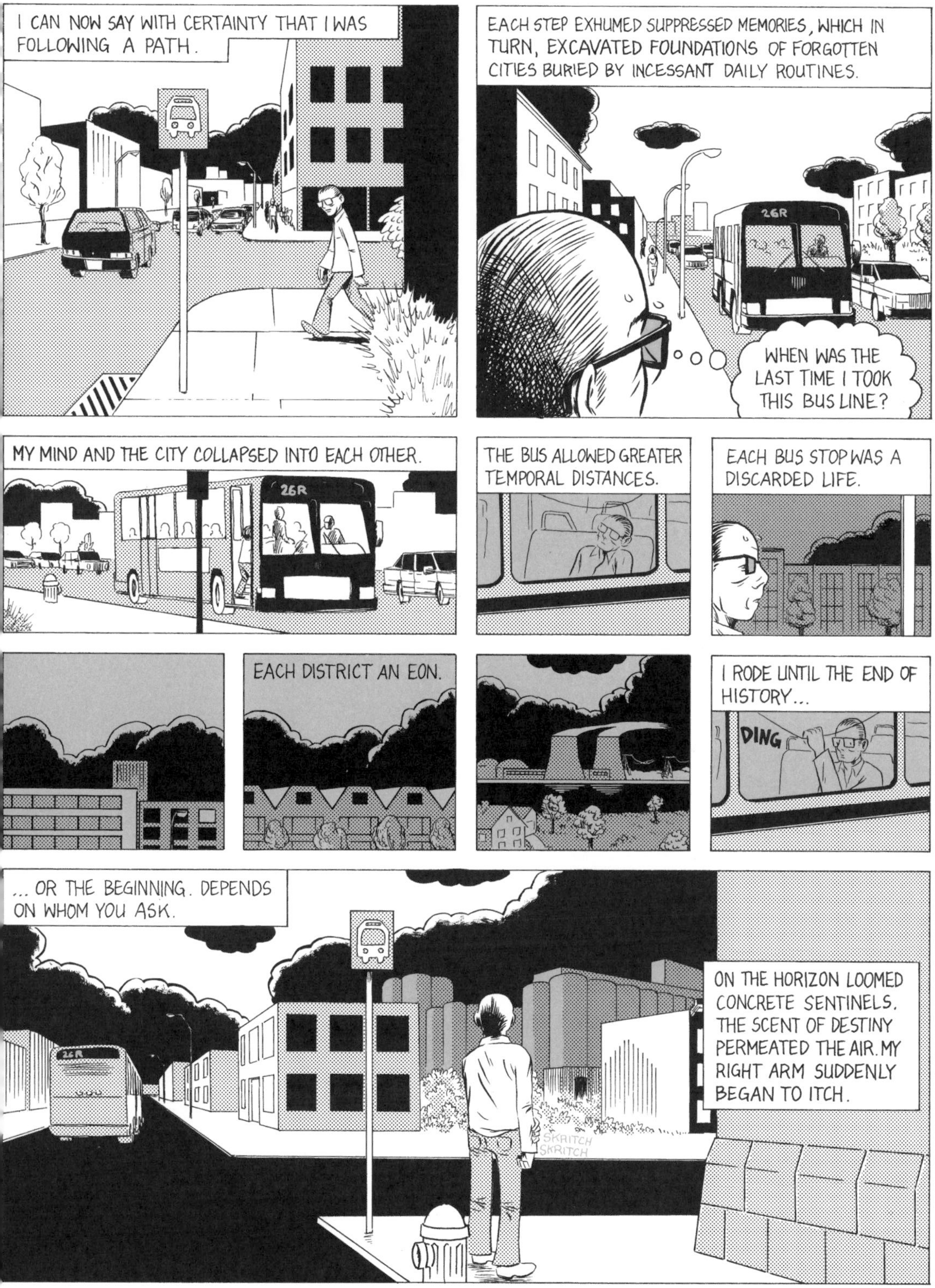
I CAN NOW SAY WITH CERTAINTY THAT I WAS FOLLOWING A PATH.
EACH STEP EXHUMED SUPPRESSED MEMORIES, WHICH IN TURN, EXCAVATED FOUNDATIONS OF FORGOTTEN CITIES BURIED BY INCESSANT DAILY ROUTINES.
26R
WHEN WAS THE LAST TIME I TOOK THIS BUS LINE?
MY MIND AND THE CITY COLLAPSED INTO EACH OTHER.
26R
THE BUS ALLOWED GREATER TEMPORAL DISTANCES.
EACH BUS STOP WAS A DISCARDED LIFE.
EACH DISTRICT AN EON.
I RODE UNTIL THE END OF HISTORY...
DING
... OR THE BEGINNING. DEPENDS ON WHOM YOU ASK.
26R
ON THE HORIZON LOOMED CONCRETE SENTINELS. THE SCENT OF DESTINY PERMEATED THE AIR. MY RIGHT ARM SUDDENLY BEGAN TO ITCH.
SKRITCH
SKRITCH

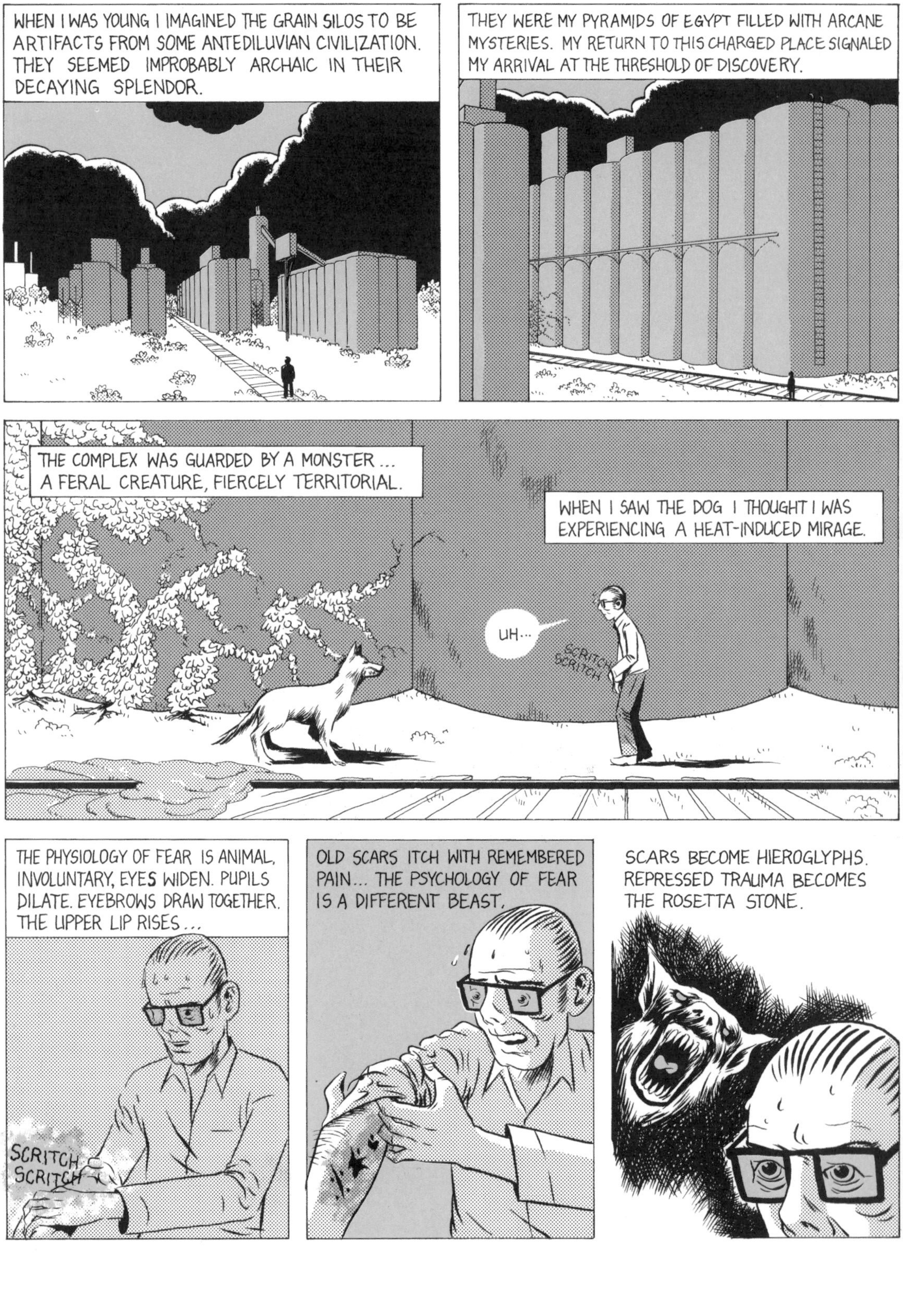
WHEN I WAS YOUNG I IMAGINED THE GRAIN SILOS TO BE ARTIFACTS FROM SOME ANTEDILUVIAN CIVILIZATION. THEY SEEMED IMPROBABLY ARCHAIC IN THEIR DECAYING SPLENDOR.
THEY WERE MY PYRAMIDS OF EGYPT FILLED WITH ARCANE MYSTERIES. MY RETURN TO THIS CHARGED PLACE SIGNALED MY ARRIVAL AT THE THRESHOLD OF DISCOVERY.
THE COMPLEX WAS GUARDED BY A MONSTER... A FERAL CREATURE, FIERCELY TERRITORIAL.
WHEN I SAW THE DOG I THOUGHT I WAS EXPERIENCING A HEAT-INDUCED MIRAGE.
UH...
SCRITCH SCRITCH
THE PHYSIOLOGY OF FEAR IS ANIMAL, INVOLUNTARY, EYES WIDEN. PUPILS DILATE. EYEBROWS DRAW TOGETHER. THE UPPER LIP RISES...
SCRITCH SCRITCH
OLD SCARS ITCH WITH REMEMBERED PAIN... THE PSYCHOLOGY OF FEAR IS A DIFFERENT BEAST.
SCARS BECOME HIEROGLYPHS. REPRESSED TRAUMA BECOMES THE ROSETTA STONE.

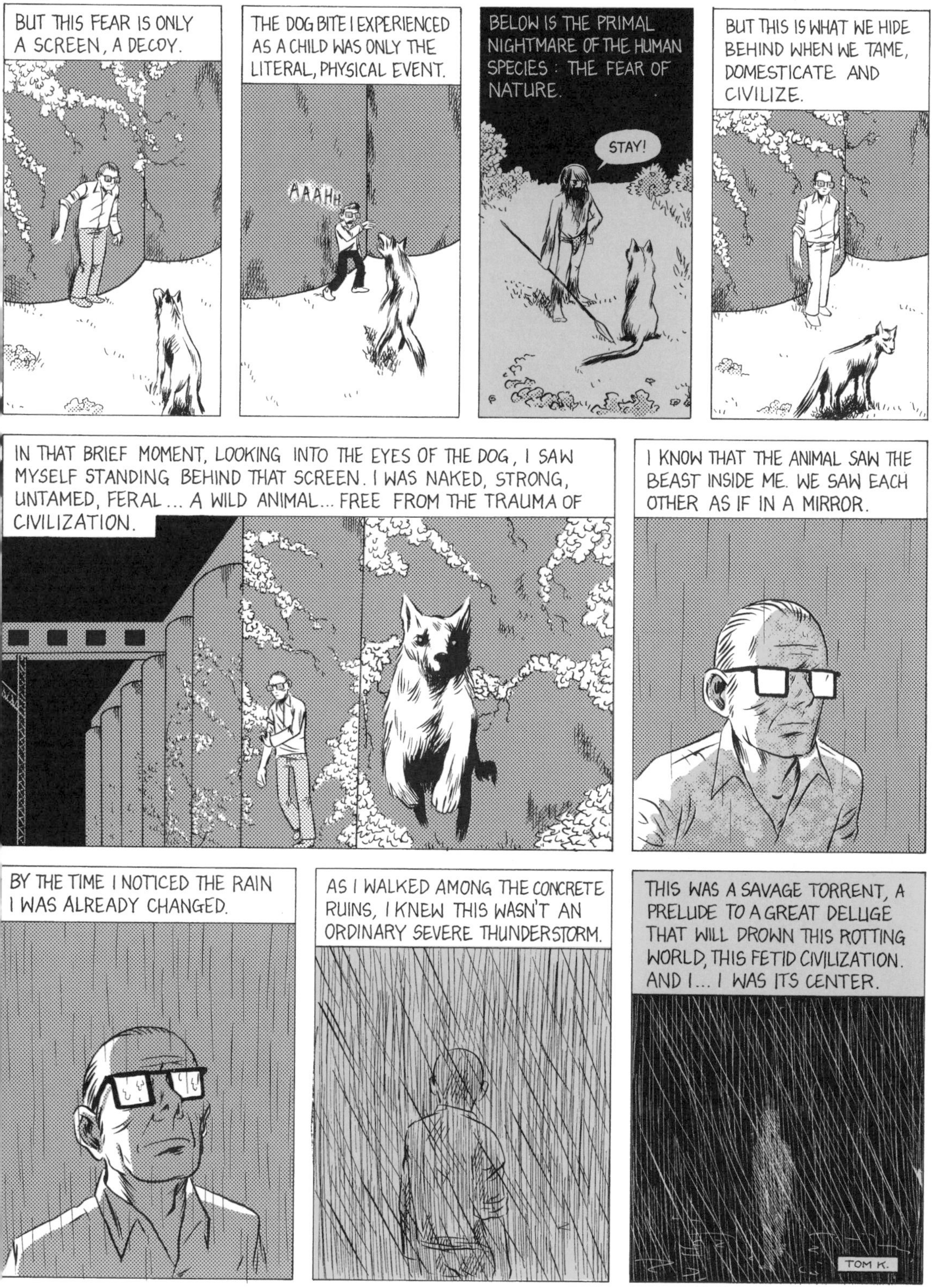
BUT THIS FEAR IS ONLY A SCREEN, A DECOY.
THE DOG BITE I EXPERIENCED AS A CHILD WAS ONLY THE LITERAL, PHYSICAL EVENT.
AAAHH
BELOW IS THE PRIMAL NIGHTMARE OF THE HUMAN SPECIES: THE FEAR OF NATURE.
STAY!
BUT THIS IS WHAT WE HIDE BEHIND WHEN WE TAME, DOMESTICATE AND CIVILIZE.
IN THAT BRIEF MOMENT, LOOKING INTO THE EYES OF THE DOG, I SAW MYSELF STANDING BEHIND THAT SCREEN. I WAS NAKED, STRONG, UNTAMED, FERAL... A WILD ANIMAL... FREE FROM THE TRAUMA OF CIVILIZATION.
I KNOW THAT THE ANIMAL SAW THE BEAST INSIDE ME. WE SAW EACH OTHER AS IF IN A MIRROR.
BY THE TIME I NOTICED THE RAIN I WAS ALREADY CHANGED.
AS I WALKED AMONG THE CONCRETE RUINS, I KNEW THIS WASN'T AN ORDINARY SEVERE THUNDERSTORM.
THIS WAS A SAVAGE TORRENT, A PRELUDE TO A GREAT DELUGE THAT WILL DROWN THIS ROTTING WORLD, THIS FETID CIVILIZATION. AND I... I WAS ITS CENTER.
TOM K.

NOISE a history

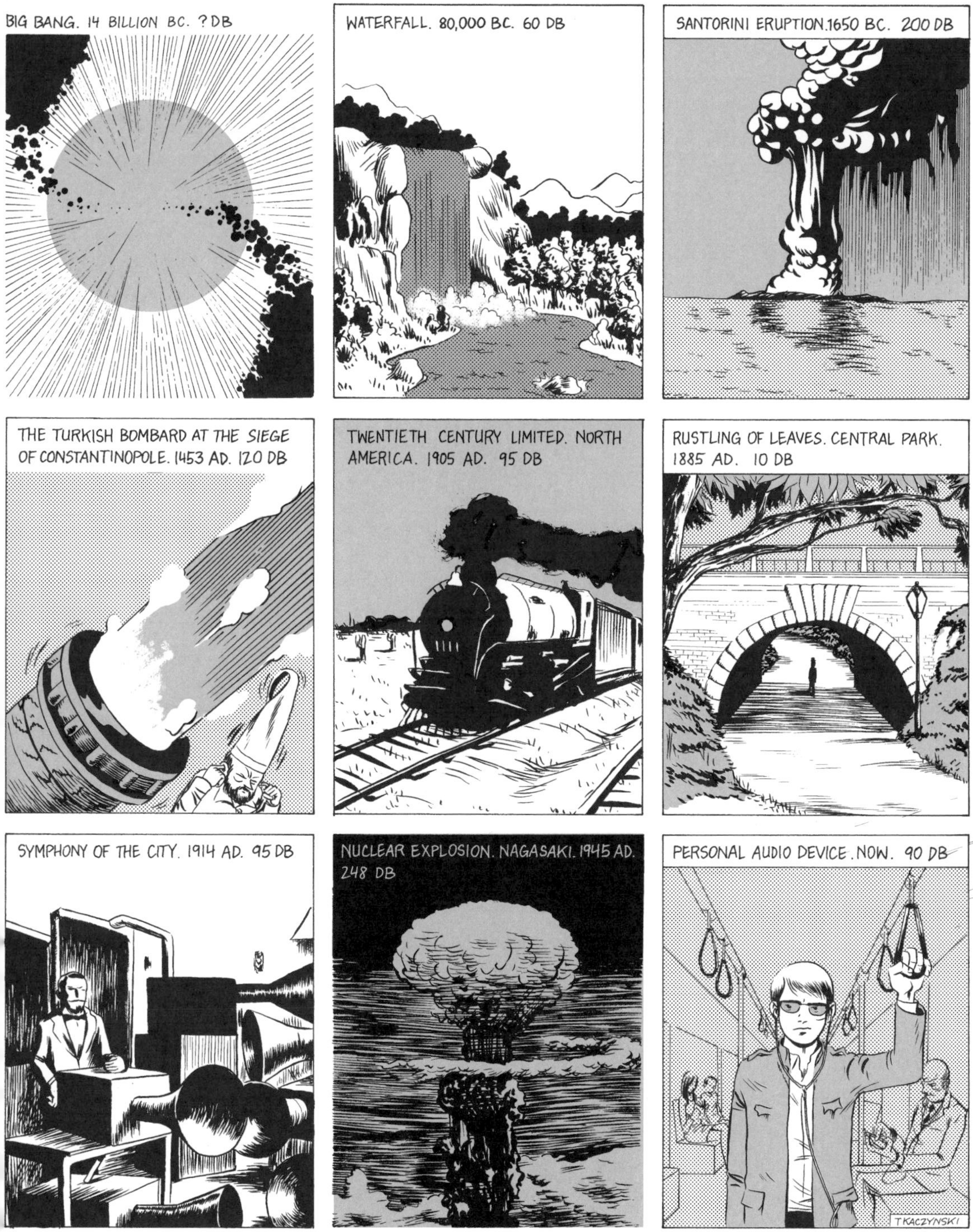
BIG BANG. 14 BILLION BC. ? DB
WATERFALL. 80,000 BC. 60 DB
SANTORINI ERUPTION. 1650 BC. 200 DB
THE TURKISH BOMBARD AT THE SIEGE OF CONSTANTINOPOLE. 1453 AD. 120 DB
TWENTIETH CENTURY LIMITED. NORTH AMERICA. 1905 AD. 95 DB
RUSTLING OF LEAVES. CENTRAL PARK. 1885 AD. 10 DB
SYMPHONY OF THE CITY. 1914 AD. 95 DB
NUCLEAR EXPLOSION. NAGASAKI. 1945 AD. 248 DB
PERSONAL AUDIO DEVICE. NOW. 90 DB
TKACZYNSKI

MILLION YEAR BOOM

First appearance: *MOME 11*, 2008
Reprinted in *Best American Nonrequired Reading 2009*

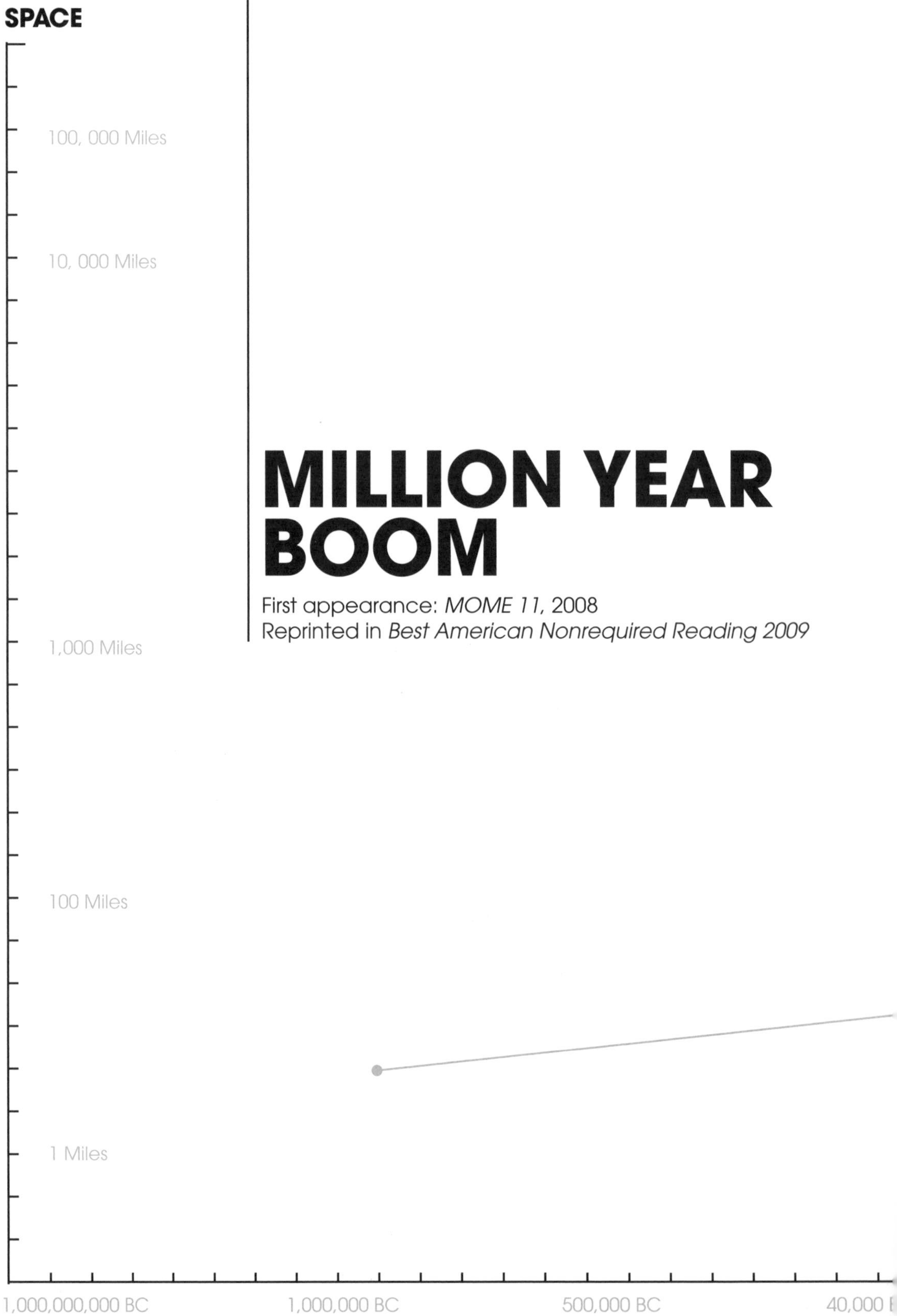

SPACE
100, 000 Miles
10, 000 Miles
1,000 Miles
100 Miles
1 Miles
1,000,000,000 BC
1,000,000 BC
500,000 BC
40,000

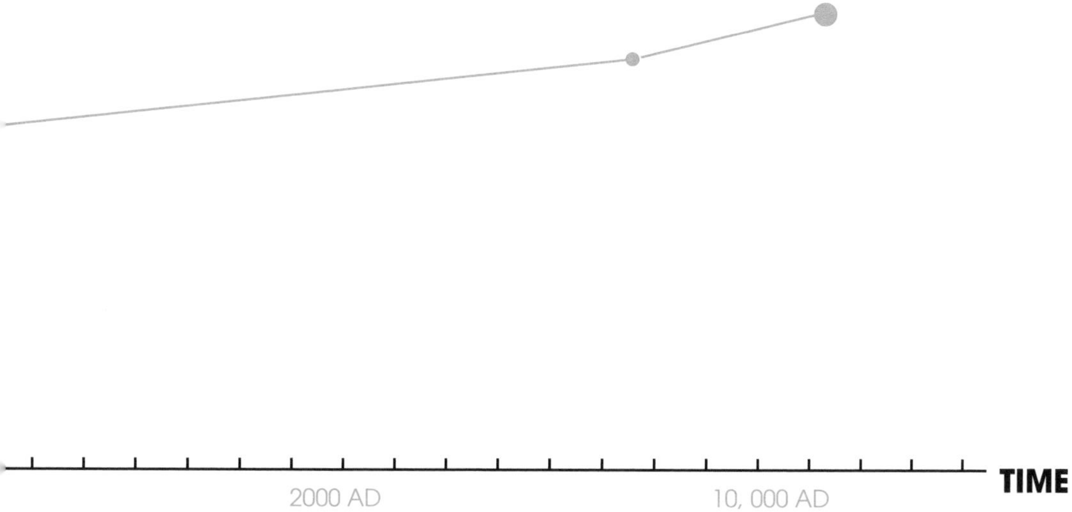

TIME
2000 AD
10, 000 AD

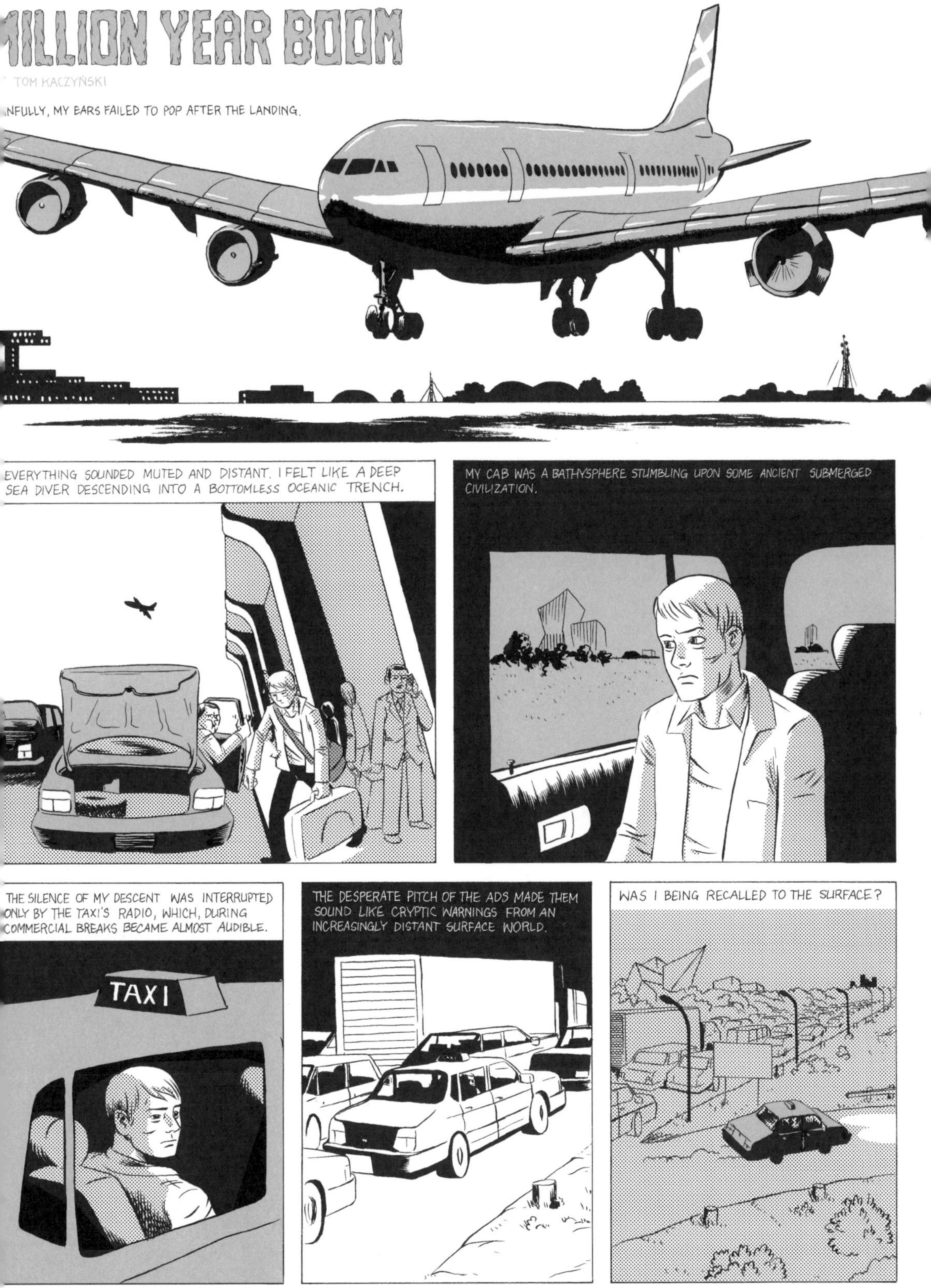

ILLION YEAR BOOM
TOM KACZYŃSKI
NFULLY, MY EARS FAILED TO POP AFTER THE LANDING.
EVERYTHING SOUNDED MUTED AND DISTANT. I FELT LIKE A DEEP SEA DIVER DESCENDING INTO A BOTTOMLESS OCEANIC TRENCH.
MY CAB WAS A BATHYSPHERE STUMBLING UPON SOME ANCIENT SUBMERGED CIVILIZATION.
THE SILENCE OF MY DESCENT WAS INTERRUPTED ONLY BY THE TAXI'S RADIO, WHICH, DURING COMMERCIAL BREAKS BECAME ALMOST AUDIBLE.
TAXI
THE DESPERATE PITCH OF THE ADS MADE THEM SOUND LIKE CRYPTIC WARNINGS FROM AN INCREASINGLY DISTANT SURFACE WORLD.
WAS I BEING RECALLED TO THE SURFACE?

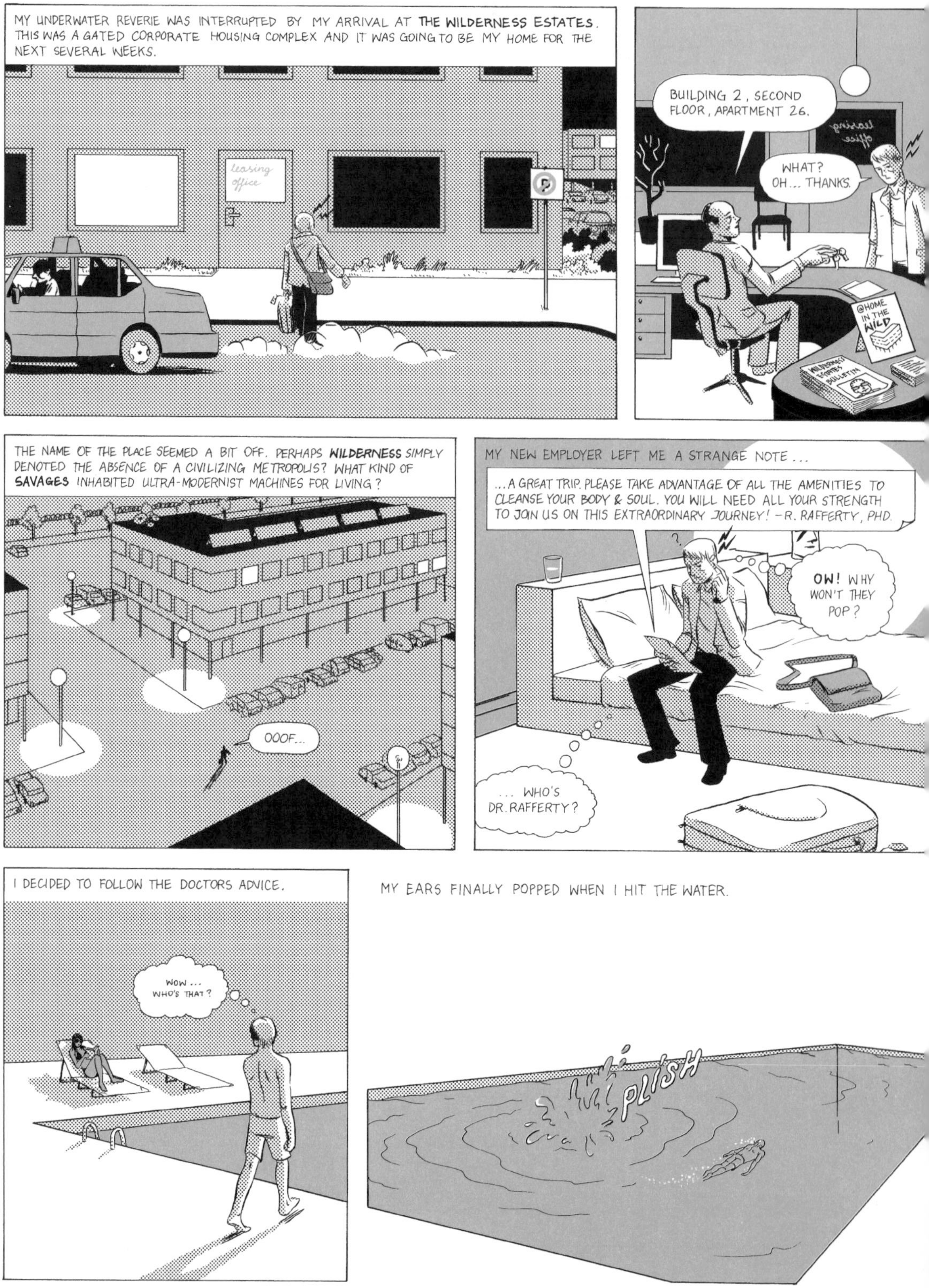
MY UNDERWATER REVERIE WAS INTERRUPTED BY MY ARRIVAL AT THE WILDERNESS ESTATES. THIS WAS A GATED CORPORATE HOUSING COMPLEX AND IT WAS GOING TO BE MY HOME FOR THE NEXT SEVERAL WEEKS.
leasing office
BUILDING 2, SECOND FLOOR, APARTMENT 26.
WHAT? OH... THANKS.
@HOME IN THE WILD
WILDERNESS ESTATES BULLETIN
THE NAME OF THE PLACE SEEMED A BIT OFF. PERHAPS WILDERNESS SIMPLY DENOTED THE ABSENCE OF A CIVILIZING METROPOLIS? WHAT KIND OF SAVAGES INHABITED ULTRA-MODERNIST MACHINES FOR LIVING?
OOOF...
MY NEW EMPLOYER LEFT ME A STRANGE NOTE...
...A GREAT TRIP. PLEASE TAKE ADVANTAGE OF ALL THE AMENITIES TO CLEANSE YOUR BODY & SOUL. YOU WILL NEED ALL YOUR STRENGTH TO JOIN US ON THIS EXTRAORDINARY JOURNEY! –R. RAFFERTY, PHD.
?
OW! WHY WON'T THEY POP?
... WHO'S DR. RAFFERTY?
I DECIDED TO FOLLOW THE DOCTORS ADVICE.
WOW... WHO'S THAT?
MY EARS FINALLY POPPED WHEN I HIT THE WATER.
PLISH

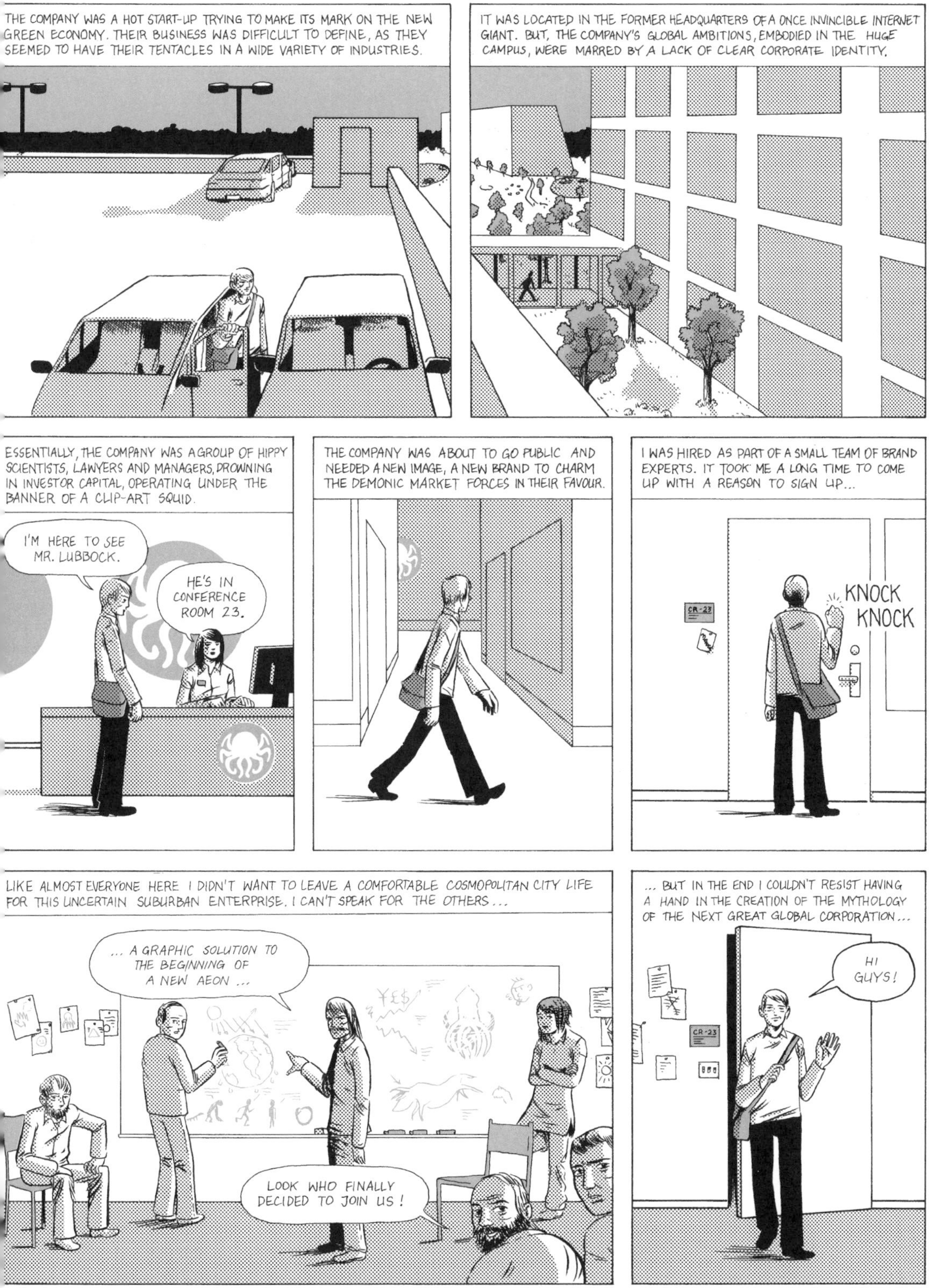
THE COMPANY WAS A HOT START-UP TRYING TO MAKE ITS MARK ON THE NEW GREEN ECONOMY. THEIR BUSINESS WAS DIFFICULT TO DEFINE, AS THEY SEEMED TO HAVE THEIR TENTACLES IN A WIDE VARIETY OF INDUSTRIES.
IT WAS LOCATED IN THE FORMER HEADQUARTERS OF A ONCE INVINCIBLE INTERNET GIANT. BUT, THE COMPANY'S GLOBAL AMBITIONS, EMBODIED IN THE HUGE CAMPUS, WERE MARRED BY A LACK OF CLEAR CORPORATE IDENTITY.
ESSENTIALLY, THE COMPANY WAS A GROUP OF HIPPY SCIENTISTS, LAWYERS AND MANAGERS, DROWNING IN INVESTOR CAPITAL, OPERATING UNDER THE BANNER OF A CLIP-ART SQUID.
I'M HERE TO SEE MR. LUBBOCK.
HE'S IN CONFERENCE ROOM 23.
THE COMPANY WAS ABOUT TO GO PUBLIC AND NEEDED A NEW IMAGE, A NEW BRAND TO CHARM THE DEMONIC MARKET FORCES IN THEIR FAVOUR.
I WAS HIRED AS PART OF A SMALL TEAM OF BRAND EXPERTS. IT TOOK ME A LONG TIME TO COME UP WITH A REASON TO SIGN UP...
CR-23
KNOCK KNOCK
LIKE ALMOST EVERYONE HERE I DIDN'T WANT TO LEAVE A COMFORTABLE COSMOPOLITAN CITY LIFE FOR THIS UNCERTAIN SUBURBAN ENTERPRISE. I CAN'T SPEAK FOR THE OTHERS...
... A GRAPHIC SOLUTION TO THE BEGINNING OF A NEW AEON ...
LOOK WHO FINALLY DECIDED TO JOIN US!
... BUT IN THE END I COULDN'T RESIST HAVING A HAND IN THE CREATION OF THE MYTHOLOGY OF THE NEXT GREAT GLOBAL CORPORATION...
CR-23
HI GUYS!

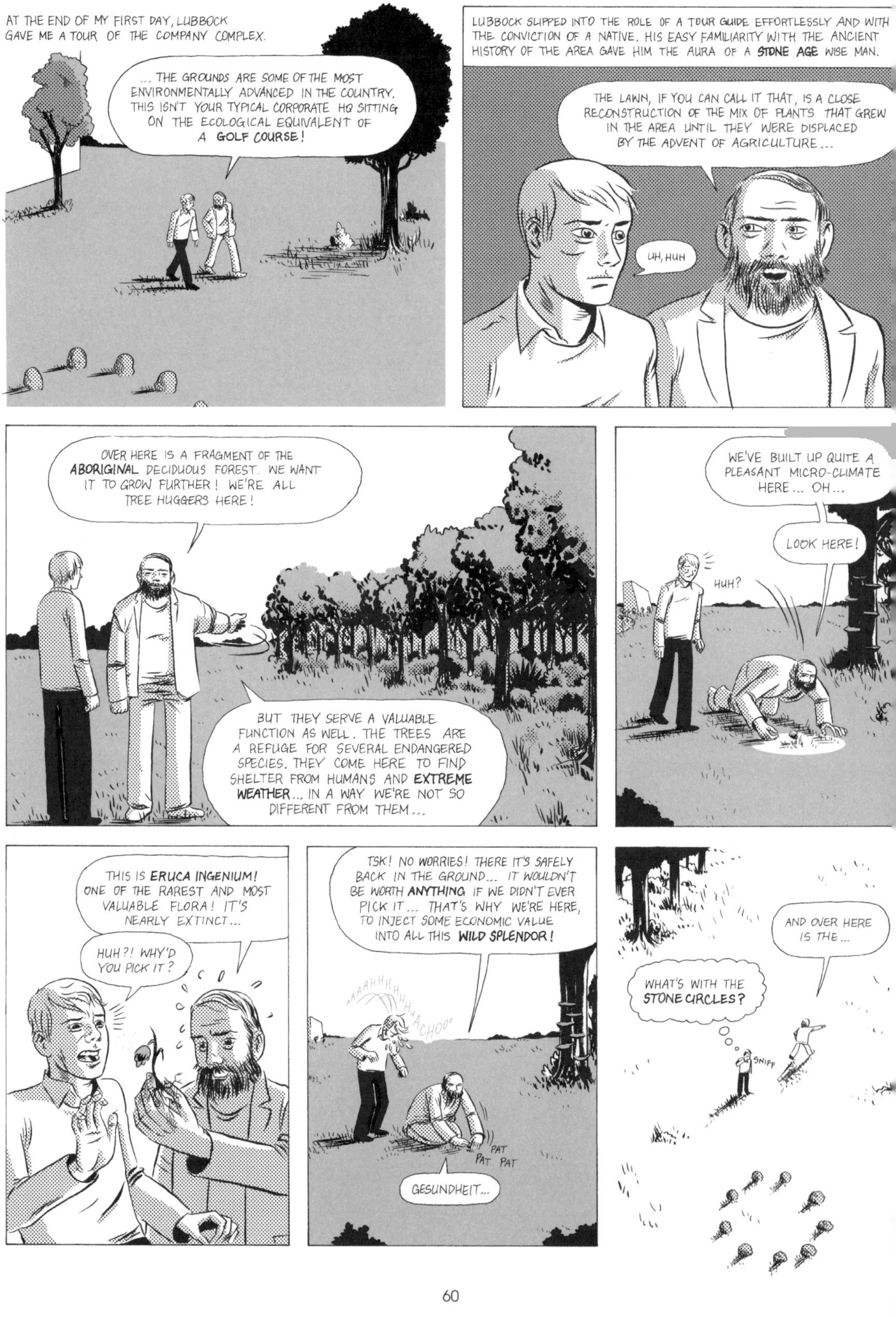

AT THE END OF MY FIRST DAY, LUBBOCK GAVE ME A TOUR OF THE COMPANY COMPLEX.
... THE GROUNDS ARE SOME OF THE MOST ENVIRONMENTALLY ADVANCED IN THE COUNTRY. THIS ISN'T YOUR TYPICAL CORPORATE HQ SITTING ON THE ECOLOGICAL EQUIVALENT OF A GOLF COURSE!
LUBBOCK SLIPPED INTO THE ROLE OF A TOUR GUIDE EFFORTLESSLY AND WITH THE CONVICTION OF A NATIVE. HIS EASY FAMILIARITY WITH THE ANCIENT HISTORY OF THE AREA GAVE HIM THE AURA OF A STONE AGE WISE MAN.
THE LAWN, IF YOU CAN CALL IT THAT, IS A CLOSE RECONSTRUCTION OF THE MIX OF PLANTS THAT GREW IN THE AREA UNTIL THEY WERE DISPLACED BY THE ADVENT OF AGRICULTURE...
UH, HUH
OVER HERE IS A FRAGMENT OF THE ABORIGINAL DECIDUOUS FOREST. WE WANT IT TO GROW FURTHER! WE'RE ALL TREE HUGGERS HERE!
BUT THEY SERVE A VALUABLE FUNCTION AS WELL. THE TREES ARE A REFUGE FOR SEVERAL ENDANGERED SPECIES. THEY COME HERE TO FIND SHELTER FROM HUMANS AND EXTREME WEATHER... IN A WAY WE'RE NOT SO DIFFERENT FROM THEM...
WE'VE BUILT UP QUITE A PLEASANT MICRO-CLIMATE HERE... OH...
LOOK HERE!
HUH?
THIS IS ERUCA INGENIUM! ONE OF THE RAREST AND MOST VALUABLE FLORA! IT'S NEARLY EXTINCT...
HUH?! WHY'D YOU PICK IT?
TSK! NO WORRIES! THERE IT'S SAFELY BACK IN THE GROUND... IT WOULDN'T BE WORTH ANYTHING IF WE DIDN'T EVER PICK IT... THAT'S WHY WE'RE HERE, TO INJECT SOME ECONOMIC VALUE INTO ALL THIS WILD SPLENDOR!
AAAAHHHHHHACHOO
PAT PAT PAT
GESUNDHEIT...
AND OVER HERE IS THE...
WHAT'S WITH THE STONE CIRCLES?
SNIFF

THE PACE OF WORK WAS INTENSE. LATE NIGHTS AND WEEKEND WORK WERE STANDARD. THE ENORMITY OF THE COMPANY'S PROJECT BECAME QUICKLY APPARENT.

...SNIFF... WE NEED A SYMBOLIC CONTAINER THAT CAN HOLD BOTH... ARCHAIC HERITAGE AND...SNIFF... THE LIMITLESS POSSIBILITIES OF THE FUTURE...

UGH... I THINK I'M GETTING A COLD...

IN SHORT THE COMPANY WAS ATTEMPTING TO MAP THE ENTIRE PRODUCTIVITY OF THE PLANET'S BIOSPHERE INTO DOLLAR TERMS... EVENTUALLY THIS WOULD LEAD TO THE CREATION OF A NEW GLOBAL **BIO-CURRENCY**...

... SO EVEN A BLADE OF GRASS WOULD HAVE, SNIFF, **EXCHANGE VALUE**?

TO GET A MORE ACCURATE MEASURE OF THE PERFORMANCE OF THE GLOBAL BIO-ECONOMY, THE COMPANY WAS RETROACTIVELY PROJECTING CONTEMPORARY MARKET ECONOMICS INTO A MILLION YEARS OF PLANETARY HISTORY.

MY COLD IS GETTING WORSE.

SNIFF

KLACK KLACK

IT WAS ENOUGH TO MAKE ANYONE'S HEAD SPIN... AND I WAS ALREADY DIZZY FROM WHAT SEEMED LIKE A NASTY SINUS INFECTION.

SMOKE BREAK?

SNIFF... SURE!

... YOU HAVEN'T COME TO ANY OF THE SPECIAL CREATIVITY SESSIONS YET...

AAHHHCHOO

GESUNDHEIT

YOU OK?

YEAH... I JUST HAVE THIS PERPETUAL CONGESTION... IT'S PROBABLY JUST A COLD OR SOMETHING...

MHMM...

SNIFF

... I HAD SOMETHING SIMILAR WHEN I STARTED HERE... TURNED OUT TO BE A RARE ALLERGY CAUSED BY AN ENDANGERED PLANT... I GUESS IT'S HAPPENED TO OTHERS TOO...

REALLY?

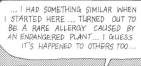

YEAH... YOU SHOULD SEE DOCTOR RAFFERTY ABOUT IT.

SNIFF, I DON'T LIKE DOCTORS... I'VE NEVER BEEN ALLERGIC TO ANYTHING BEFORE... BESIDES ISN'T HE A SHRINK?

I HADN'T MET DOCTOR RAFFERTY YET, BUT I NOTICED HOW HIS NAME WAS ALWAYS INVOKED WITH A HUSHED AWE...

YEAH HE'S A SHRINK... BUT HE'S ALSO MUCH MORE THAN THAT... GO SEE HIM.

I'M SURE I'LL GET BETTER SOON...

SNIFF

OVER THE NEXT FEW DAYS I WAS REMINDED OF MY INITIAL MISGIVINGS ABOUT LEAVING THE RELATIVE SAFETY OF THE BIG CITY.

UGH... THESE MEDS AREN'T HELPING MUCH... MAYBE THIS **IS** SOME KIND OF WEIRD ALLERGY ..?

SNIFF

THE CORPORATE HOUSING COMPLEX ACTED AS A KIND OF STERILE DEPRIVATION CHAMBER IN CONTRAST TO THE SENSORY RICHNESS OF THE ECOLOGICAL EDEN SURROUNDING THE COMPANY CAMPUS.

THAT LAMP GIVES ME THE CREEPS...

COLD & SINUS

THE COCKTAIL OF SUBURBAN ISOLATION AND **NON-DROWSY** COLD MEDICATION WAS DEADLY. I WAS SLOWLY GOING OUT OF MY MIND.

WHO WOULD EVER NAME THIS PLACE THE WILDERNESS ESTATES ...!?

CLICK CLICK CLICK

THE ONLY ANTIDOTE AGAINST CRUSHING BOREDOM WAS PHYSICAL EXERTION. I BECAME OBSESSED WITH SWIMMING.

I WOULD SWIM UNTIL COMPLETE EXHAUSTION... THEN, DRAINED I WOULD FLOAT, *SUSPENDED* PRECARIOUSLY IN THE MIDDLE OF A GENTLE TUG OF WAR BETWEEN GRAVITY AND WATER ... THE FAINT, CHEMICAL ODOR OF CHLORINE KEEPING MY CONGESTION AT BAY...

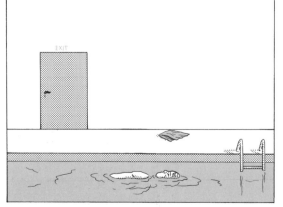

EXIT

MY ONLY SPECTATOR WAS A BEAUTIFUL WOMAN WHO REGARDED MY PRESENCE WITH THE KIND OF ATTENTION USUALLY RESERVED FOR DRIFTWOOD.

WHAT'S HER STORY ?

STILL SUFFERING?

SNIFF... YEAH... UM... I THINK YOU MIGHT BE RIGHT.

LISTEN, HERE'S WHAT RAFFERTY GAVE ME FOR THIS ALLERGY. I HAVE A COUPLE OF PILLS LEFT. YOU SHOULD TRY THEM.

BUT DON'T YOU NEED THEM?

I CAN ALWAYS GET MORE.

YOU WON'T REGRET IT! AND GO SEE THE DOCTOR!

THANKS

A COUPLE OF HOURS LATER THE MEDICATION KICKED IN. ALL SYMPTOMS VANISHED.

...ODD, MY FINGERS ARE TINGLING...

KLACK KLACK KLACK

MORE THAN THAT, ONCE THE SINUS HAZE CLEARED, MY BODY WENT INTO SENSORY OVERDRIVE.

I THINK I'M GETTING HIGH FROM THESE DRY ERASE MARKERS

SQUEEEEK

HA HA HA

SIMPLE ACTIVITIES LIKE EATING ACQUIRED NEW IMPORTANCE. I CHEWED WITH DETERMINATION.

TASTES LIKE SHIT... BUT I CAN TASTE IT...

CHEW CHEW

VMMMMM...

vmmmmm

PENETRATED THE STILL SURFACE OF THE POOL EAGER TO IMMERSE MYSELF IN THE COOL DEPTHS.

PLISH

MY LIMBS FLAILED WITH WILD ABANDON IN AN ATTEMPT TO AGITATE NOT ONLY THE STAGNANT WATER BUT ALSO MY INERT AUDIENCE.

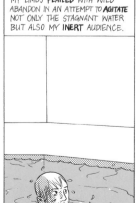

BUT SHE WAS UNMOVED BY MY PHYSICAL DISPLAYS. WHAT WOULD IT TAKE TO DISTURB HER UNBREAKABLE POISE?

I WOKE UP TIRED AND DRAINED. THE ALLERGY SYMPTOMS RETURNED.

I HAVE TO GET MORE OF THAT MEDICATION.

SNIFF

SCRITCH SCRITCH

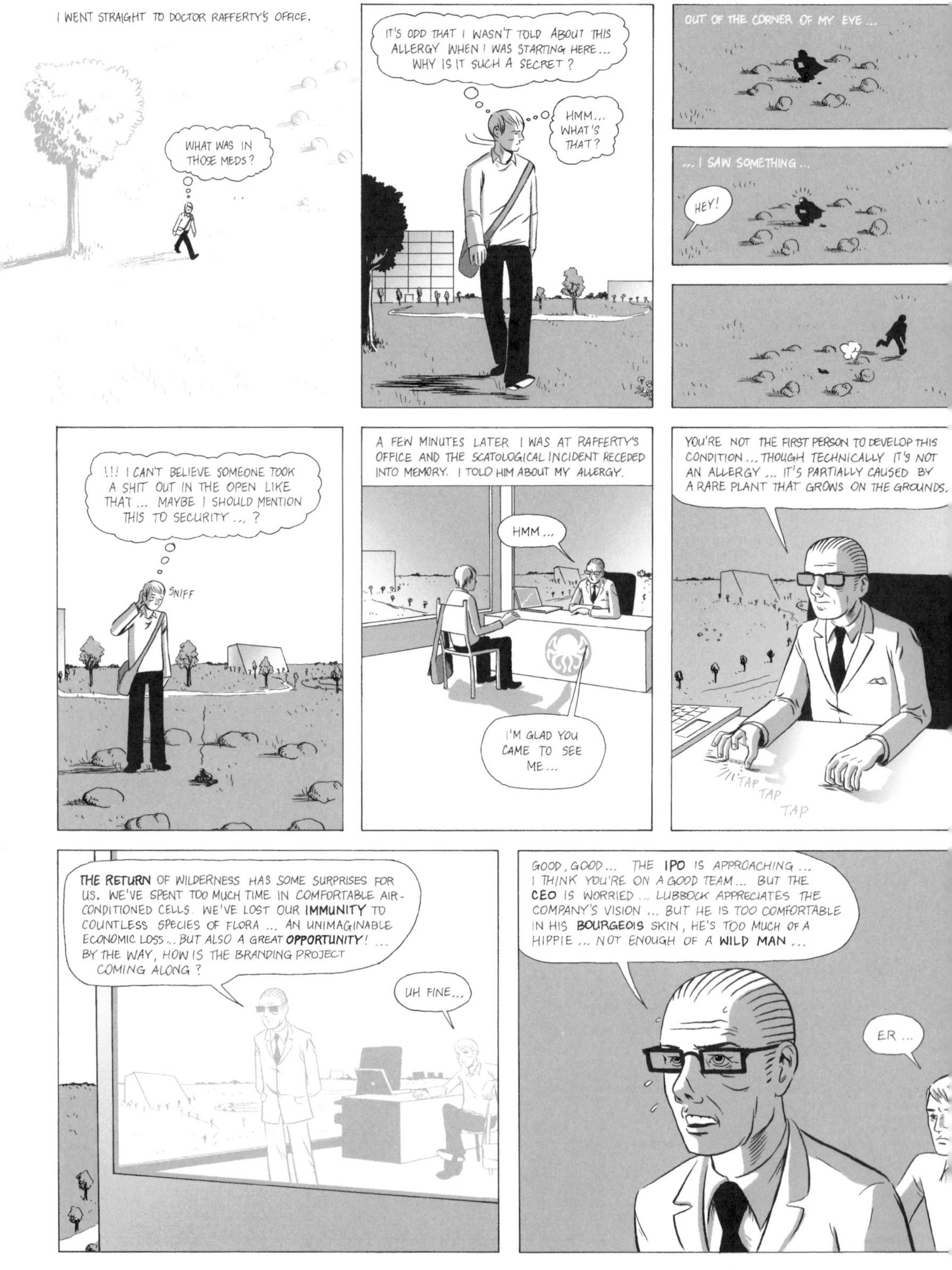
I WENT STRAIGHT TO DOCTOR RAFFERTY'S OFFICE.
WHAT WAS IN THOSE MEDS?
IT'S ODD THAT I WASN'T TOLD ABOUT THIS ALLERGY WHEN I WAS STARTING HERE... WHY IS IT SUCH A SECRET?
HMM... WHAT'S THAT?
OUT OF THE CORNER OF MY EYE...
... I SAW SOMETHING...
HEY!
!!! I CAN'T BELIEVE SOMEONE TOOK A SHIT OUT IN THE OPEN LIKE THAT... MAYBE I SHOULD MENTION THIS TO SECURITY...?
SNIFF
A FEW MINUTES LATER I WAS AT RAFFERTY'S OFFICE AND THE SCATOLOGICAL INCIDENT RECEDED INTO MEMORY. I TOLD HIM ABOUT MY ALLERGY.
HMM...
I'M GLAD YOU CAME TO SEE ME...
YOU'RE NOT THE FIRST PERSON TO DEVELOP THIS CONDITION... THOUGH TECHNICALLY IT'S NOT AN ALLERGY... IT'S PARTIALLY CAUSED BY A RARE PLANT THAT GROWS ON THE GROUNDS.
TAP TAP TAP
THE RETURN OF WILDERNESS HAS SOME SURPRISES FOR US. WE'VE SPENT TOO MUCH TIME IN COMFORTABLE AIR-CONDITIONED CELLS. WE'VE LOST OUR IMMUNITY TO COUNTLESS SPECIES OF FLORA... AN UNIMAGINABLE ECONOMIC LOSS... BUT ALSO A GREAT OPPORTUNITY! ... BY THE WAY, HOW IS THE BRANDING PROJECT COMING ALONG?
UH FINE...
GOOD, GOOD... THE IPO IS APPROACHING... I THINK YOU'RE ON A GOOD TEAM... BUT THE CEO IS WORRIED... LUBBOCK APPRECIATES THE COMPANY'S VISION... BUT HE IS TOO COMFORTABLE IN HIS BOURGEOIS SKIN, HE'S TOO MUCH OF A HIPPIE... NOT ENOUGH OF A WILD MAN...
ER...

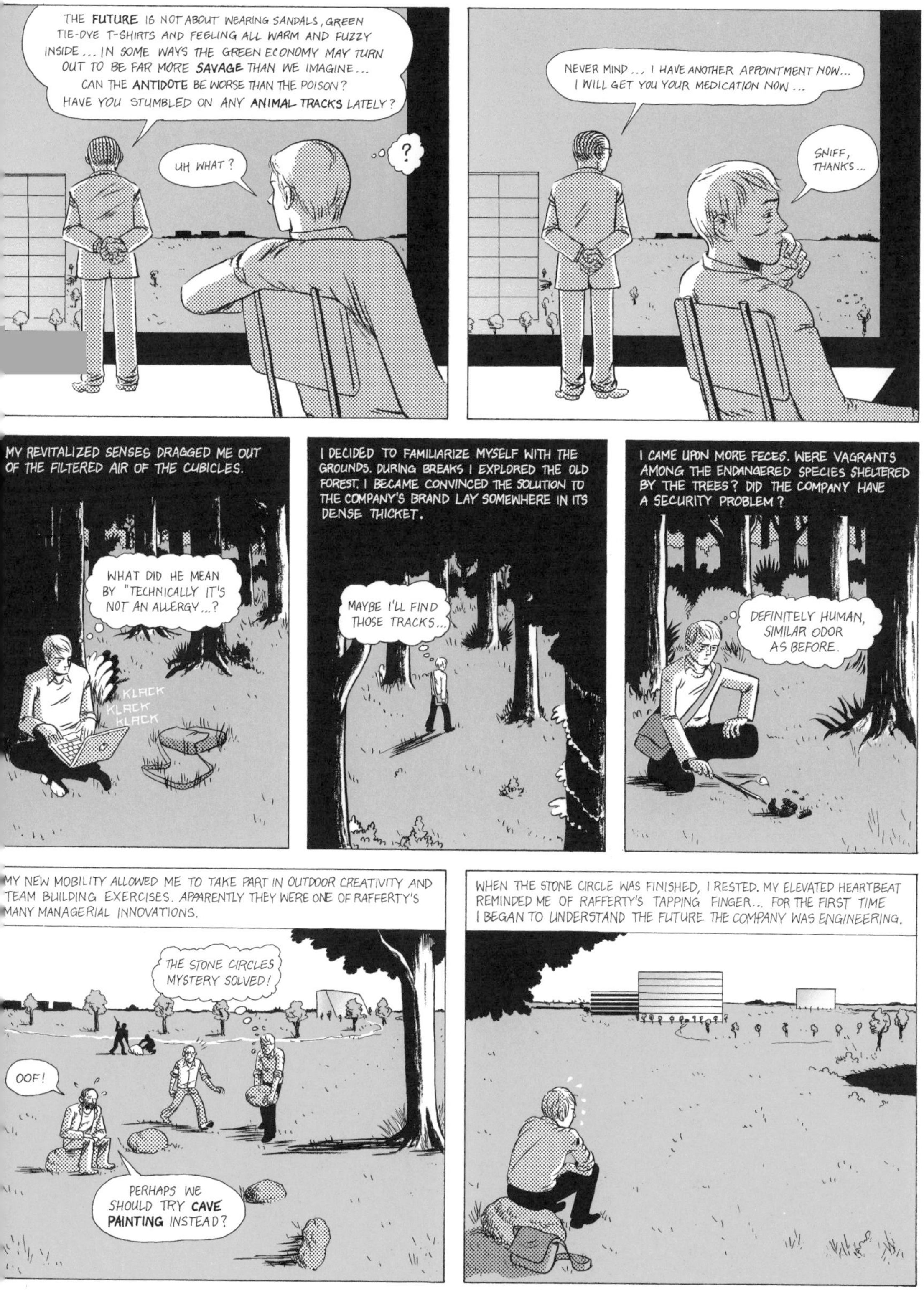
THE FUTURE IS NOT ABOUT WEARING SANDALS, GREEN TIE-DYE T-SHIRTS AND FEELING ALL WARM AND FUZZY INSIDE... IN SOME WAYS THE GREEN ECONOMY MAY TURN OUT TO BE FAR MORE SAVAGE THAN WE IMAGINE... CAN THE ANTIDOTE BE WORSE THAN THE POISON? HAVE YOU STUMBLED ON ANY ANIMAL TRACKS LATELY?
UH WHAT?
?
NEVER MIND... I HAVE ANOTHER APPOINTMENT NOW... I WILL GET YOU YOUR MEDICATION NOW...
SNIFF, THANKS...
MY REVITALIZED SENSES DRAGGED ME OUT OF THE FILTERED AIR OF THE CUBICLES.
WHAT DID HE MEAN BY "TECHNICALLY IT'S NOT AN ALLERGY..?
KLACK
KLACK
KLACK
I DECIDED TO FAMILIARIZE MYSELF WITH THE GROUNDS. DURING BREAKS I EXPLORED THE OLD FOREST. I BECAME CONVINCED THE SOLUTION TO THE COMPANY'S BRAND LAY SOMEWHERE IN ITS DENSE THICKET.
MAYBE I'LL FIND THOSE TRACKS...
I CAME UPON MORE FECES. WERE VAGRANTS AMONG THE ENDANGERED SPECIES SHELTERED BY THE TREES? DID THE COMPANY HAVE A SECURITY PROBLEM?
DEFINITELY HUMAN, SIMILAR ODOR AS BEFORE.
MY NEW MOBILITY ALLOWED ME TO TAKE PART IN OUTDOOR CREATIVITY AND TEAM BUILDING EXERCISES. APPARENTLY THEY WERE ONE OF RAFFERTY'S MANY MANAGERIAL INNOVATIONS.
THE STONE CIRCLES MYSTERY SOLVED!
OOF!
PERHAPS WE SHOULD TRY CAVE PAINTING INSTEAD?
WHEN THE STONE CIRCLE WAS FINISHED, I RESTED. MY ELEVATED HEARTBEAT REMINDED ME OF RAFFERTY'S TAPPING FINGER... FOR THE FIRST TIME I BEGAN TO UNDERSTAND THE FUTURE THE COMPANY WAS ENGINEERING.

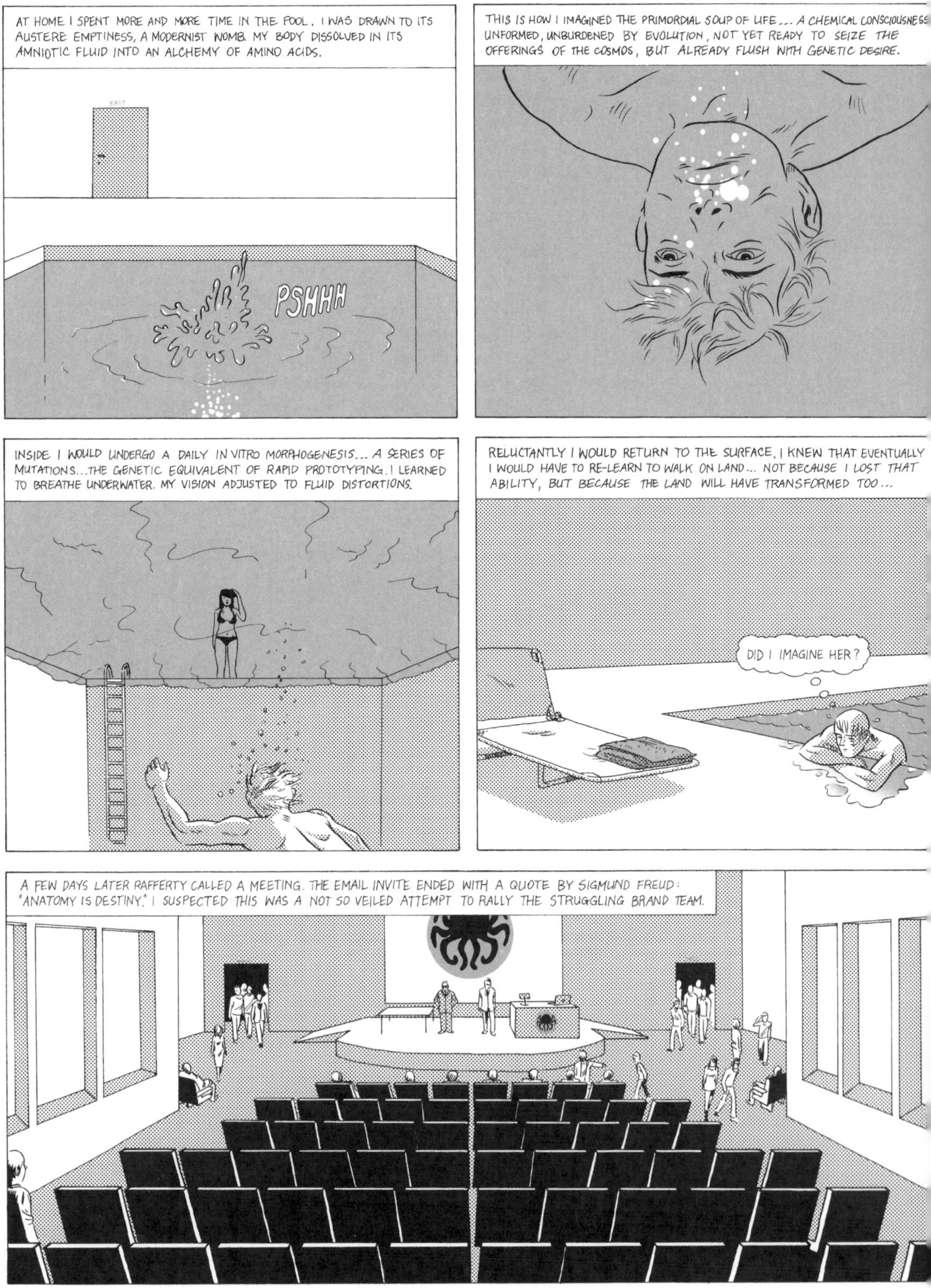
AT HOME I SPENT MORE AND MORE TIME IN THE POOL. I WAS DRAWN TO ITS AUSTERE EMPTINESS, A MODERNIST WOMB. MY BODY DISSOLVED IN ITS AMNIOTIC FLUID INTO AN ALCHEMY OF AMINO ACIDS.
EXIT
PSHHH
THIS IS HOW I IMAGINED THE PRIMORDIAL SOUP OF LIFE... A CHEMICAL CONSCIOUSNESS UNFORMED, UNBURDENED BY EVOLUTION, NOT YET READY TO SEIZE THE OFFERINGS OF THE COSMOS, BUT ALREADY FLUSH WITH GENETIC DESIRE.
INSIDE I WOULD UNDERGO A DAILY IN VITRO MORPHOGENESIS... A SERIES OF MUTATIONS...THE GENETIC EQUIVALENT OF RAPID PROTOTYPING. I LEARNED TO BREATHE UNDERWATER. MY VISION ADJUSTED TO FLUID DISTORTIONS.
RELUCTANTLY I WOULD RETURN TO THE SURFACE. I KNEW THAT EVENTUALLY I WOULD HAVE TO RE-LEARN TO WALK ON LAND... NOT BECAUSE I LOST THAT ABILITY, BUT BECAUSE THE LAND WILL HAVE TRANSFORMED TOO...
DID I IMAGINE HER?
A FEW DAYS LATER RAFFERTY CALLED A MEETING. THE EMAIL INVITE ENDED WITH A QUOTE BY SIGMUND FREUD: "ANATOMY IS DESTINY." I SUSPECTED THIS WAS A NOT SO VEILED ATTEMPT TO RALLY THE STRUGGLING BRAND TEAM.

THE DOCTOR TRANSFORMED ON STAGE...

SUCCESS. VISION. ENERGY. ASK YOURSELVES THIS: WHO ARE YOUR **ANCESTORS**? GENERAL ELECTRIC, FORD, IBM, APPLE, SONY, MICROSOFT GOOGLE? **NO!** YOUR ANCESTORS ARE THE **HUNTER-GATHERERS** OF THE PALEOLITHIC WHO INVENTED LANGUAGE, MUSIC AND ART!

THE AUDIENCE WAS MESMERIZED BY THE PERFORMANCE. I BECAME AWARE OF FAINT DRUMMING.

WE'RE ON THE VERGE OF THE GREATEST COMMERCIAL **OPPORTUNITY** IN HUMAN HISTORY. CARBON TRADE, BIO-FUELS, SOLAR ENERGY, THESE ARE ALL INSIGNIFICANT PUDDLES COMPARED TO THE VAST OCEANS OF **PROFITS** TO BE **EXTRACTED** FROM THIS PLANET...

WAS I HEARING A RECORDED SOUNDTRACK OR THE **THROBBING BLOOD** IN RAFFERTY'S VEINS?

THE COMING AGE OF CLIMATE DISASTERS WILL TEST THE INGENUITY OF THE SPECIES. WILL WE ACCEPT EXTINCTION LIKE THE NEADERTHALS?

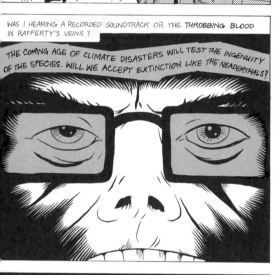

AT SOME POINT I STOPPED LISTENING. I ALREADY KNEW WHAT RAFFERTY WAS GOING TO SAY, I HEARD IT BEFORE... IN THE POOL... WHEN THE WATERS FLOODED MY EARS WITH **KNOWING WHISPERS**.

INVEST IN EVOLUTION REVERSE THE GENETIC CREDIT CRUNCH COMPOUND THE INTEREST OF BIODIVERSITY

...RE-WILD THE HUMAN MIND, GET PAST THIS **DOMESTICATED** CREATIVITY... NO MORE iPODS, iPHONES, iHUMANS ... WE NEED TO REINVENT **FIRE! IGNITE** YOUR **SAVAGE INTELLIGENCE** ... PREPARE FOR THE MILLION YEAR **PROFIT CYCLES**...

THE APPLAUSE RESEMBLED A **STAMPEDE** OF NORTH AMERICAN BISON. I ALMOST PEED MY PANTS.

CLAP CLAP CLAP CLAP CLAP CLAP CLAP CLAP CLAP CLAP CLAP CLAP CLAP CLAP CLAP CLAP! CLAP CLAP CLAP CLAP CLAP CLAP CLAP CLAP CLAP CLAP CLAP CLAP CLAP CLAP CLAP

YOU'RE WELCOME...

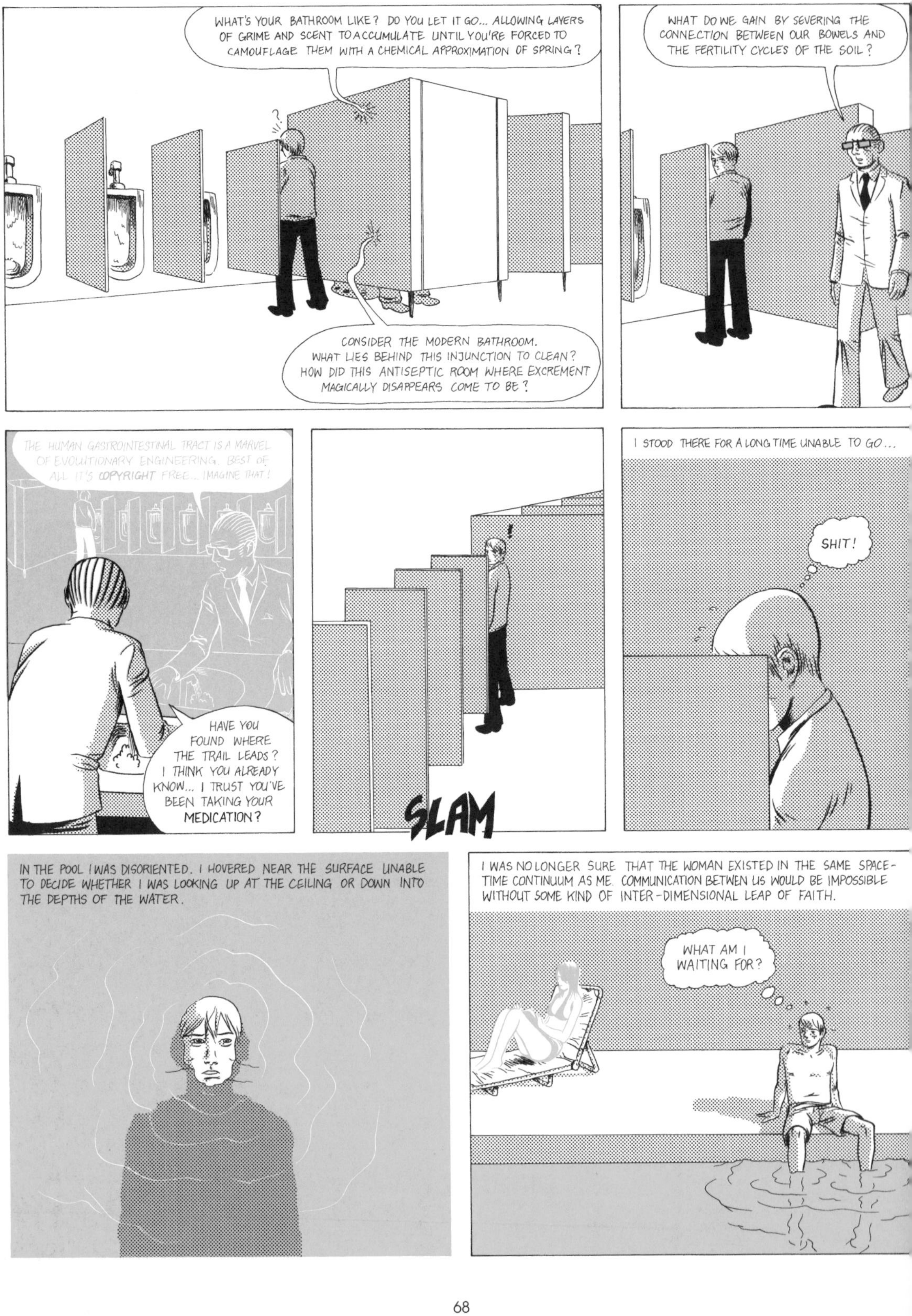
WHAT'S YOUR BATHROOM LIKE? DO YOU LET IT GO... ALLOWING LAYERS OF GRIME AND SCENT TO ACCUMULATE UNTIL YOU'RE FORCED TO CAMOUFLAGE THEM WITH A CHEMICAL APPROXIMATION OF SPRING?
?
CONSIDER THE MODERN BATHROOM. WHAT LIES BEHIND THIS INJUNCTION TO CLEAN? HOW DID THIS ANTISEPTIC ROOM WHERE EXCREMENT MAGICALLY DISAPPEARS COME TO BE?
WHAT DO WE GAIN BY SEVERING THE CONNECTION BETWEEN OUR BOWELS AND THE FERTILITY CYCLES OF THE SOIL?
THE HUMAN GASTROINTESTINAL TRACT IS A MARVEL OF EVOLUTIONARY ENGINEERING. BEST OF ALL IT'S COPYRIGHT FREE... IMAGINE THAT!
HAVE YOU FOUND WHERE THE TRAIL LEADS? I THINK YOU ALREADY KNOW... I TRUST YOU'VE BEEN TAKING YOUR MEDICATION?
!
SLAM
I STOOD THERE FOR A LONG TIME UNABLE TO GO...
SHIT!
IN THE POOL I WAS DISORIENTED. I HOVERED NEAR THE SURFACE UNABLE TO DECIDE WHETHER I WAS LOOKING UP AT THE CEILING OR DOWN INTO THE DEPTHS OF THE WATER.
I WAS NO LONGER SURE THAT THE WOMAN EXISTED IN THE SAME SPACE-TIME CONTINUUM AS ME. COMMUNICATION BETWEN US WOULD BE IMPOSSIBLE WITHOUT SOME KIND OF INTER-DIMENSIONAL LEAP OF FAITH.
WHAT AM I WAITING FOR?

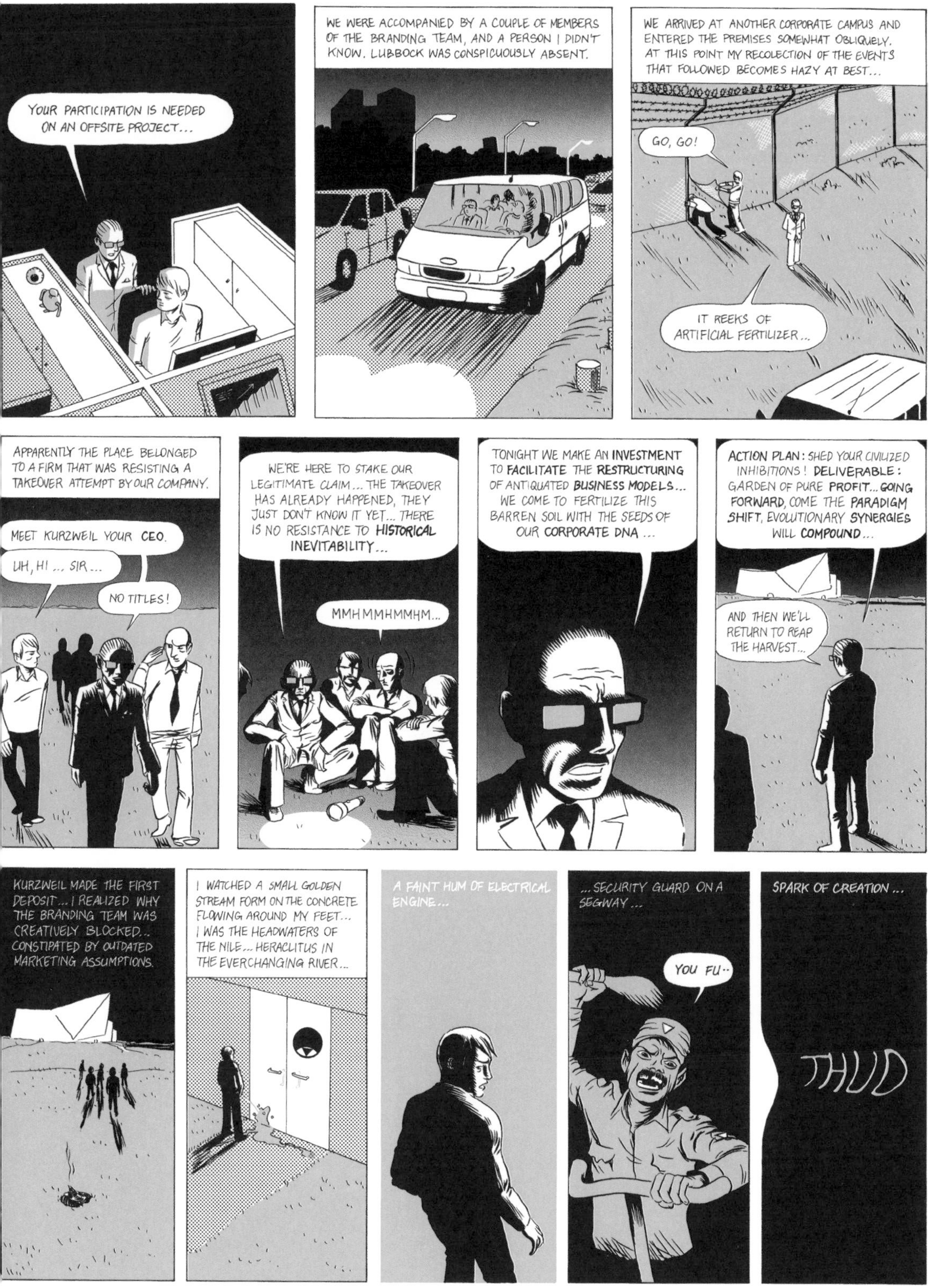
YOUR PARTICIPATION IS NEEDED ON AN OFFSITE PROJECT...
WE WERE ACCOMPANIED BY A COUPLE OF MEMBERS OF THE BRANDING TEAM, AND A PERSON I DIDN'T KNOW. LUBBOCK WAS CONSPICUOUSLY ABSENT.
WE ARRIVED AT ANOTHER CORPORATE CAMPUS AND ENTERED THE PREMISES SOMEWHAT OBLIQUELY. AT THIS POINT MY RECOLECTION OF THE EVENTS THAT FOLLOWED BECOMES HAZY AT BEST...
GO, GO!
IT REEKS OF ARTIFICIAL FERTILIZER...
APPARENTLY THE PLACE BELONGED TO A FIRM THAT WAS RESISTING A TAKEOVER ATTEMPT BY OUR COMPANY.
MEET KURZWEIL YOUR CEO.
UH, HI ... SIR ...
NO TITLES!
WE'RE HERE TO STAKE OUR LEGITIMATE CLAIM ... THE TAKEOVER HAS ALREADY HAPPENED, THEY JUST DON'T KNOW IT YET... THERE IS NO RESISTANCE TO HISTORICAL INEVITABILITY...
MMHMMHMMHM...
TONIGHT WE MAKE AN INVESTMENT TO FACILITATE THE RESTRUCTURING OF ANTIQUATED BUSINESS MODELS... WE COME TO FERTILIZE THIS BARREN SOIL WITH THE SEEDS OF OUR CORPORATE DNA ...
ACTION PLAN: SHED YOUR CIVILIZED INHIBITIONS! DELIVERABLE: GARDEN OF PURE PROFIT... GOING FORWARD, COME THE PARADIGM SHIFT, EVOLUTIONARY SYNERGIES WILL COMPOUND...
AND THEN WE'LL RETURN TO REAP THE HARVEST...
KURZWEIL MADE THE FIRST DEPOSIT... I REALIZED WHY THE BRANDING TEAM WAS CREATIVELY BLOCKED... CONSTIPATED BY OUTDATED MARKETING ASSUMPTIONS.
I WATCHED A SMALL GOLDEN STREAM FORM ON THE CONCRETE FLOWING AROUND MY FEET... I WAS THE HEADWATERS OF THE NILE... HERACLITUS IN THE EVERCHANGING RIVER...
A FAINT HUM OF ELECTRICAL ENGINE...
...SECURITY GUARD ON A SEGWAY...
YOU FU..
SPARK OF CREATION ...
THUD

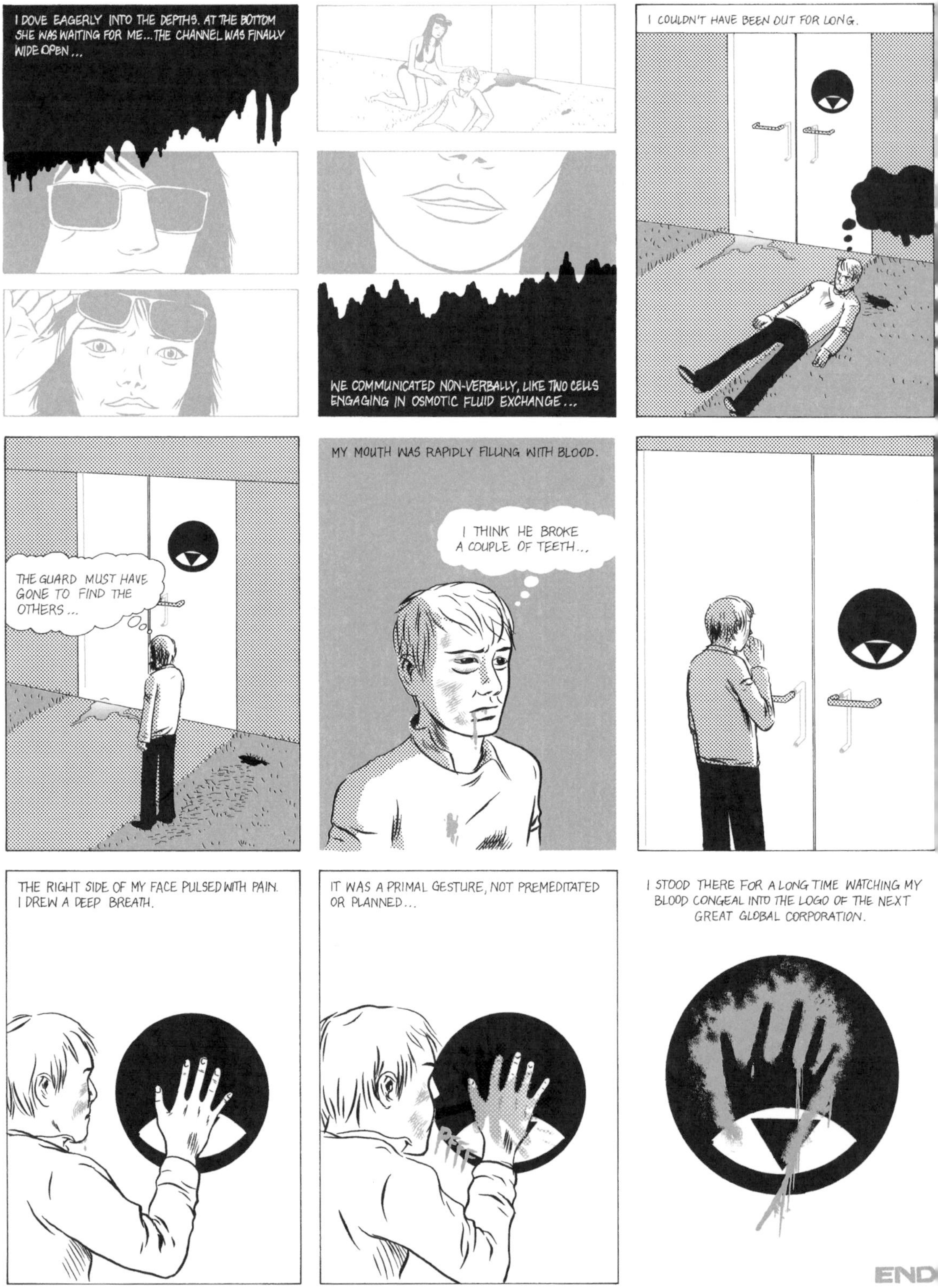
I DOVE EAGERLY INTO THE DEPTHS. AT THE BOTTOM SHE WAS WAITING FOR ME... THE CHANNEL WAS FINALLY WIDE OPEN...
WE COMMUNICATED NON-VERBALLY, LIKE TWO CELLS ENGAGING IN OSMOTIC FLUID EXCHANGE...
I COULDN'T HAVE BEEN OUT FOR LONG.
THE GUARD MUST HAVE GONE TO FIND THE OTHERS...
MY MOUTH WAS RAPIDLY FILLING WITH BLOOD.
I THINK HE BROKE A COUPLE OF TEETH...
THE RIGHT SIDE OF MY FACE PULSED WITH PAIN. I DREW A DEEP BREATH.
IT WAS A PRIMAL GESTURE, NOT PREMEDITATED OR PLANNED...
I STOOD THERE FOR A LONG TIME WATCHING MY BLOOD CONGEAL INTO THE LOGO OF THE NEXT GREAT GLOBAL CORPORATION.
END

100, 000 Miles

10, 000 Miles

COZY
APOCALYPSE

First appearance: *MOME 21*, 2011

1,000 Miles

100 Miles

1 Miles

1,000,000,000 BC   1,000,000 BC   500,000 BC   40,000 B

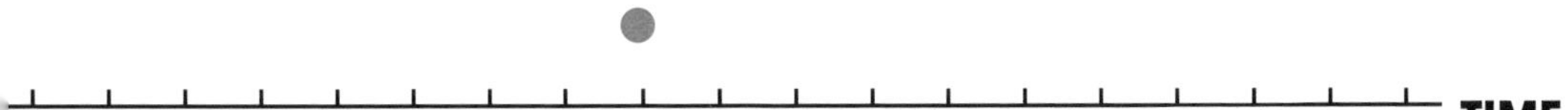
TIME
2000 AD
10, 000 AD

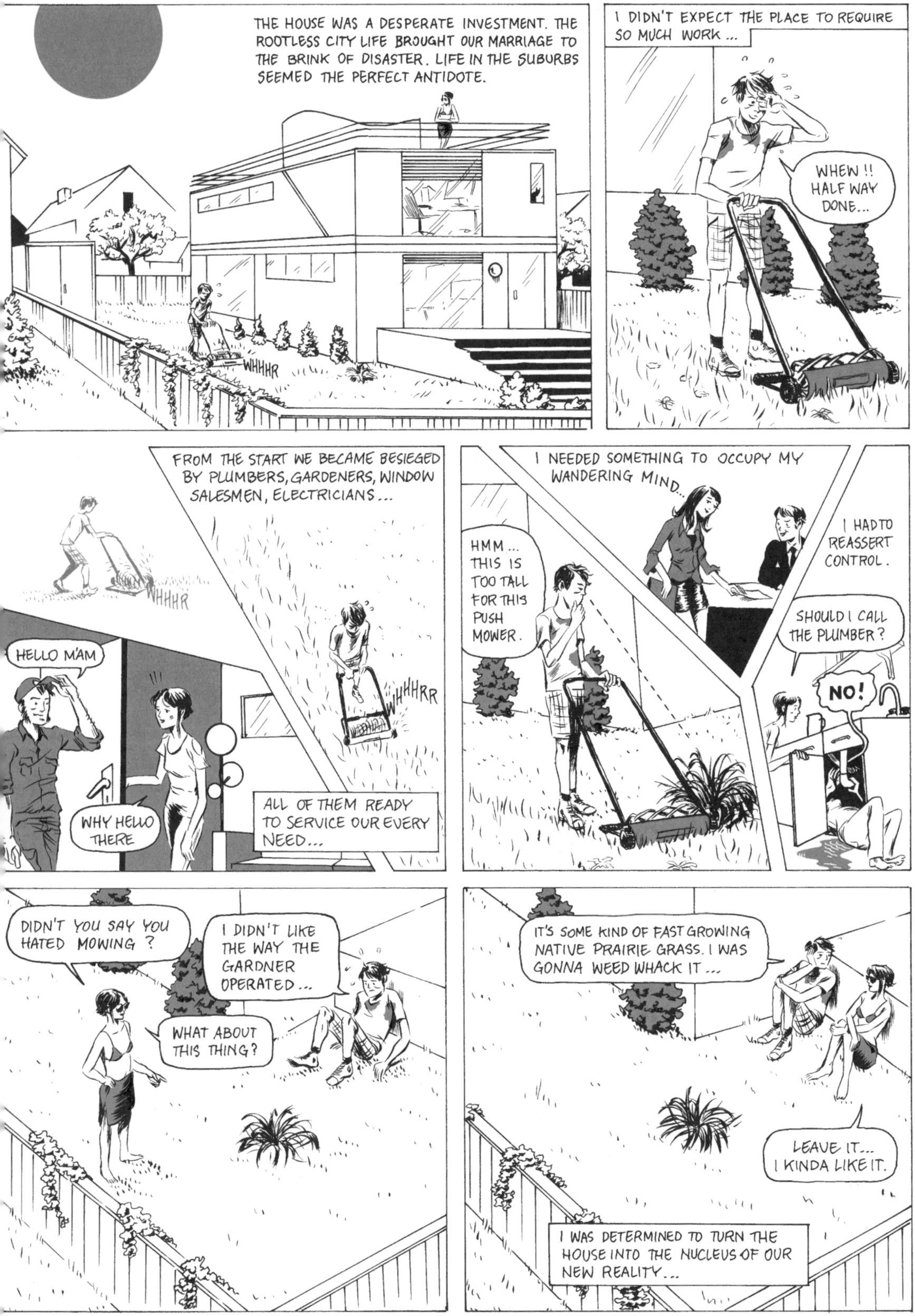
THE HOUSE WAS A DESPERATE INVESTMENT. THE ROOTLESS CITY LIFE BROUGHT OUR MARRIAGE TO THE BRINK OF DISASTER. LIFE IN THE SUBURBS SEEMED THE PERFECT ANTIDOTE.
WHHHR
I DIDN'T EXPECT THE PLACE TO REQUIRE SO MUCH WORK ...
WHEW !! HALF WAY DONE...
FROM THE START WE BECAME BESIEGED BY PLUMBERS, GARDENERS, WINDOW SALESMEN, ELECTRICIANS...
WHHHR
WHHHRR
HELLO M'AM
WHY HELLO THERE
ALL OF THEM READY TO SERVICE OUR EVERY NEED...
I NEEDED SOMETHING TO OCCUPY MY WANDERING MIND...
HMM... THIS IS TOO TALL FOR THIS PUSH MOWER.
I HAD TO REASSERT CONTROL.
SHOULD I CALL THE PLUMBER?
NO!
DIDN'T YOU SAY YOU HATED MOWING ?
I DIDN'T LIKE THE WAY THE GARDNER OPERATED...
WHAT ABOUT THIS THING?
IT'S SOME KIND OF FAST GROWING NATIVE PRAIRIE GRASS. I WAS GONNA WEED WHACK IT...
LEAVE IT... I KINDA LIKE IT.
I WAS DETERMINED TO TURN THE HOUSE INTO THE NUCLEUS OF OUR NEW REALITY...

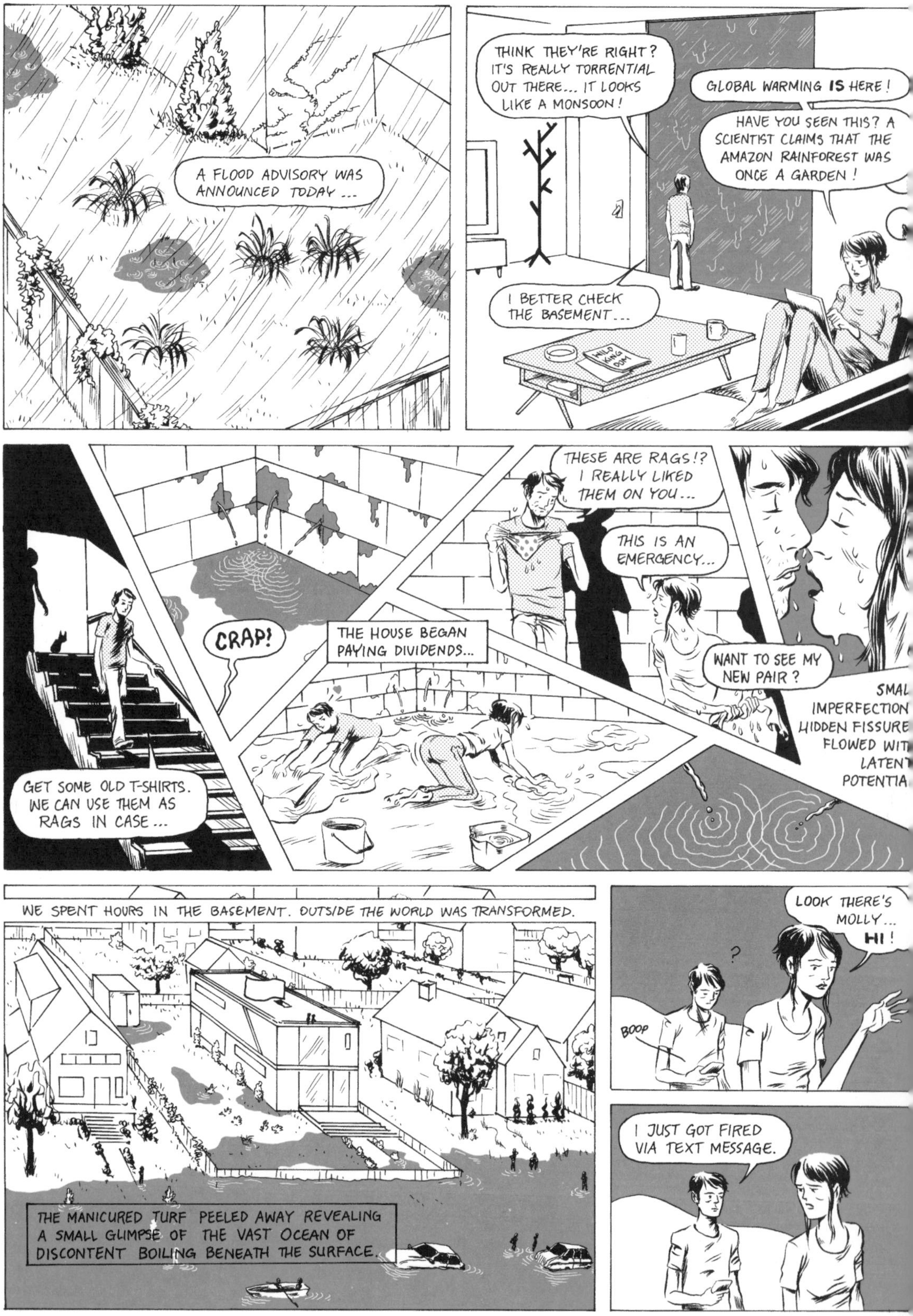
A FLOOD ADVISORY WAS ANNOUNCED TODAY ...
THINK THEY'RE RIGHT? IT'S REALLY TORRENTIAL OUT THERE... IT LOOKS LIKE A MONSOON!
GLOBAL WARMING IS HERE!
HAVE YOU SEEN THIS? A SCIENTIST CLAIMS THAT THE AMAZON RAINFOREST WAS ONCE A GARDEN!
I BETTER CHECK THE BASEMENT...
WILD KINGDOM
GET SOME OLD T-SHIRTS. WE CAN USE THEM AS RAGS IN CASE...
CRAP!
THE HOUSE BEGAN PAYING DIVIDENDS...
THESE ARE RAGS!? I REALLY LIKED THEM ON YOU...
THIS IS AN EMERGENCY...
WANT TO SEE MY NEW PAIR?
SMAL
IMPERFECTION
HIDDEN FISSURE
FLOWED WIT
LATEN
POTENTIA
WE SPENT HOURS IN THE BASEMENT. OUTSIDE THE WORLD WAS TRANSFORMED.
THE MANICURED TURF PEELED AWAY REVEALING A SMALL GLIMPSE OF THE VAST OCEAN OF DISCONTENT BOILING BENEATH THE SURFACE.
LOOK THERE'S MOLLY... HI!
?
BOOP
I JUST GOT FIRED VIA TEXT MESSAGE.

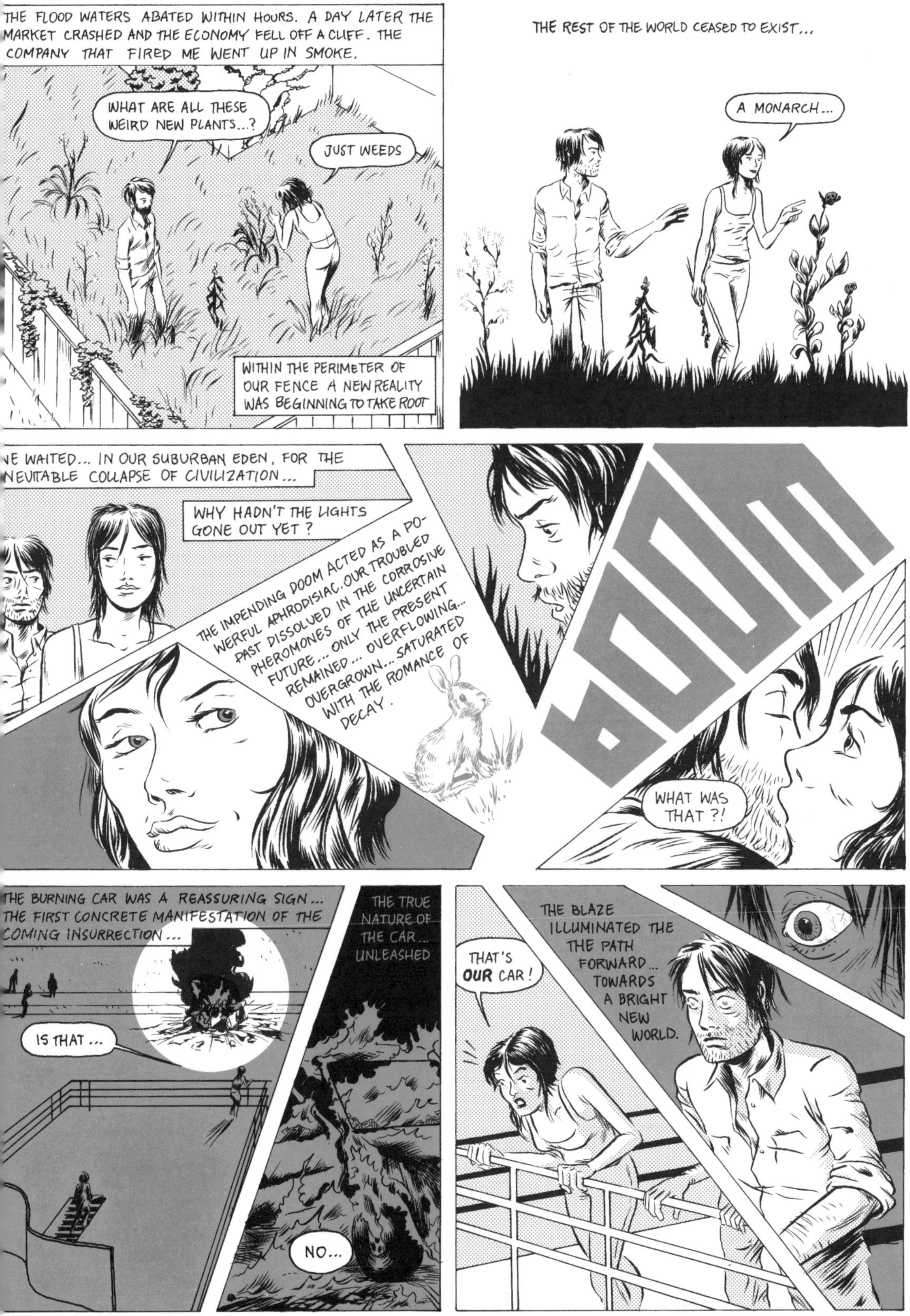

THE FLOOD WATERS ABATED WITHIN HOURS. A DAY LATER THE MARKET CRASHED AND THE ECONOMY FELL OFF A CLIFF. THE COMPANY THAT FIRED ME WENT UP IN SMOKE.
WHAT ARE ALL THESE WEIRD NEW PLANTS...?
JUST WEEDS
WITHIN THE PERIMETER OF OUR FENCE A NEW REALITY WAS BEGINNING TO TAKE ROOT
THE REST OF THE WORLD CEASED TO EXIST...
A MONARCH...
VE WAITED... IN OUR SUBURBAN EDEN, FOR THE NEVITABLE COLLAPSE OF CIVILIZATION...
WHY HADN'T THE LIGHTS GONE OUT YET?
THE IMPENDING DOOM ACTED AS A POWERFUL APHRODISIAC. OUR TROUBLED PAST DISSOLVED IN THE CORROSIVE PHEROMONES OF THE UNCERTAIN FUTURE... ONLY THE PRESENT REMAINED... OVERFLOWING... OVERGROWN... SATURATED WITH THE ROMANCE OF DECAY.
WHAT WAS THAT?!
THE BURNING CAR WAS A REASSURING SIGN... THE FIRST CONCRETE MANIFESTATION OF THE COMING INSURRECTION...
IS THAT...
THE TRUE NATURE OF THE CAR... UNLEASHED
NO...
THE BLAZE ILLUMINATED THE THE PATH FORWARD... TOWARDS A BRIGHT NEW WORLD.
THAT'S OUR CAR!

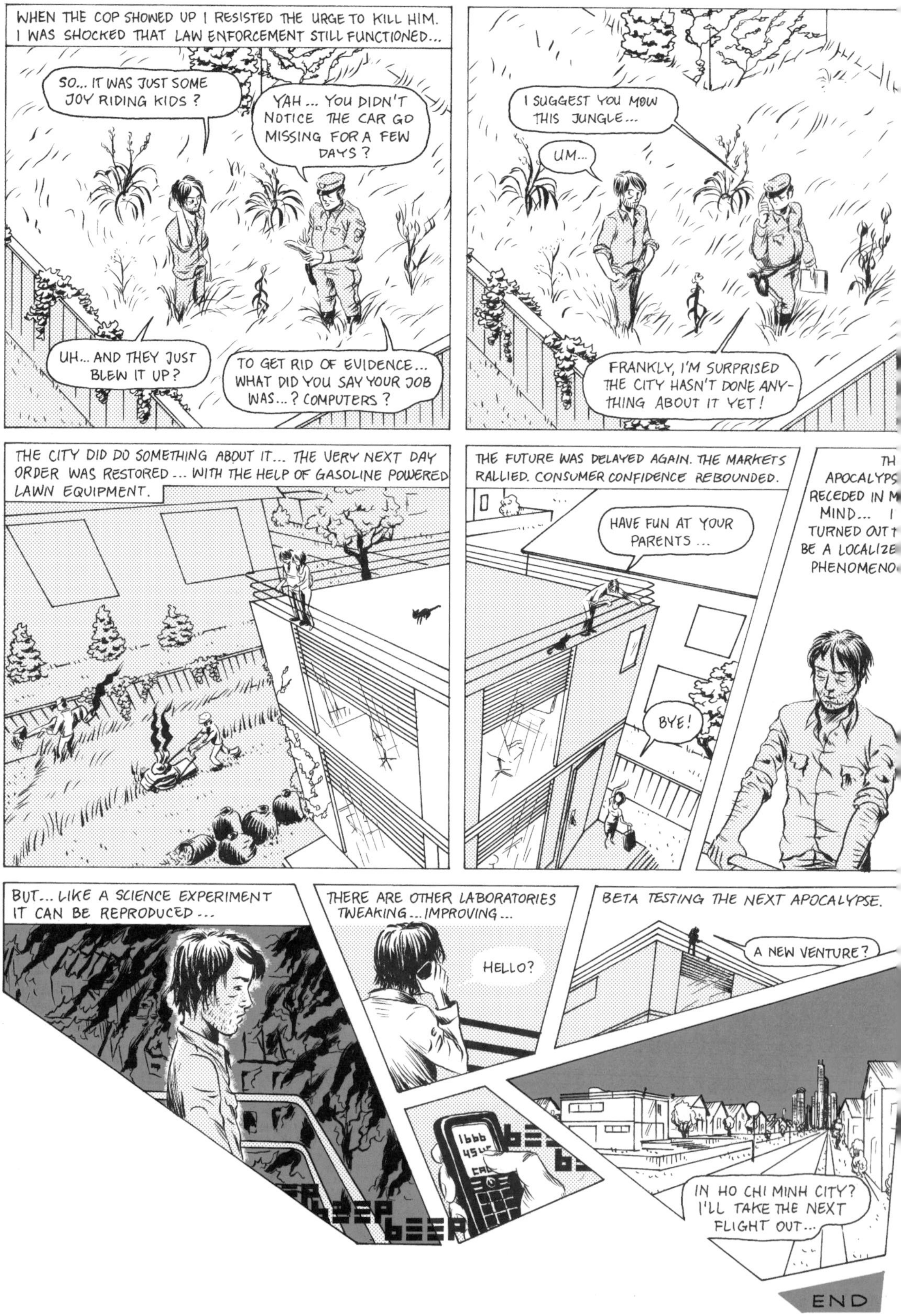
WHEN THE COP SHOWED UP I RESISTED THE URGE TO KILL HIM. I WAS SHOCKED THAT LAW ENFORCEMENT STILL FUNCTIONED...
SO... IT WAS JUST SOME JOY RIDING KIDS?
YAH... YOU DIDN'T NOTICE THE CAR GO MISSING FOR A FEW DAYS?
UH... AND THEY JUST BLEW IT UP?
TO GET RID OF EVIDENCE... WHAT DID YOU SAY YOUR JOB WAS...? COMPUTERS?
I SUGGEST YOU MOW THIS JUNGLE...
UM...
FRANKLY, I'M SURPRISED THE CITY HASN'T DONE ANYTHING ABOUT IT YET!
THE CITY DID DO SOMETHING ABOUT IT... THE VERY NEXT DAY ORDER WAS RESTORED... WITH THE HELP OF GASOLINE POWERED LAWN EQUIPMENT.
THE FUTURE WAS DELAYED AGAIN. THE MARKETS RALLIED. CONSUMER CONFIDENCE REBOUNDED.
HAVE FUN AT YOUR PARENTS...
BYE!
TH
APOCALYPS
RECEDED IN M
MIND... I
TURNED OUT T
BE A LOCALIZE
PHENOMENO
BUT... LIKE A SCIENCE EXPERIMENT IT CAN BE REPRODUCED...
THERE ARE OTHER LABORATORIES TWEAKING... IMPROVING...
HELLO?
BETA TESTING THE NEXT APOCALYPSE.
A NEW VENTURE?
IN HO CHI MINH CITY? I'LL TAKE THE NEXT FLIGHT OUT...
END

THE IDEA CAME TO JACOB JENAS WHILE STAYING AT A HOTEL UNDERGOING MAJOR RENOVATION.
THUD
BANG
BLAH, BLAH, BLAH, BLAH!
WHAM
KLANG
HOTEL SILENCIO
WITHIN WEEKS A SUITABLE LOCATION WAS FOUND.
BOOM BOX
EACH ROOM WAS OUTFITTED WITH STATE OF THE ART SOUND PROOFING MATERIALS.
THE OPENING OF HOTEL SILENCIO MADE JACOB INTO A MINOR CELEBRITY IN THE ACADEMIC WORLD.
THE SOLUTION TO 'NOISE POLLUTION' IS NOT EVASION BY ZONING, IT IS NEW GOODS AND SERVICES: NEW ACOUSTICAL MATERIALS, NEW EQUIPMENT, ETC.
EXCESSIVE NOISE IS NOT A PROBLEM OF PROGRESS, BUT EVIDENCE OF STAGNATION!
ALL MANNER OF ANTI-NOISE DEVICES WENT INTO PRODUCTION.
EXPENSIVE EAR PLUGS WERE INTRODUCED AS FASHION ACCESSORIES.
LIBRARIES BECAME POPULAR DATING DESTINATIONS.
SILENT FILMS SAW A BRIEF RESURGENCE ON TV.
A DOCUMENTARY ABOUT MONKS UNDER THE VOW OF SILENCE BECAME A SURPRIZE HIT THAT SAME SUMMER.
BUT, IT SOON BECAME APPARENT THAT MOST GUESTS FOUND EXTREME SILENCE TO BE A DISCONCERTING EXPERIENCE.
WHAT WAS THAT!?
GURGLE
A FEW MONTHS LATER THE HOTEL WAS CONVERTED INTO A RECORDING STUDIO FOR AVANT GARDE MUSICIANS.
UH
STUDIO PINDROP
HERE FOR THE RADIATOR SESSIONS? SECOND FLOOR, ROOM TWENTY SIX.
T. KACZYNSKI '08

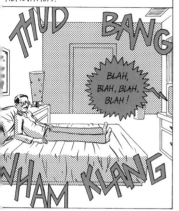

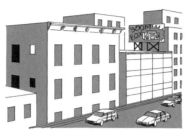

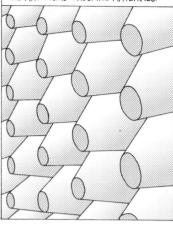

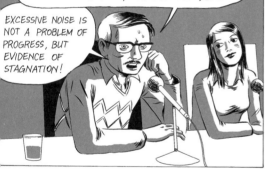

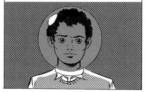

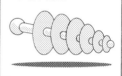

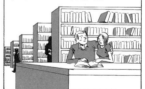

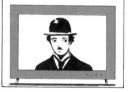

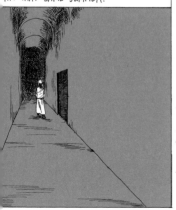

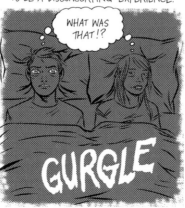

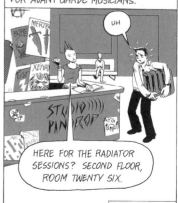

100, 000 Miles

10, 000 Miles

MUSIC FOR NEANDERTHALS

First appearance: *MOME 22,* 2011

1,000 Miles

100 Miles

1 Miles

1,000,000,000 BC   1,000,000 BC   500,000 BC   40,000

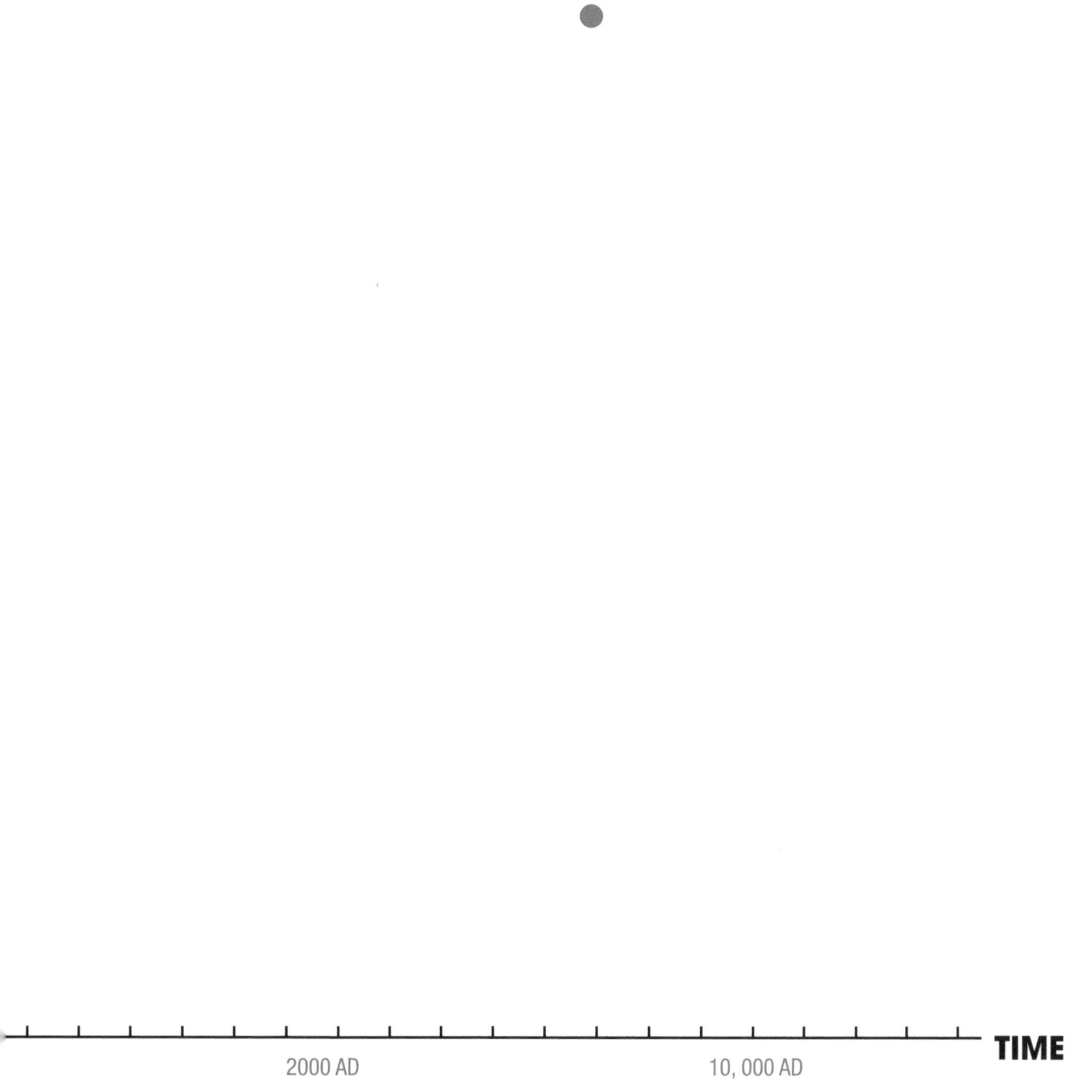
TIME
2000 AD
10, 000 AD

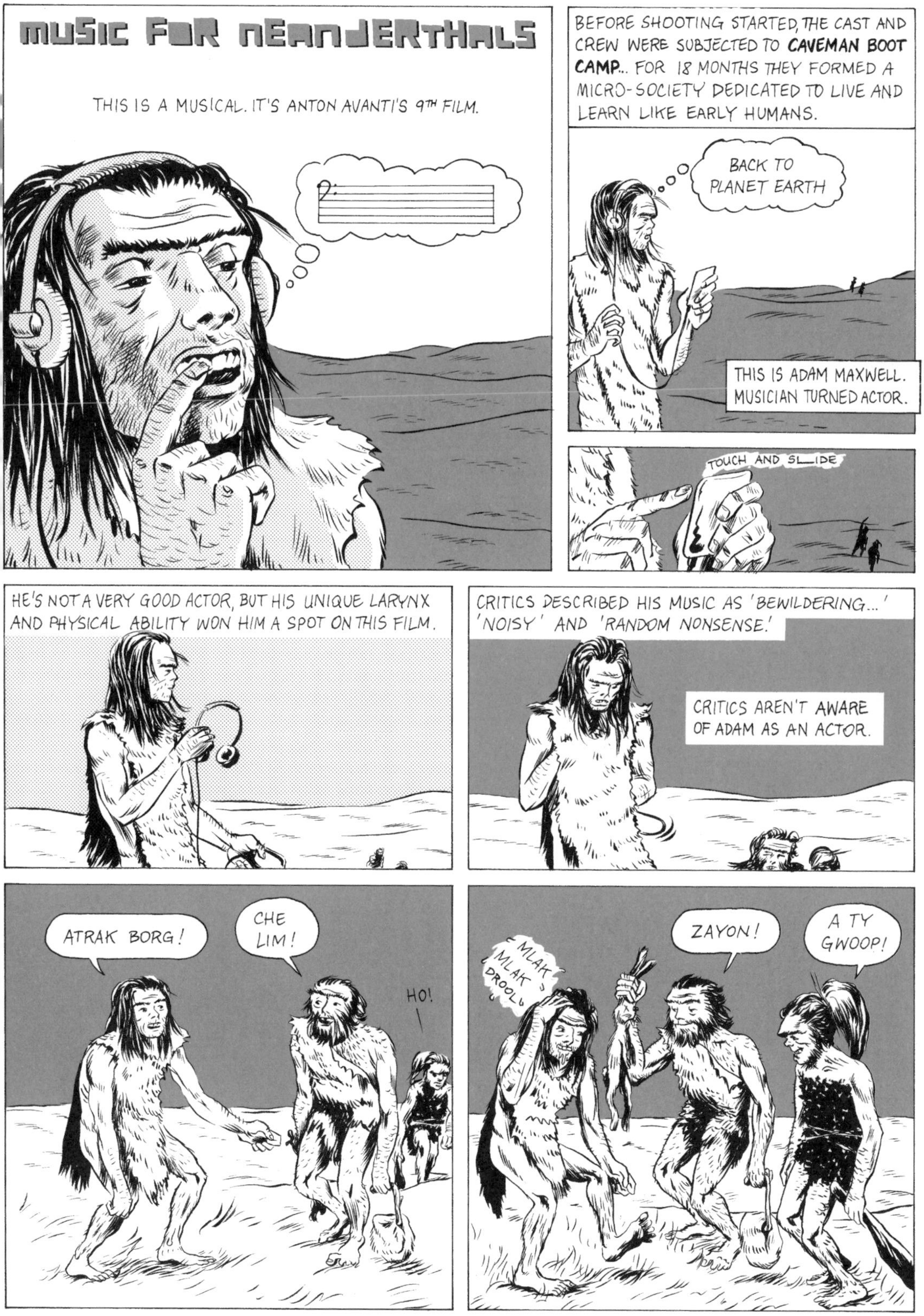
MUSIC FOR NEANDERTHALS
THIS IS A MUSICAL. IT'S ANTON AVANTI'S 9TH FILM.
BEFORE SHOOTING STARTED, THE CAST AND CREW WERE SUBJECTED TO CAVEMAN BOOT CAMP.. FOR 18 MONTHS THEY FORMED A MICRO-SOCIETY DEDICATED TO LIVE AND LEARN LIKE EARLY HUMANS.
BACK TO PLANET EARTH
THIS IS ADAM MAXWELL. MUSICIAN TURNED ACTOR.
TOUCH AND SL—IDE
HE'S NOT A VERY GOOD ACTOR, BUT HIS UNIQUE LARYNX AND PHYSICAL ABILITY WON HIM A SPOT ON THIS FILM.
CRITICS DESCRIBED HIS MUSIC AS 'BEWILDERING...' 'NOISY' AND 'RANDOM NONSENSE.'
CRITICS AREN'T AWARE OF ADAM AS AN ACTOR.
ATRAK BORG!
CHE LIM!
HO!
MLAK MLAK DROOL
ZAYON!
A TY GWOOP!

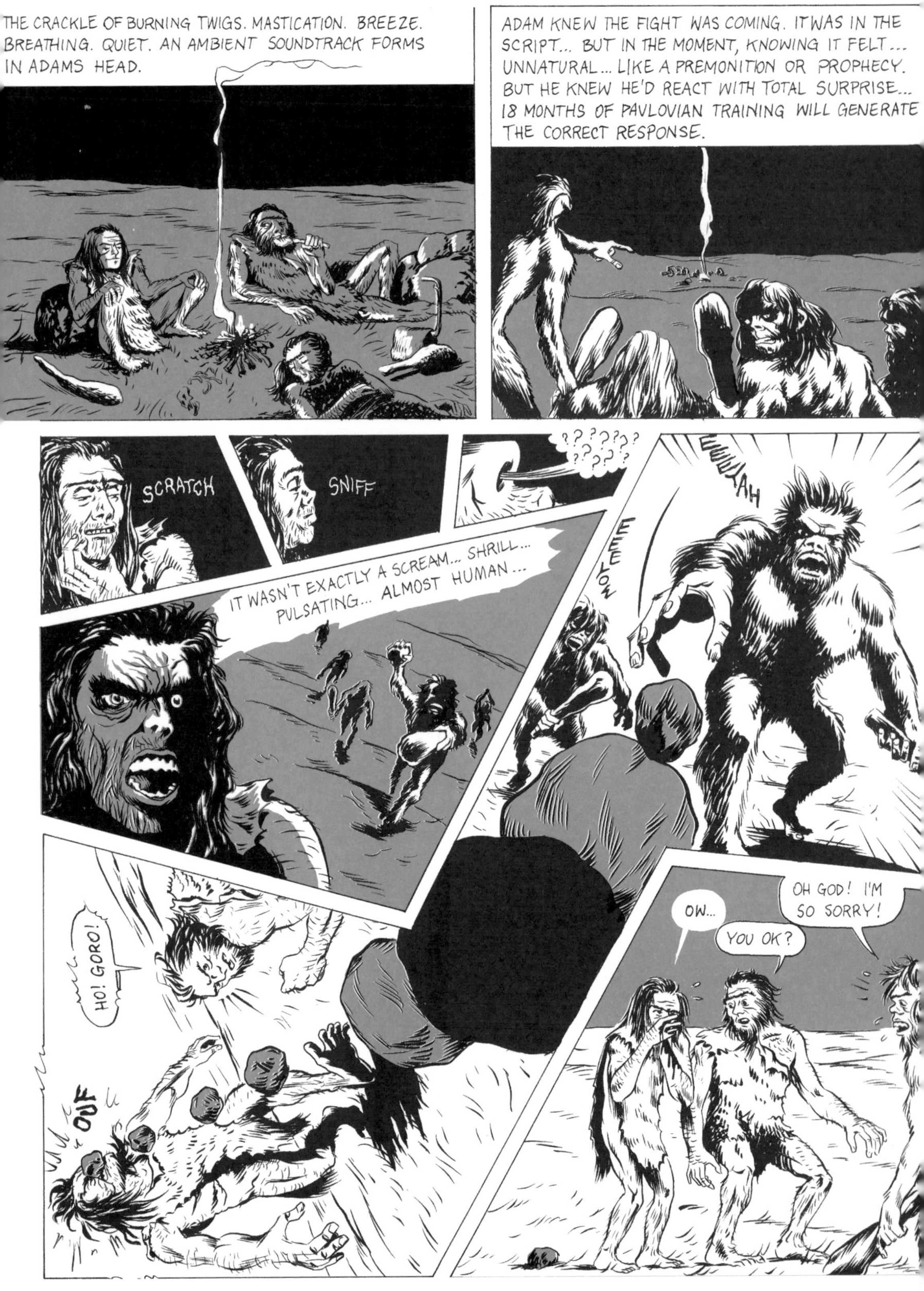
THE CRACKLE OF BURNING TWIGS. MASTICATION. BREEZE. BREATHING. QUIET. AN AMBIENT SOUNDTRACK FORMS IN ADAMS HEAD.
ADAM KNEW THE FIGHT WAS COMING. IT WAS IN THE SCRIPT... BUT IN THE MOMENT, KNOWING IT FELT... UNNATURAL... LIKE A PREMONITION OR PROPHECY. BUT HE KNEW HE'D REACT WITH TOTAL SURPRISE... 18 MONTHS OF PAVLOVIAN TRAINING WILL GENERATE THE CORRECT RESPONSE.
SCRATCH
SNIFF
??????
????
EEEEYAH
EEEEOW
IT WASN'T EXACTLY A SCREAM... SHRILL... PULSATING... ALMOST HUMAN...
HO! GORO!
OUF
OW...
YOU OK?
OH GOD! I'M SO SORRY!

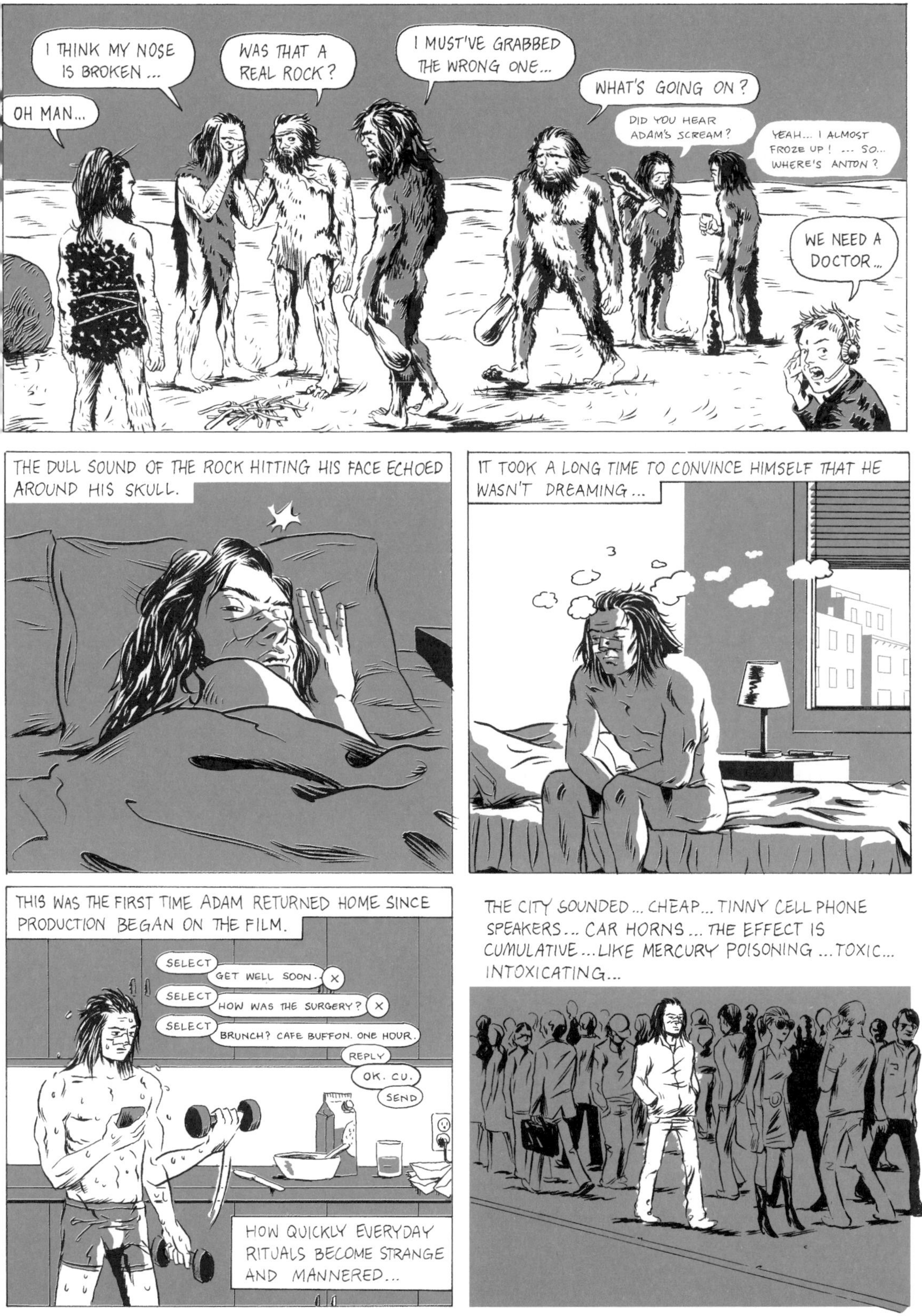
OH MAN...
I THINK MY NOSE IS BROKEN...
WAS THAT A REAL ROCK?
I MUST'VE GRABBED THE WRONG ONE...
WHAT'S GOING ON?
DID YOU HEAR ADAM'S SCREAM?
YEAH... I ALMOST FROZE UP! ... SO... WHERE'S ANTON?
WE NEED A DOCTOR...
THE DULL SOUND OF THE ROCK HITTING HIS FACE ECHOED AROUND HIS SKULL.
IT TOOK A LONG TIME TO CONVINCE HIMSELF THAT HE WASN'T DREAMING...
3
THIS WAS THE FIRST TIME ADAM RETURNED HOME SINCE PRODUCTION BEGAN ON THE FILM.
SELECT
GET WELL SOON.
X
SELECT
HOW WAS THE SURGERY?
X
SELECT
BRUNCH? CAFE BUFFON. ONE HOUR.
REPLY
OK. CU.
SEND
HOW QUICKLY EVERYDAY RITUALS BECOME STRANGE AND MANNERED...
THE CITY SOUNDED... CHEAP... TINNY CELL PHONE SPEAKERS... CAR HORNS... THE EFFECT IS CUMULATIVE... LIKE MERCURY POISONING... TOXIC... INTOXICATING...

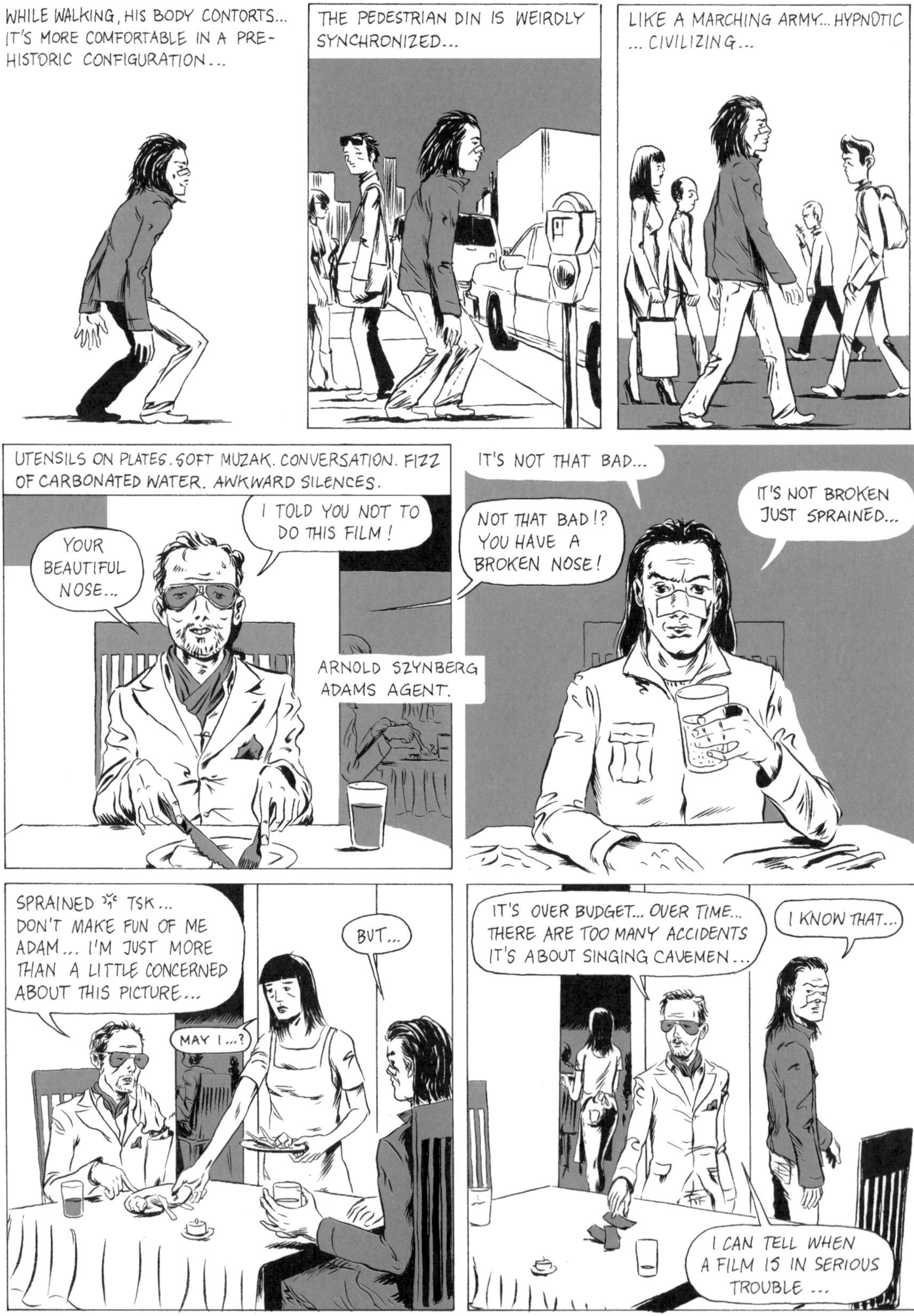
WHILE WALKING, HIS BODY CONTORTS... IT'S MORE COMFORTABLE IN A PRE-HISTORIC CONFIGURATION...
THE PEDESTRIAN DIN IS WEIRDLY SYNCHRONIZED...
LIKE A MARCHING ARMY... HYPNOTIC ... CIVILIZING...
UTENSILS ON PLATES. SOFT MUZAK. CONVERSATION. FIZZ OF CARBONATED WATER. AWKWARD SILENCES.
YOUR BEAUTIFUL NOSE...
I TOLD YOU NOT TO DO THIS FILM!
ARNOLD SZYNBERG ADAMS AGENT.
IT'S NOT THAT BAD...
NOT THAT BAD!? YOU HAVE A BROKEN NOSE!
IT'S NOT BROKEN JUST SPRAINED...
SPRAINED TSK... DON'T MAKE FUN OF ME ADAM... I'M JUST MORE THAN A LITTLE CONCERNED ABOUT THIS PICTURE...
BUT...
MAY I...?
IT'S OVER BUDGET... OVER TIME... THERE ARE TOO MANY ACCIDENTS IT'S ABOUT SINGING CAVEMEN...
I KNOW THAT...
I CAN TELL WHEN A FILM IS IN SERIOUS TROUBLE...

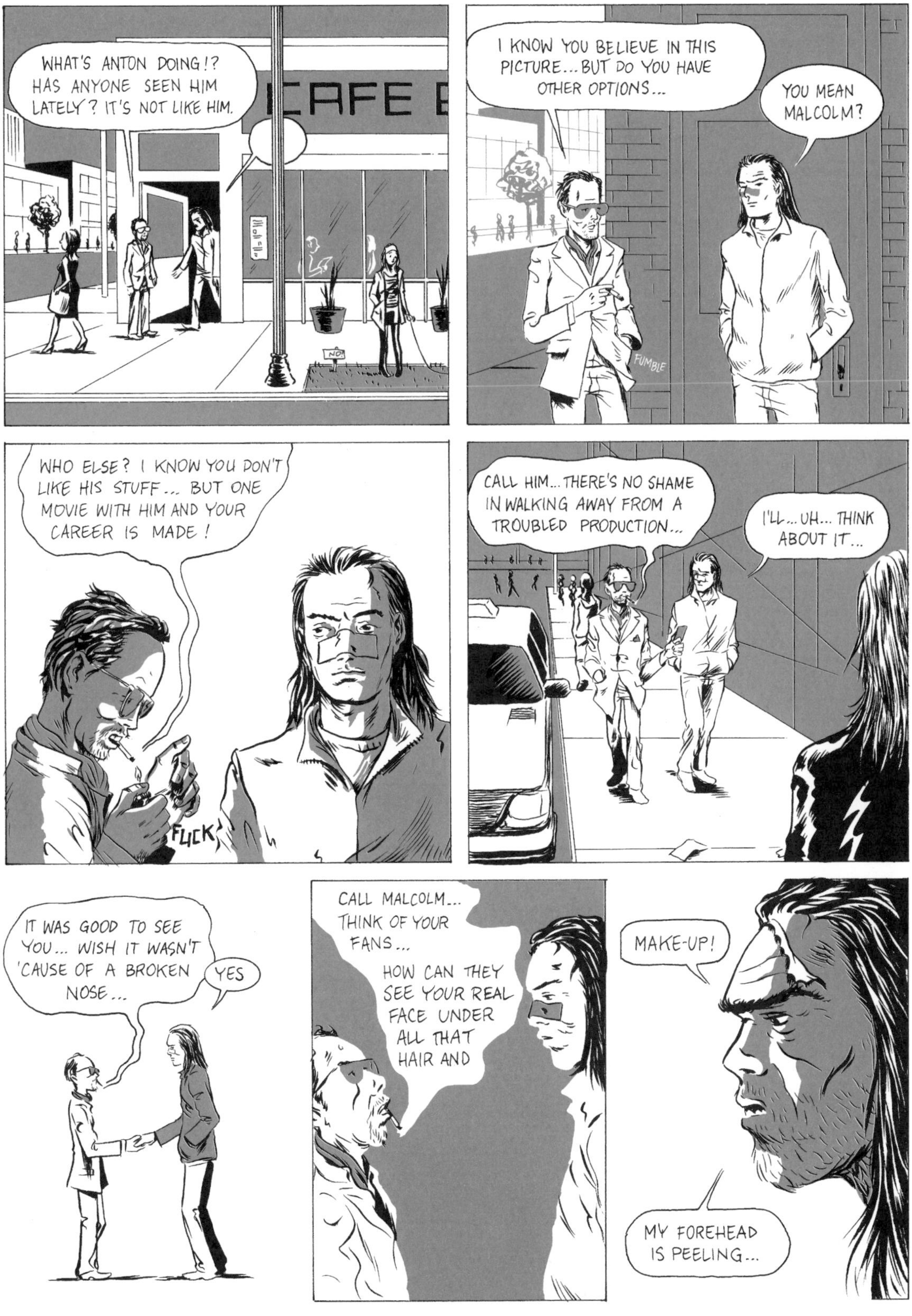
WHAT'S ANTON DOING!? HAS ANYONE SEEN HIM LATELY? IT'S NOT LIKE HIM.
CAFE
NO!
I KNOW YOU BELIEVE IN THIS PICTURE... BUT DO YOU HAVE OTHER OPTIONS...
YOU MEAN MALCOLM?
FUMBLE
WHO ELSE? I KNOW YOU DON'T LIKE HIS STUFF... BUT ONE MOVIE WITH HIM AND YOUR CAREER IS MADE!
FLICK
CALL HIM... THERE'S NO SHAME IN WALKING AWAY FROM A TROUBLED PRODUCTION...
I'LL... UH... THINK ABOUT IT...
IT WAS GOOD TO SEE YOU... WISH IT WASN'T 'CAUSE OF A BROKEN NOSE...
YES
CALL MALCOLM... THINK OF YOUR FANS...
HOW CAN THEY SEE YOUR REAL FACE UNDER ALL THAT HAIR AND
MAKE-UP!
MY FOREHEAD IS PEELING...

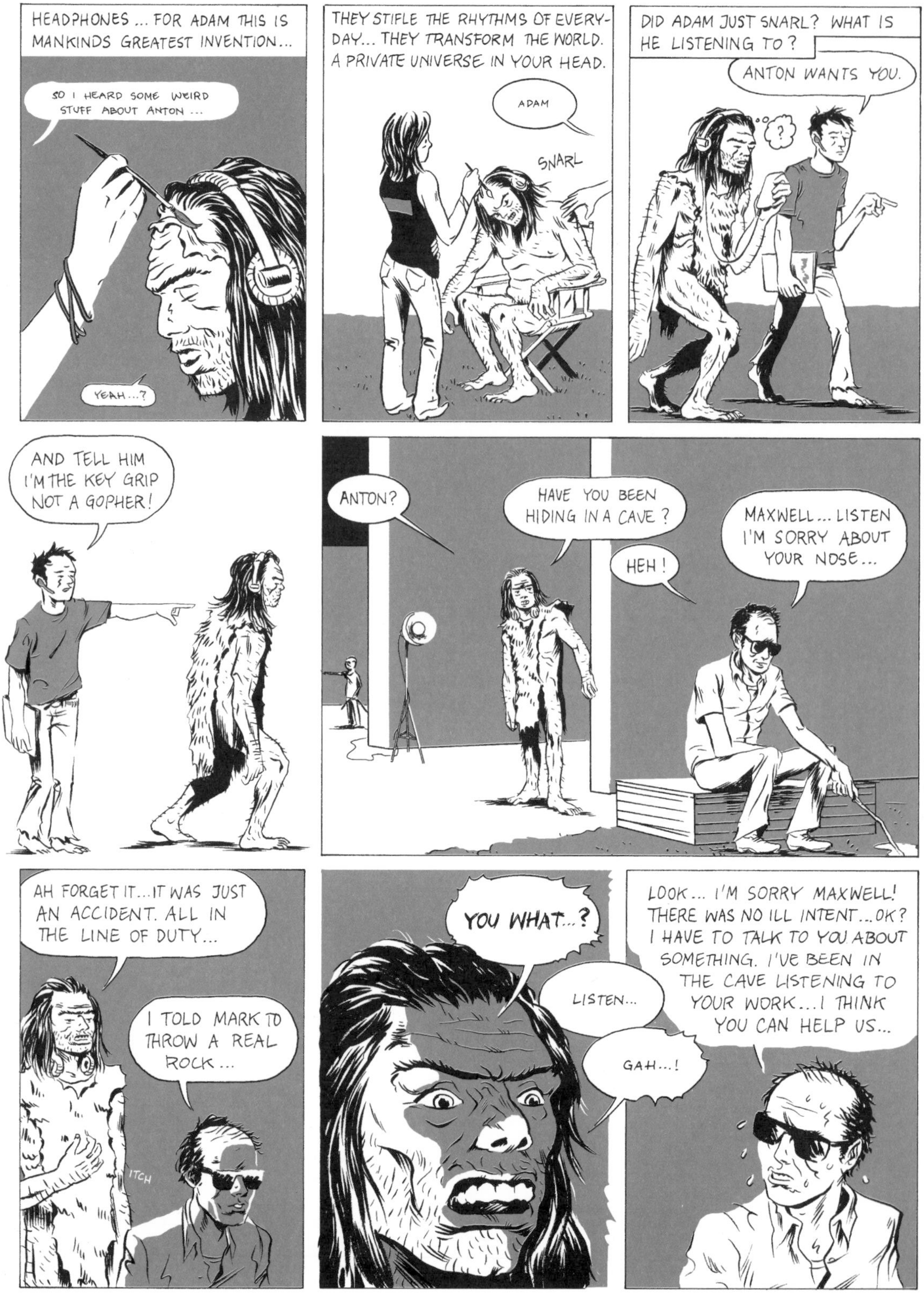
HEADPHONES ... FOR ADAM THIS IS MANKINDS GREATEST INVENTION...
SO I HEARD SOME WEIRD STUFF ABOUT ANTON ...
YEAH...?
THEY STIFLE THE RHYTHMS OF EVERY-DAY... THEY TRANSFORM THE WORLD. A PRIVATE UNIVERSE IN YOUR HEAD.
ADAM
SNARL
DID ADAM JUST SNARL? WHAT IS HE LISTENING TO?
ANTON WANTS YOU.
?
AND TELL HIM I'M THE KEY GRIP NOT A GOPHER!
ANTON?
HAVE YOU BEEN HIDING IN A CAVE?
HEH!
MAXWELL... LISTEN I'M SORRY ABOUT YOUR NOSE...
AH FORGET IT...IT WAS JUST AN ACCIDENT. ALL IN THE LINE OF DUTY...
I TOLD MARK TO THROW A REAL ROCK...
ITCH
YOU WHAT...?
LISTEN...
GAH...!
LOOK... I'M SORRY MAXWELL! THERE WAS NO ILL INTENT...OK? I HAVE TO TALK TO YOU ABOUT SOMETHING. I'VE BEEN IN THE CAVE LISTENING TO YOUR WORK...I THINK YOU CAN HELP US...

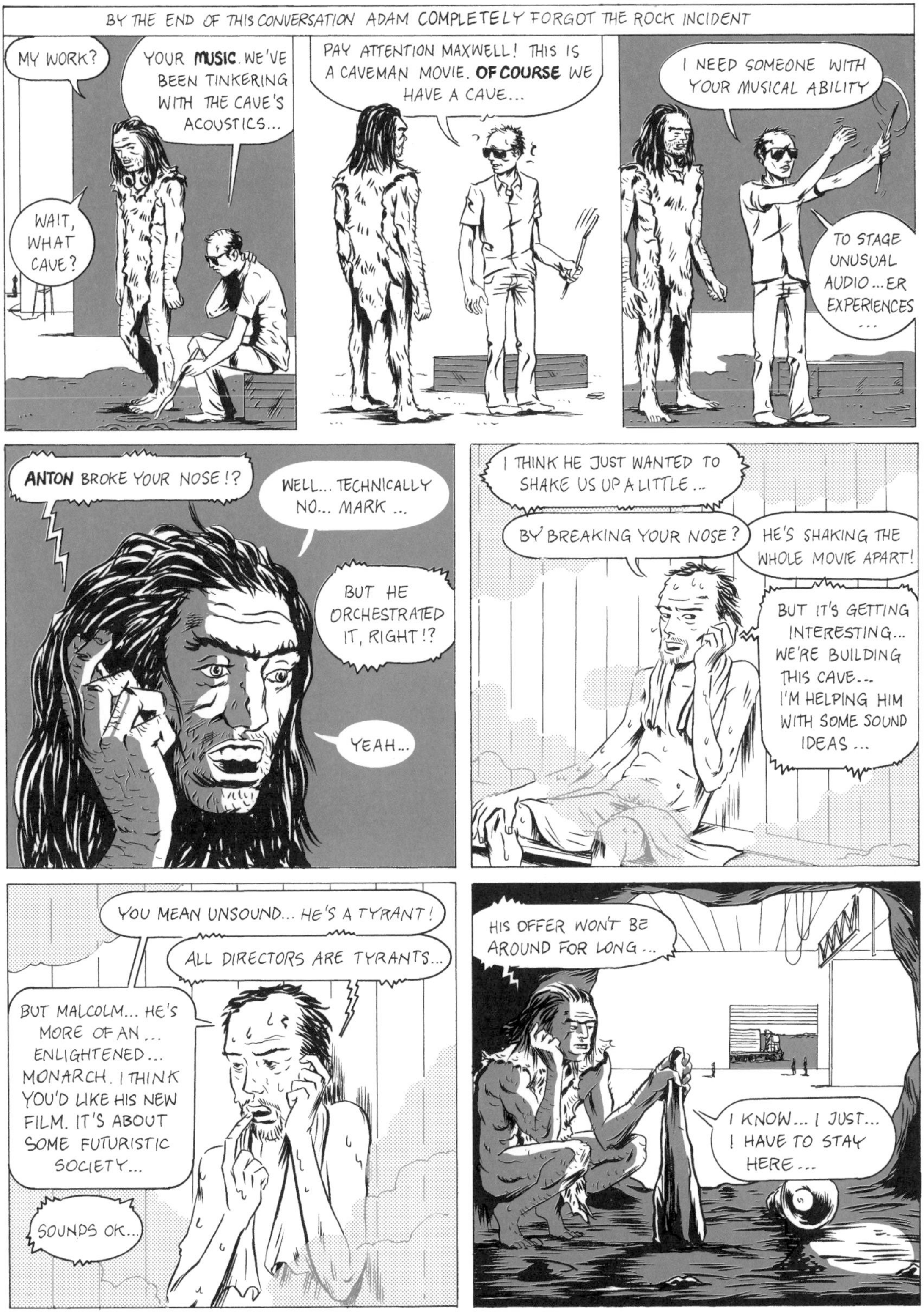

BY THE END OF THIS CONVERSATION ADAM COMPLETELY FORGOT THE ROCK INCIDENT
MY WORK?
YOUR MUSIC. WE'VE BEEN TINKERING WITH THE CAVE'S ACOUSTICS...
WAIT, WHAT CAVE?
PAY ATTENTION MAXWELL! THIS IS A CAVEMAN MOVIE. OF COURSE WE HAVE A CAVE...
I NEED SOMEONE WITH YOUR MUSICAL ABILITY
TO STAGE UNUSUAL AUDIO... ER EXPERIENCES ...
ANTON BROKE YOUR NOSE!?
WELL... TECHNICALLY NO... MARK ...
BUT HE ORCHESTRATED IT, RIGHT!?
YEAH...
I THINK HE JUST WANTED TO SHAKE US UP A LITTLE ...
BY BREAKING YOUR NOSE?
HE'S SHAKING THE WHOLE MOVIE APART!
BUT IT'S GETTING INTERESTING... WE'RE BUILDING THIS CAVE... I'M HELPING HIM WITH SOME SOUND IDEAS ...
YOU MEAN UNSOUND... HE'S A TYRANT!
ALL DIRECTORS ARE TYRANTS...
BUT MALCOLM... HE'S MORE OF AN... ENLIGHTENED... MONARCH. I THINK YOU'D LIKE HIS NEW FILM. IT'S ABOUT SOME FUTURISTIC SOCIETY...
SOUNDS OK...
HIS OFFER WON'T BE AROUND FOR LONG ...
I KNOW... I JUST... I HAVE TO STAY HERE ...

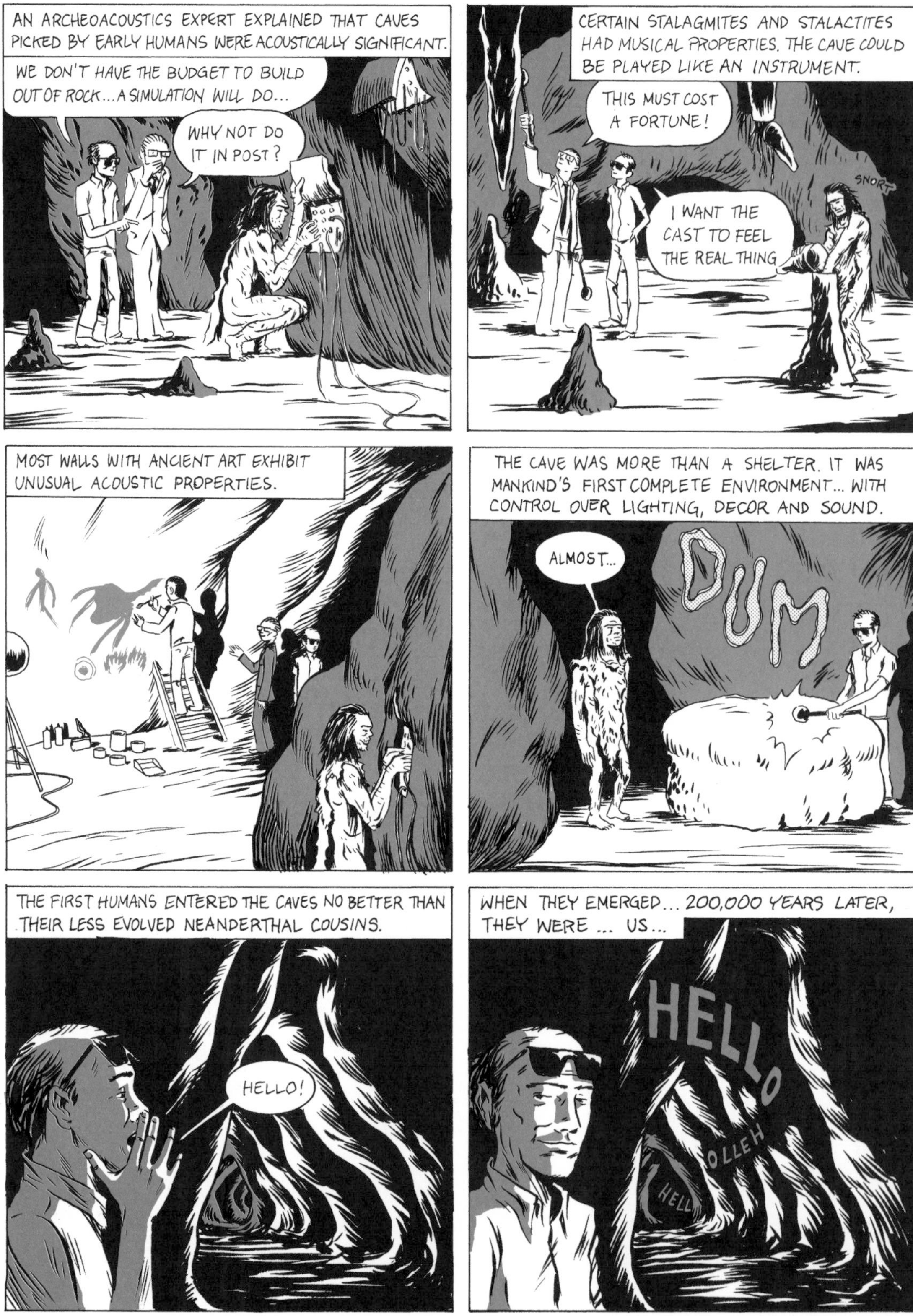
AN ARCHEOACOUSTICS EXPERT EXPLAINED THAT CAVES PICKED BY EARLY HUMANS WERE ACOUSTICALLY SIGNIFICANT.
WE DON'T HAVE THE BUDGET TO BUILD OUT OF ROCK... A SIMULATION WILL DO...
WHY NOT DO IT IN POST?
CERTAIN STALAGMITES AND STALACTITES HAD MUSICAL PROPERTIES. THE CAVE COULD BE PLAYED LIKE AN INSTRUMENT.
THIS MUST COST A FORTUNE!
SNORT
I WANT THE CAST TO FEEL THE REAL THING
MOST WALLS WITH ANCIENT ART EXHIBIT UNUSUAL ACOUSTIC PROPERTIES.
THE CAVE WAS MORE THAN A SHELTER. IT WAS MANKIND'S FIRST COMPLETE ENVIRONMENT... WITH CONTROL OVER LIGHTING, DECOR AND SOUND.
ALMOST...
DUM
THE FIRST HUMANS ENTERED THE CAVES NO BETTER THAN THEIR LESS EVOLVED NEANDERTHAL COUSINS.
HELLO!
WHEN THEY EMERGED... 200,000 YEARS LATER, THEY WERE ... US...
HELLO
OLLEH
HELL

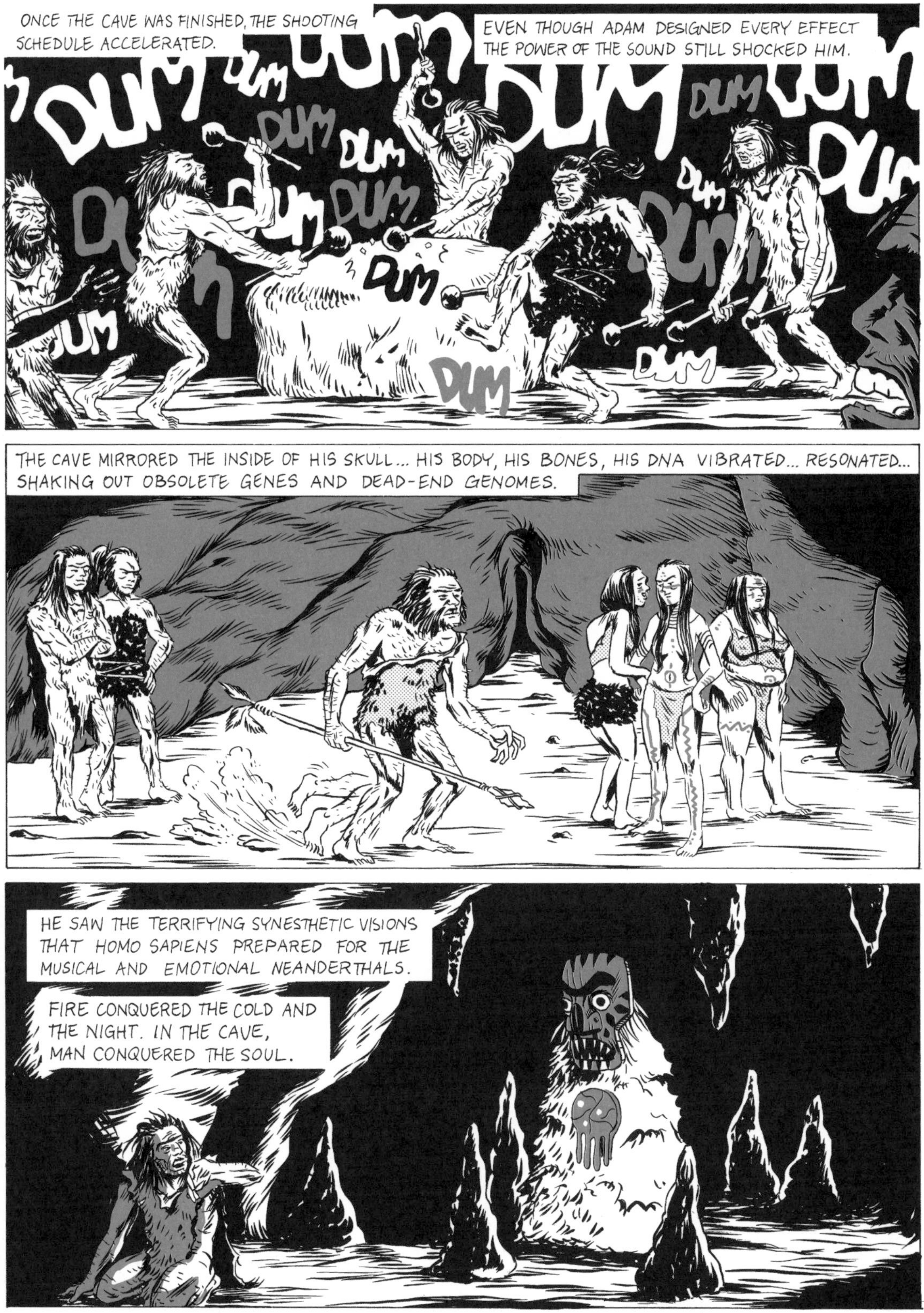
ONCE THE CAVE WAS FINISHED, THE SHOOTING SCHEDULE ACCELERATED.
EVEN THOUGH ADAM DESIGNED EVERY EFFECT THE POWER OF THE SOUND STILL SHOCKED HIM.
DUM DUM DUM DUM DUM DUM DUM DUM DUM DUM DUM
THE CAVE MIRRORED THE INSIDE OF HIS SKULL... HIS BODY, HIS BONES, HIS DNA VIBRATED... RESONATED... SHAKING OUT OBSOLETE GENES AND DEAD-END GENOMES.
HE SAW THE TERRIFYING SYNESTHETIC VISIONS THAT HOMO SAPIENS PREPARED FOR THE MUSICAL AND EMOTIONAL NEANDERTHALS.
FIRE CONQUERED THE COLD AND THE NIGHT. IN THE CAVE, MAN CONQUERED THE SOUL.

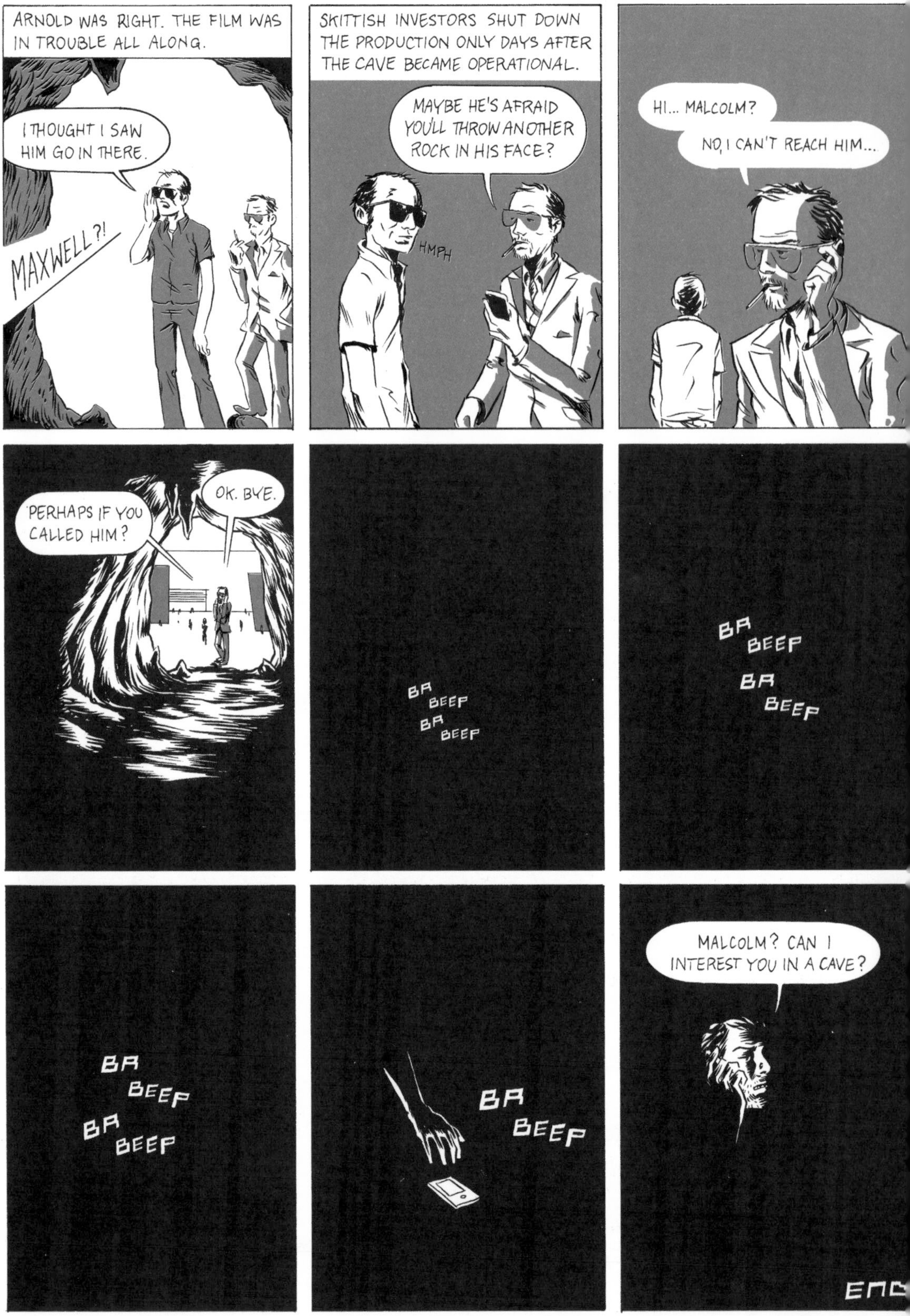
ARNOLD WAS RIGHT. THE FILM WAS IN TROUBLE ALL ALONG.
I THOUGHT I SAW HIM GO IN THERE.
MAXWELL?!
SKITTISH INVESTORS SHUT DOWN THE PRODUCTION ONLY DAYS AFTER THE CAVE BECAME OPERATIONAL.
MAYBE HE'S AFRAID YOU'LL THROW ANOTHER ROCK IN HIS FACE?
HMPH
HI... MALCOLM?
NO, I CAN'T REACH HIM...
PERHAPS IF YOU CALLED HIM?
OK. BYE.
BA BEEP BA BEEP
BA BEEP BA BEEP
BA BEEP BA BEEP
BA BEEP
MALCOLM? CAN I INTEREST YOU IN A CAVE?
END

SPACE

100, 000 Miles

10, 000 Miles

THE NEW
Previously unpublished.

1,000 Miles

100 Miles

1 Miles

1,000,000,000 BC   1,000,000 BC   500,000 BC   40,000

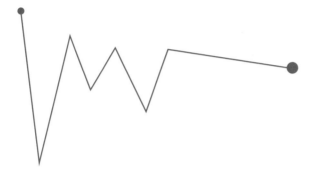

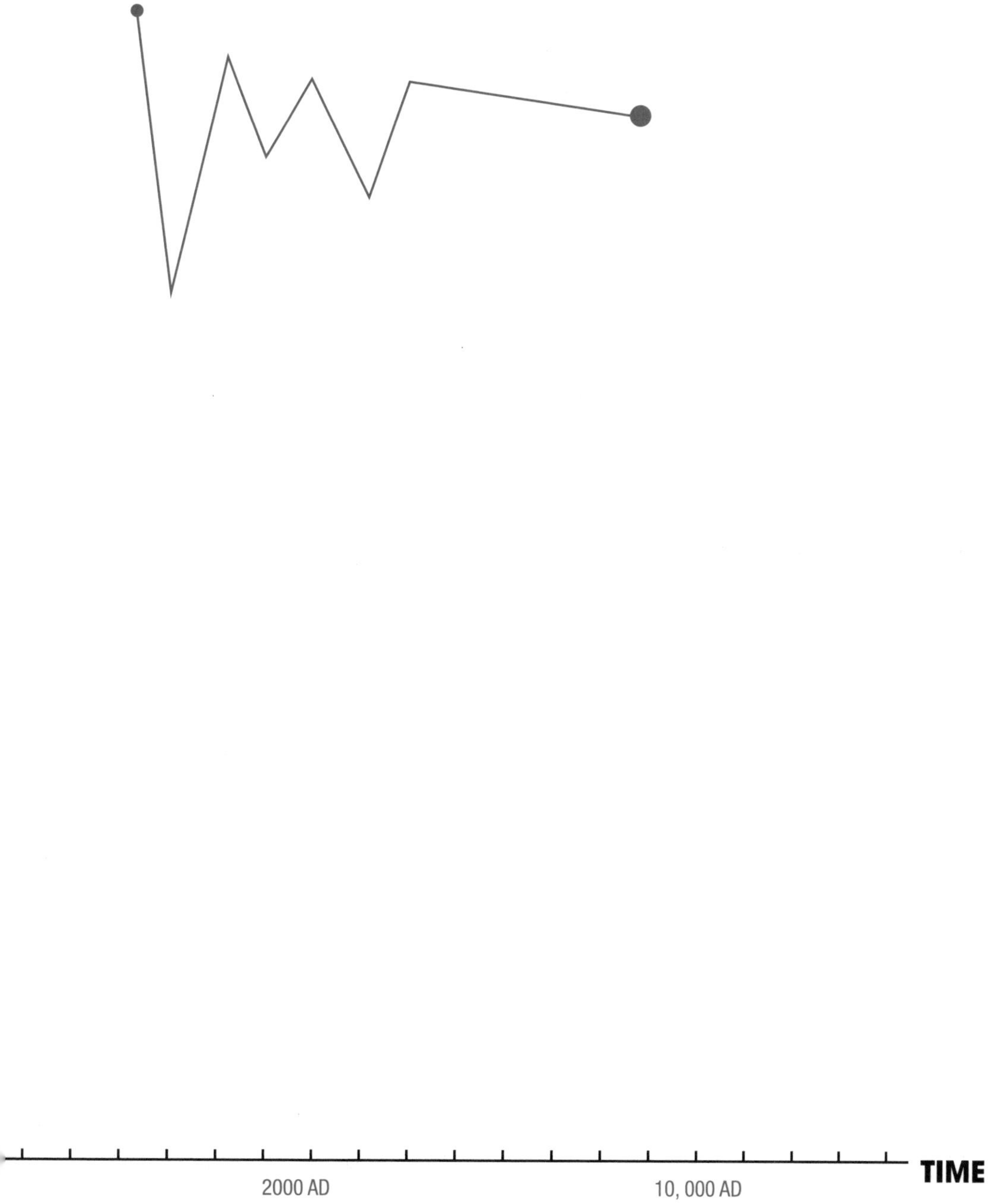

2000 AD   10, 000 AD   **TIME**

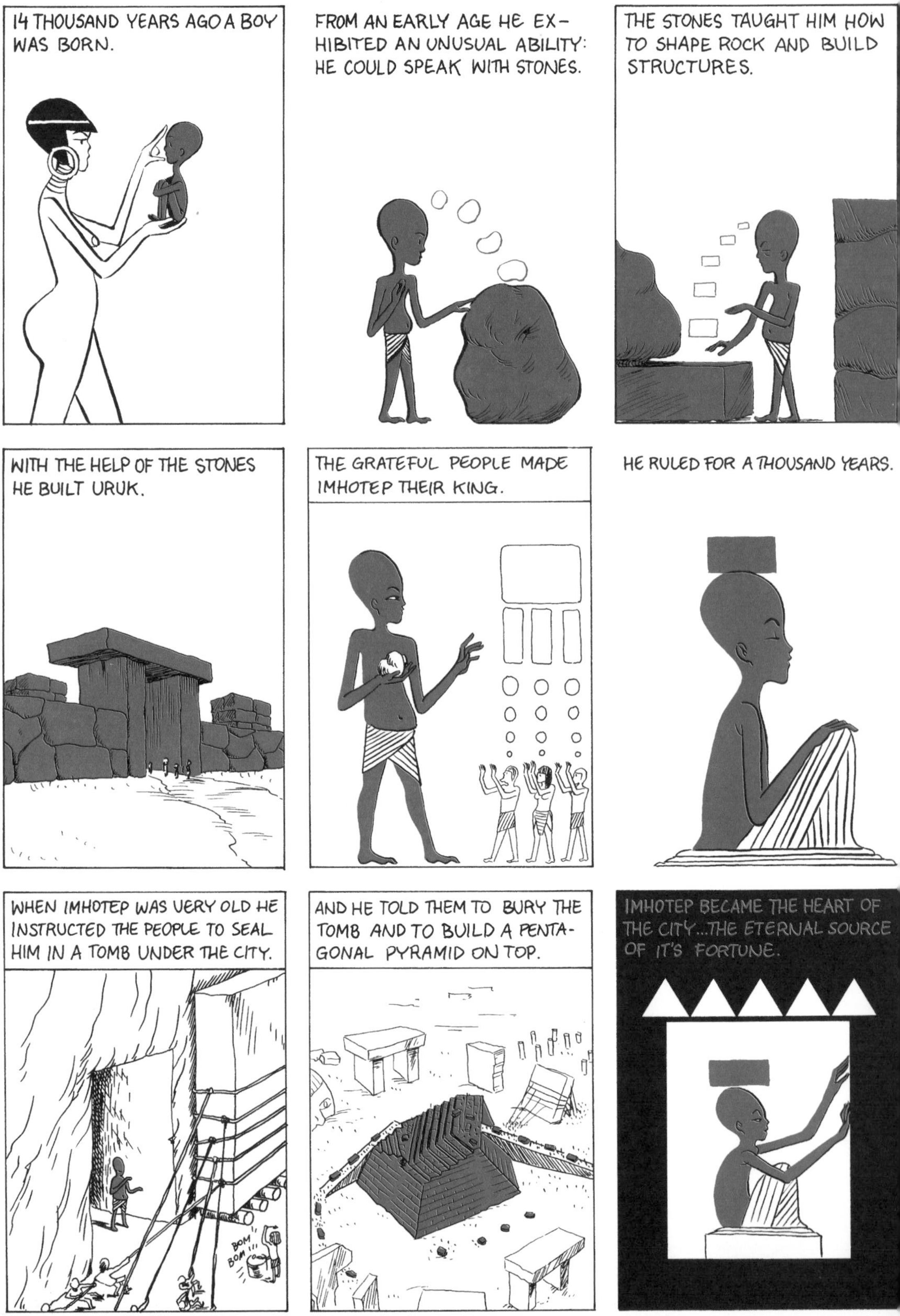
14 THOUSAND YEARS AGO A BOY WAS BORN.
FROM AN EARLY AGE HE EXHIBITED AN UNUSUAL ABILITY: HE COULD SPEAK WITH STONES.
THE STONES TAUGHT HIM HOW TO SHAPE ROCK AND BUILD STRUCTURES.
WITH THE HELP OF THE STONES HE BUILT URUK.
THE GRATEFUL PEOPLE MADE IMHOTEP THEIR KING.
HE RULED FOR A THOUSAND YEARS.
WHEN IMHOTEP WAS VERY OLD HE INSTRUCTED THE PEOPLE TO SEAL HIM IN A TOMB UNDER THE CITY.
BOM BOM !!!
AND HE TOLD THEM TO BURY THE TOMB AND TO BUILD A PENTAGONAL PYRAMID ON TOP.
IMHOTEP BECAME THE HEART OF THE CITY...THE ETERNAL SOURCE OF IT'S FORTUNE.

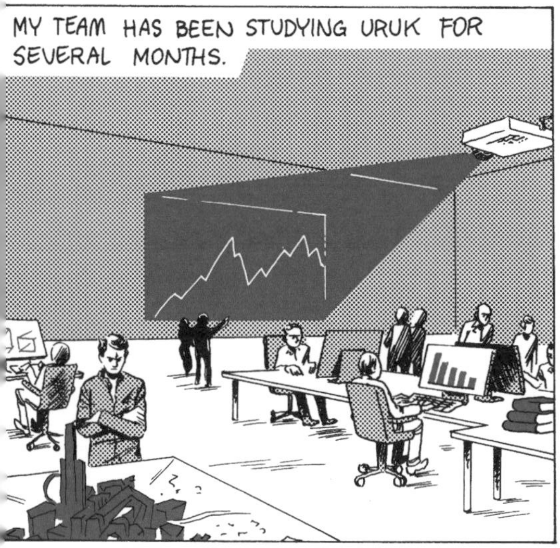
MY TEAM HAS BEEN STUDYING URUK FOR SEVERAL MONTHS.

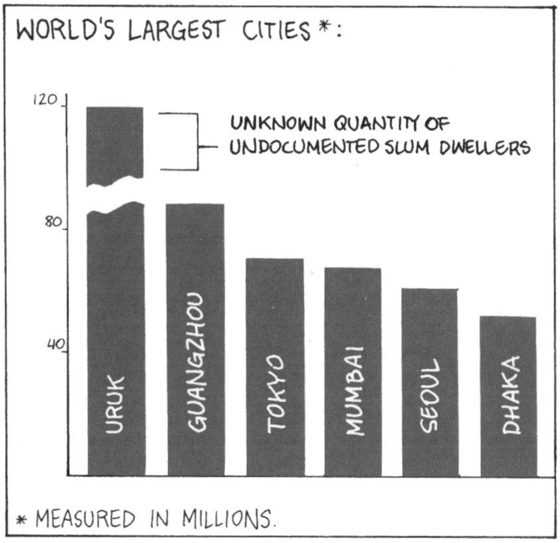
WORLD'S LARGEST CITIES *:
120
80
40
UNKNOWN QUANTITY OF UNDOCUMENTED SLUM DWELLERS
URUK
GUANGZHOU
TOKYO
MUMBAI
SEOUL
DHAKA
* MEASURED IN MILLIONS.

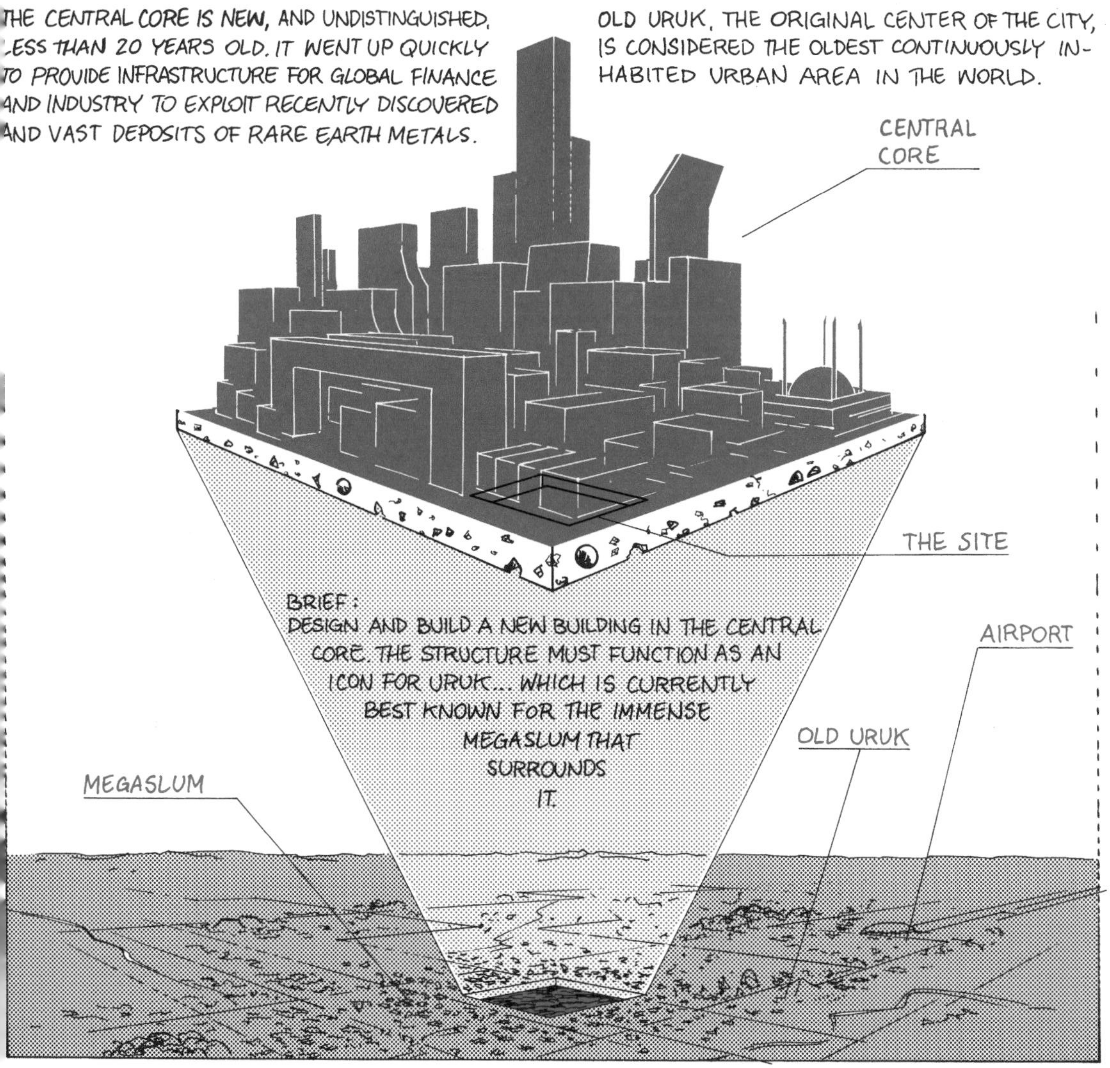
THE CENTRAL CORE IS NEW, AND UNDISTINGUISHED. ESS THAN 20 YEARS OLD. IT WENT UP QUICKLY O PROVIDE INFRASTRUCTURE FOR GLOBAL FINANCE AND INDUSTRY TO EXPLOIT RECENTLY DISCOVERED AND VAST DEPOSITS OF RARE EARTH METALS.
OLD URUK, THE ORIGINAL CENTER OF THE CITY, IS CONSIDERED THE OLDEST CONTINUOUSLY INHABITED URBAN AREA IN THE WORLD.
CENTRAL CORE
THE SITE
BRIEF:
DESIGN AND BUILD A NEW BUILDING IN THE CENTRAL CORE. THE STRUCTURE MUST FUNCTION AS AN ICON FOR URUK... WHICH IS CURRENTLY BEST KNOWN FOR THE IMMENSE MEGASLUM THAT SURROUNDS IT.
AIRPORT
OLD URUK
MEGASLUM

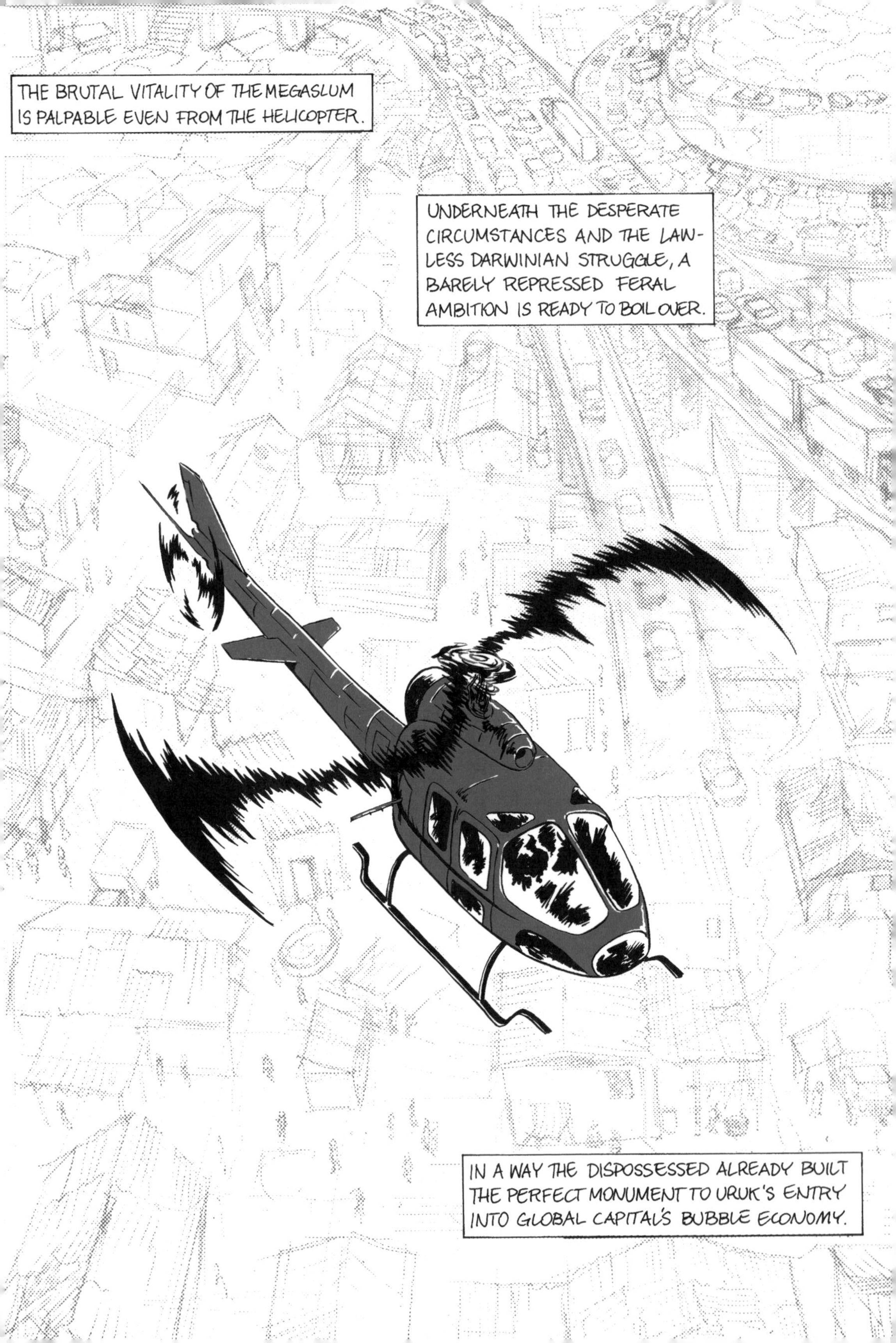
THE BRUTAL VITALITY OF THE MEGASLUM IS PALPABLE EVEN FROM THE HELICOPTER.
UNDERNEATH THE DESPERATE CIRCUMSTANCES AND THE LAWLESS DARWINIAN STRUGGLE, A BARELY REPRESSED FERAL AMBITION IS READY TO BOIL OVER.
IN A WAY THE DISPOSSESSED ALREADY BUILT THE PERFECT MONUMENT TO URUK'S ENTRY INTO GLOBAL CAPITAL'S BUBBLE ECONOMY.

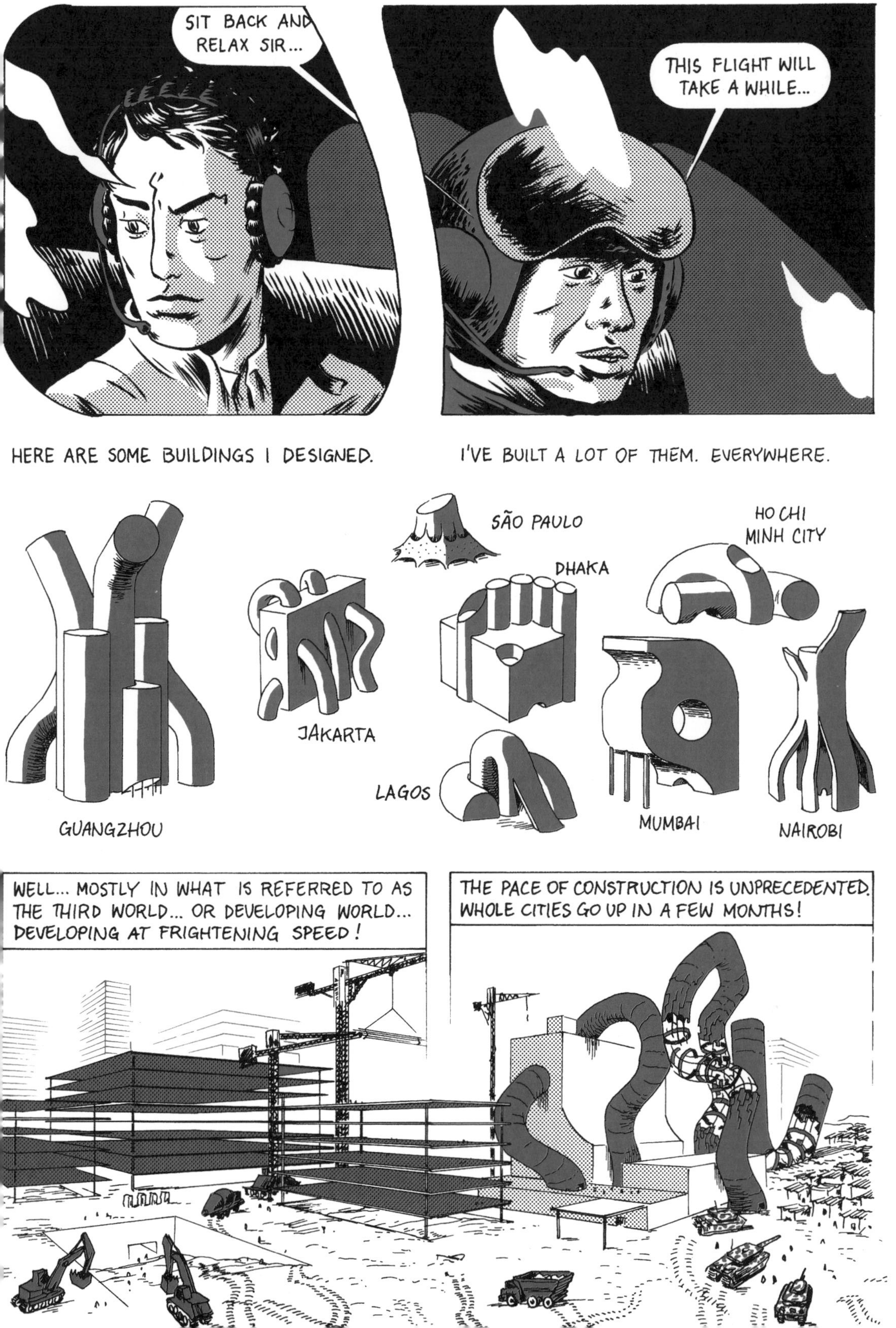
SIT BACK AND RELAX SIR...
THIS FLIGHT WILL TAKE A WHILE...
HERE ARE SOME BUILDINGS I DESIGNED.
I'VE BUILT A LOT OF THEM. EVERYWHERE.
GUANGZHOU
JAKARTA
SÃO PAULO
DHAKA
HO CHI MINH CITY
LAGOS
MUMBAI
NAIROBI
WELL... MOSTLY IN WHAT IS REFERRED TO AS THE THIRD WORLD... OR DEVELOPING WORLD... DEVELOPING AT FRIGHTENING SPEED!
THE PACE OF CONSTRUCTION IS UNPRECEDENTED. WHOLE CITIES GO UP IN A FEW MONTHS!

IT'S NOT LIKE THAT WHERE I'M FROM, THE WEST... NOT ANYMORE. NOT SINCE THE CRISIS...

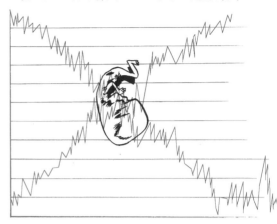

THE OIL CRISIS (WHEN, INCIDENTALLY, I WAS CONCEIVED) WAS THE MOMENT WHEN THE BLOOD OF WESTERN CIVILIZATION STOPPED FLOWING.

THE CRISIS LED TO THE DEMISE OF A SMALL EXPERIMENTAL VILLAGE, CUTTING SHORT MY IDYLLIC CHILDHOOD AND WESTERN FLIRTATION WITH THE POSSIBILITY OF UTOPIA.

MY ADOLESCENCE SPANNED CONTINENTS AND IDEOLOGIES. I SPENT A BRIEF TIME IN THE EASTERN BLOC...LONG ENOUGH TO REALIZE THAT ALL REVOLUTIONARY ENERGY DISSIPATED A LONG TIME AGO. IT'S PART OF THE WEST NOW. AGAIN.

EVEN THE NEW WORLD COULD BE EXPERIENCED PRIMARILY AS A MUSEUM OF AN ABANDONED FUTURE...

IN THE BLUR OF TRANSATLANTIC MEMORIES, ONE MOMENT STANDS OUT IN SHARP RELIEF...MY FIRST ENCOUNTER WITH THE STRUCTURE...

IT'S ...

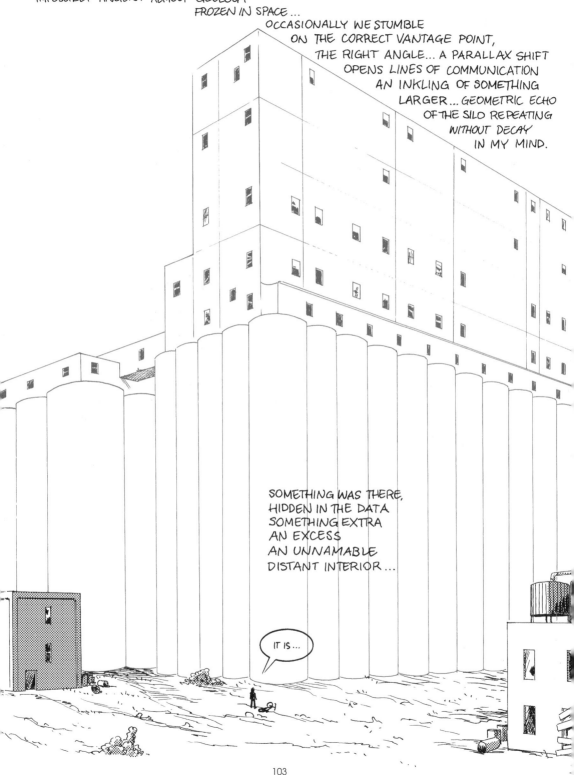

I CALL IT THE STRUCTURE... IT WAS A MASSIVE GRAIN SILO...
UTILITARIAN, A SEED OF MODERNIST ARCHITECTURE
IMPOSSIBLY ANCIENT ALMOST GEOLOGY
FROZEN IN SPACE...
OCCASIONALLY WE STUMBLE
ON THE CORRECT VANTAGE POINT,
THE RIGHT ANGLE... A PARALLAX SHIFT
OPENS LINES OF COMMUNICATION
AN INKLING OF SOMETHING
LARGER... GEOMETRIC ECHO
OF THE SILO REPEATING
WITHOUT DECAY
IN MY MIND.

SOMETHING WAS THERE,
HIDDEN IN THE DATA
SOMETHING EXTRA
AN EXCESS
AN UNNAMABLE
DISTANT INTERIOR...

IT IS...

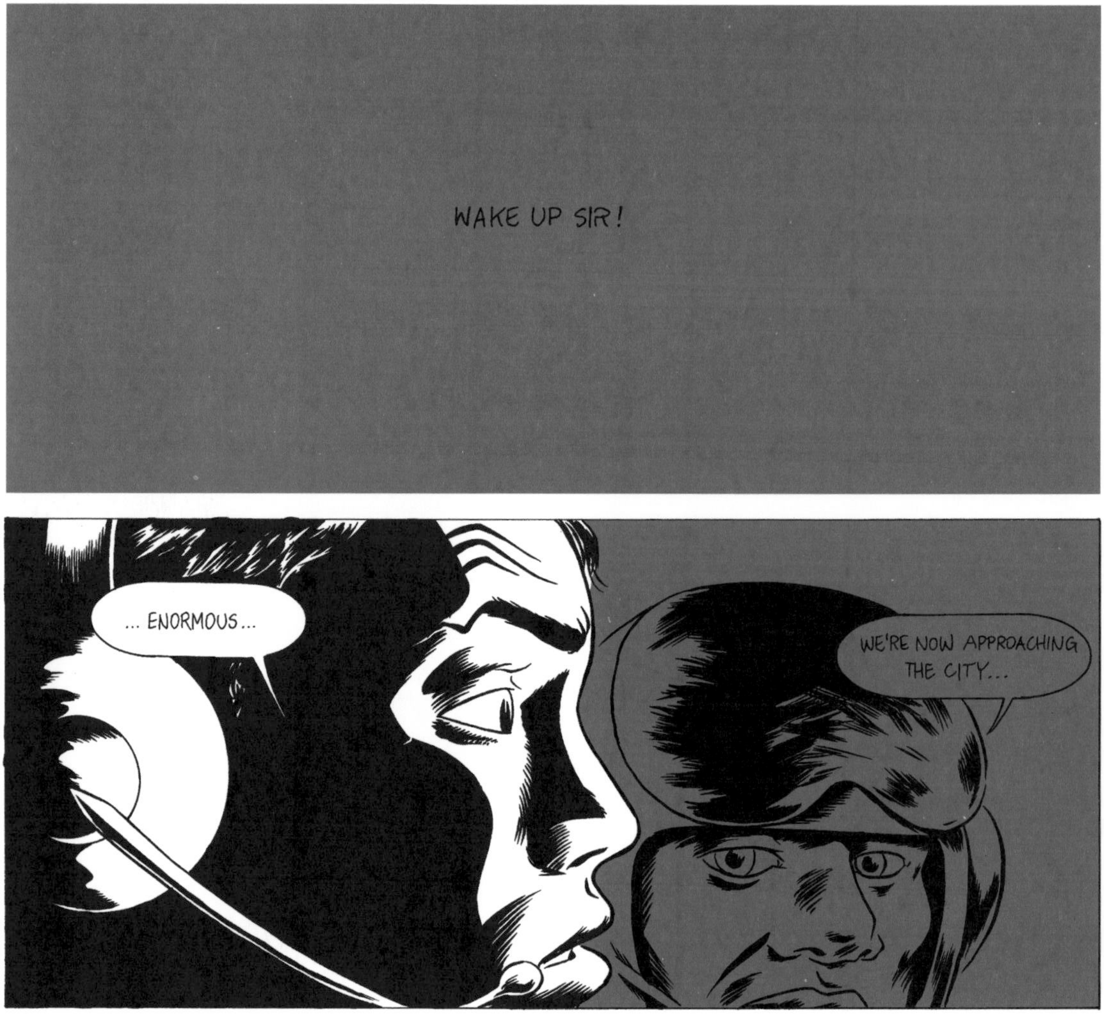
WAKE UP SIR!
... ENORMOUS ...
WE'RE NOW APPROACHING THE CITY...

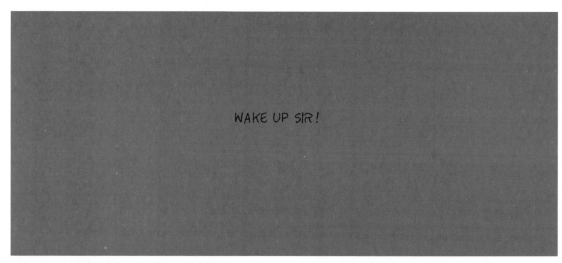

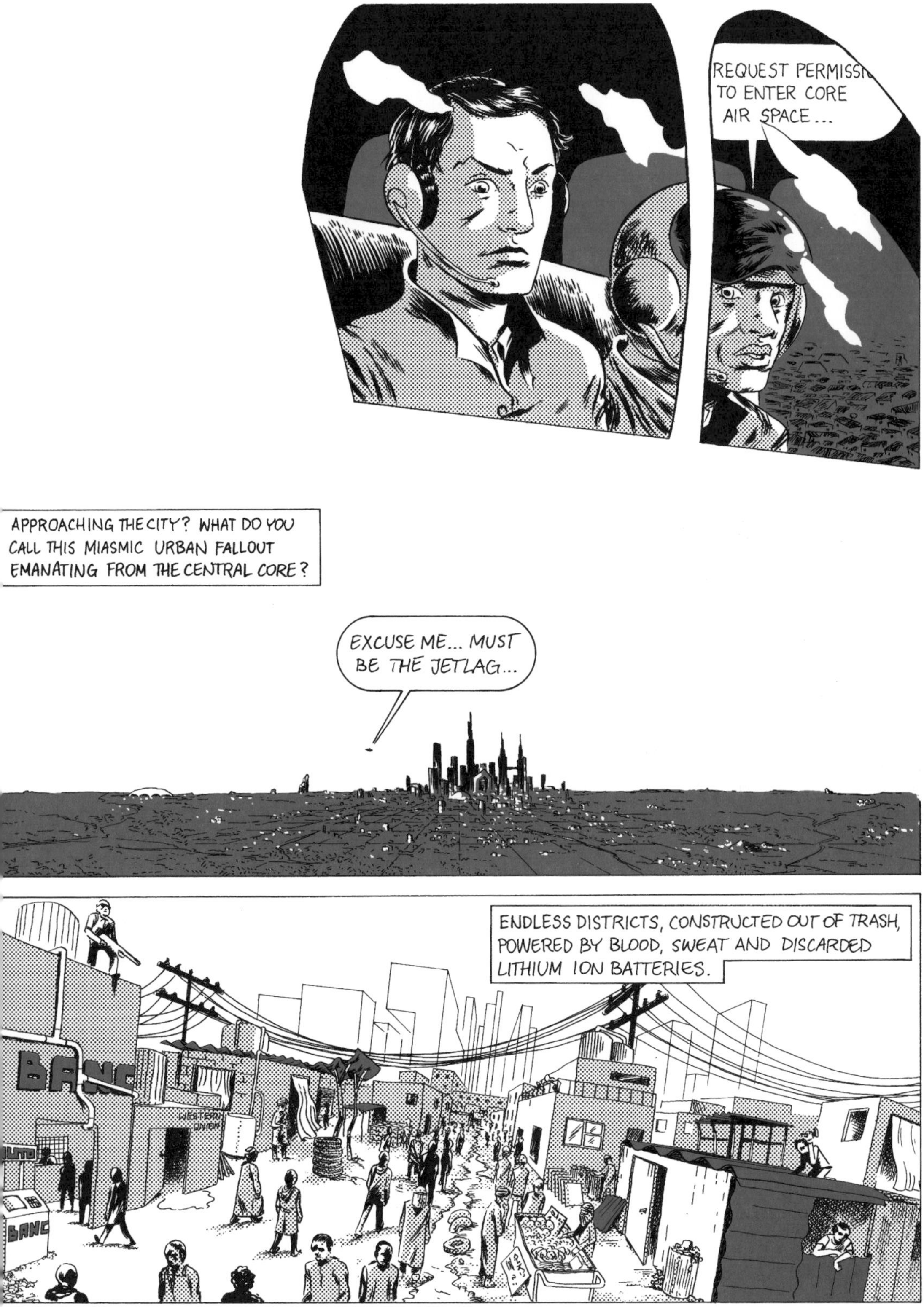
REQUEST PERMISSI
TO ENTER CORE
AIR SPACE...
APPROACHING THE CITY? WHAT DO YOU CALL THIS MIASMIC URBAN FALLOUT EMANATING FROM THE CENTRAL CORE?
EXCUSE ME... MUST BE THE JETLAG...
ENDLESS DISTRICTS, CONSTRUCTED OUT OF TRASH, POWERED BY BLOOD, SWEAT AND DISCARDED LITHIUM ION BATTERIES.
BANC
BANC

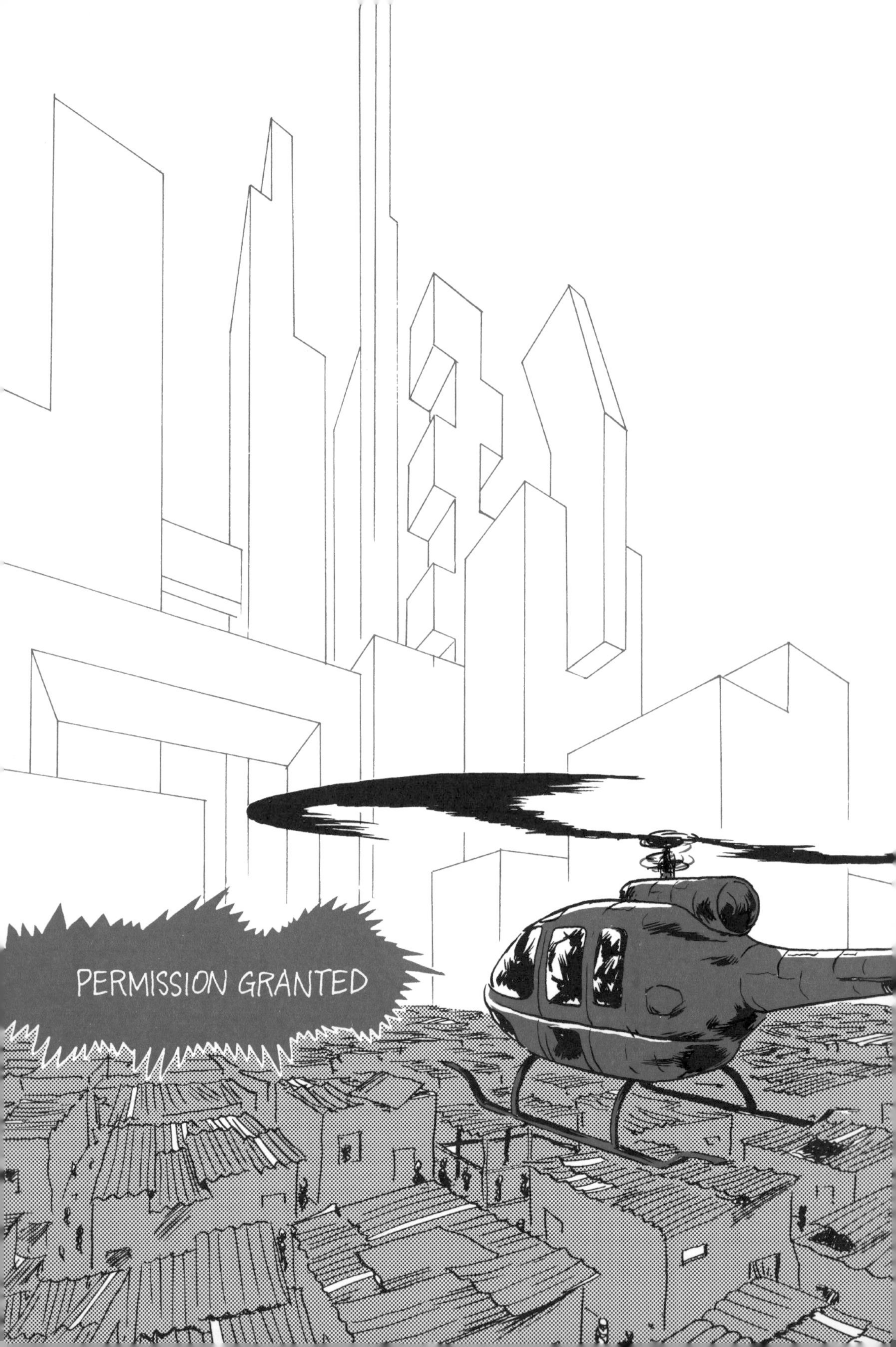
PERMISSION GRANTED

THE HELICOPTER TURNED SLIGTHTLY AND
FOR A MOMENT
THE CENTRAL CORE OF
URUK REVEALED
ITS SINISTER GEOMETRY.

THE SLUMS DESPERATELY CIRCLED
THE INVISIBLE PERIMETER
MOTH-LIKE
FEEDING ON
EMPTY LUMINESCENCE.

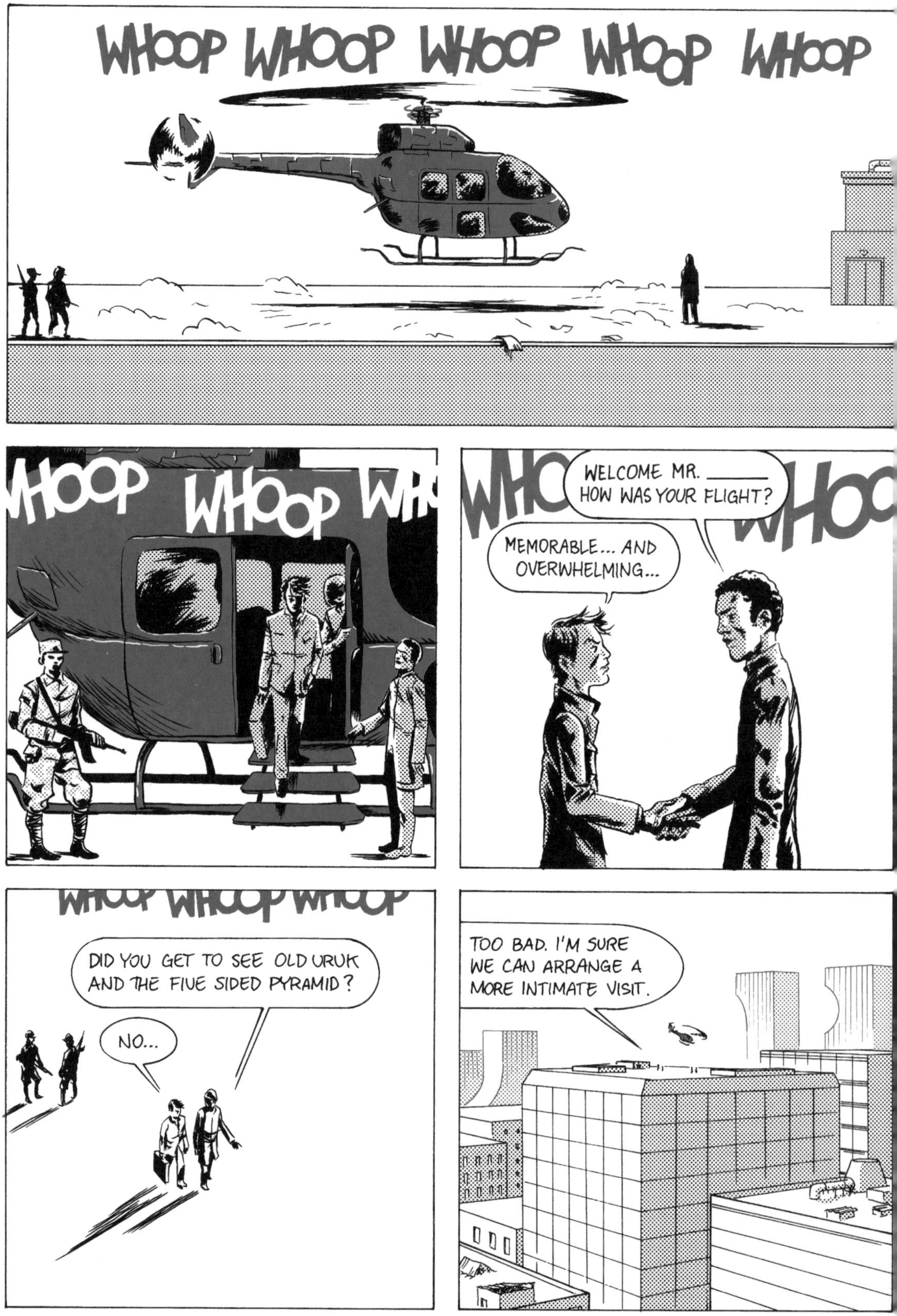
WHOOP WHOOP WHOOP WHOOP WHOOP
WHOOP WHOOP
WELCOME MR. ______ HOW WAS YOUR FLIGHT?
MEMORABLE... AND OVERWHELMING...
WHOOP WHOOP WHOOP
DID YOU GET TO SEE OLD URUK AND THE FIVE SIDED PYRAMID?
NO...
TOO BAD. I'M SURE WE CAN ARRANGE A MORE INTIMATE VISIT.

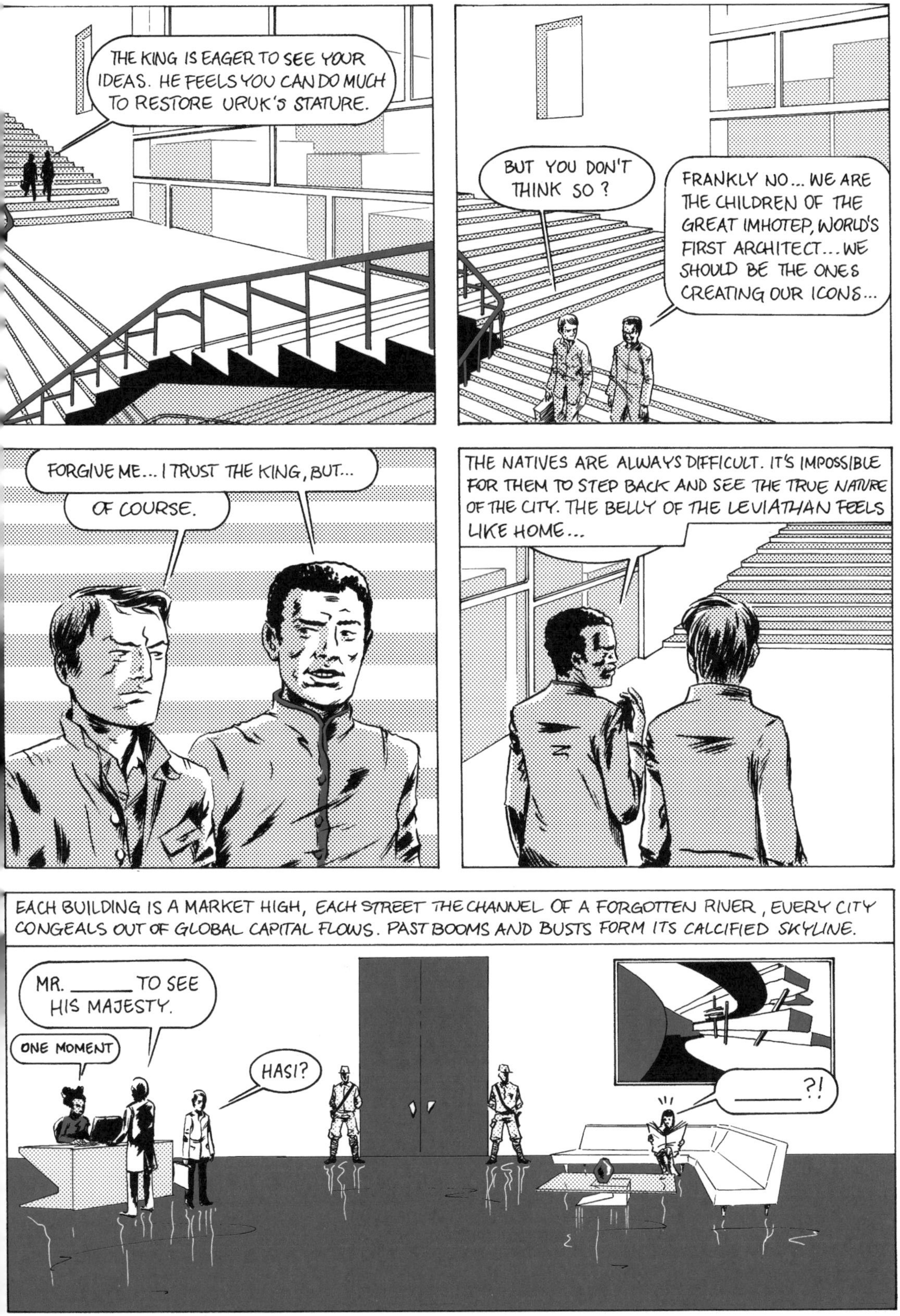
THE KING IS EAGER TO SEE YOUR IDEAS. HE FEELS YOU CAN DO MUCH TO RESTORE URUK'S STATURE.
BUT YOU DON'T THINK SO?
FRANKLY NO... WE ARE THE CHILDREN OF THE GREAT IMHOTEP, WORLD'S FIRST ARCHITECT... WE SHOULD BE THE ONES CREATING OUR ICONS...
FORGIVE ME... I TRUST THE KING, BUT...
OF COURSE.
THE NATIVES ARE ALWAYS DIFFICULT. IT'S IMPOSSIBLE FOR THEM TO STEP BACK AND SEE THE TRUE NATURE OF THE CITY. THE BELLY OF THE LEVIATHAN FEELS LIKE HOME...
EACH BUILDING IS A MARKET HIGH, EACH STREET THE CHANNEL OF A FORGOTTEN RIVER, EVERY CITY CONGEALS OUT OF GLOBAL CAPITAL FLOWS. PAST BOOMS AND BUSTS FORM ITS CALCIFIED SKYLINE.
MR. ______ TO SEE HIS MAJESTY.
ONE MOMENT
HASI?
______?!

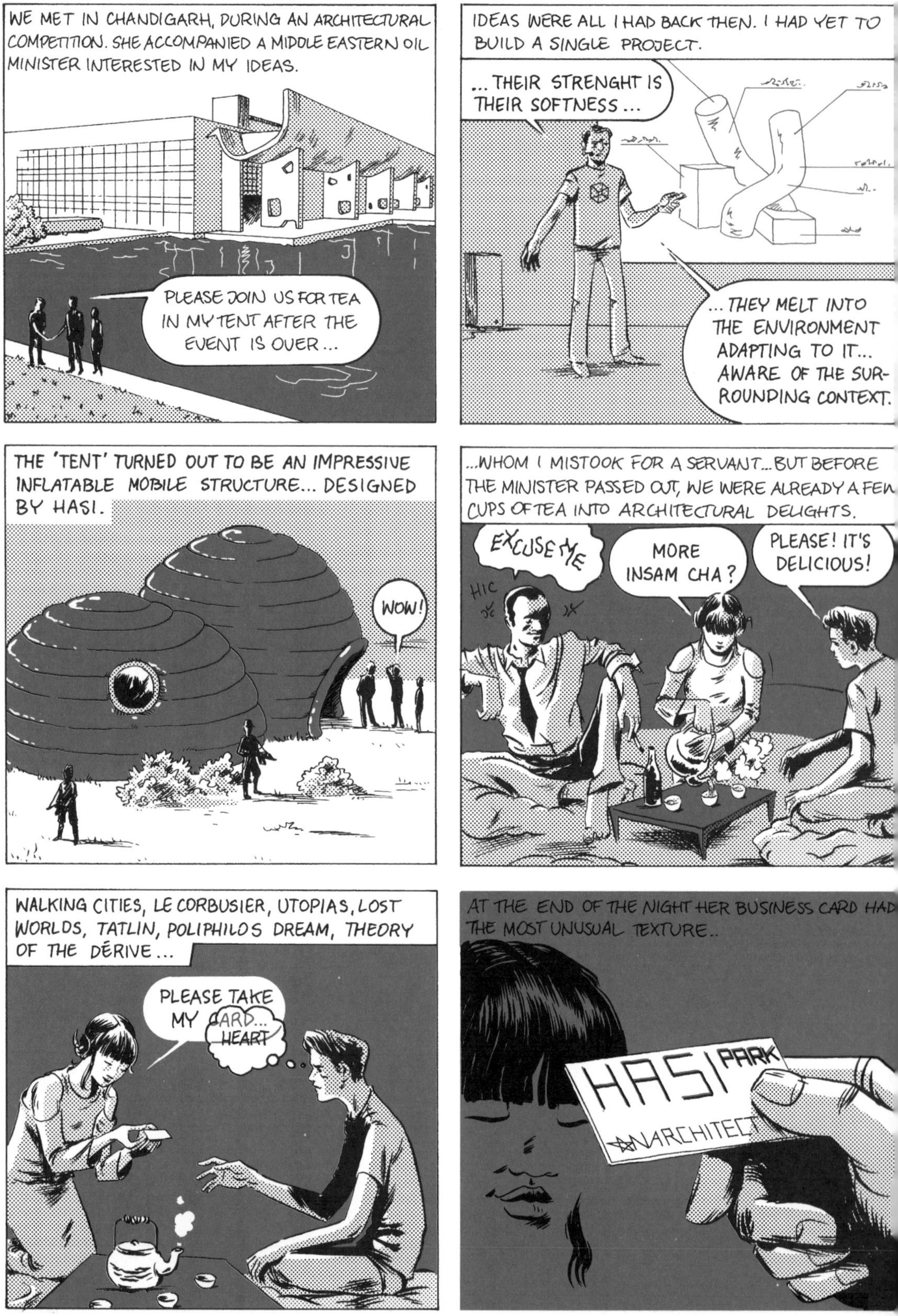

WE MET IN CHANDIGARH, DURING AN ARCHITECTURAL COMPETITION. SHE ACCOMPANIED A MIDDLE EASTERN OIL MINISTER INTERESTED IN MY IDEAS.
PLEASE JOIN US FOR TEA IN MY TENT AFTER THE EVENT IS OVER...
IDEAS WERE ALL I HAD BACK THEN. I HAD YET TO BUILD A SINGLE PROJECT.
...THEIR STRENGHT IS THEIR SOFTNESS...
...THEY MELT INTO THE ENVIRONMENT ADAPTING TO IT... AWARE OF THE SURROUNDING CONTEXT.
THE 'TENT' TURNED OUT TO BE AN IMPRESSIVE INFLATABLE MOBILE STRUCTURE... DESIGNED BY HASI.
WOW!
...WHOM I MISTOOK FOR A SERVANT... BUT BEFORE THE MINISTER PASSED OUT, WE WERE ALREADY A FEW CUPS OF TEA INTO ARCHITECTURAL DELIGHTS.
EXCUSE ME
HIC
MORE INSAM CHA?
PLEASE! IT'S DELICIOUS!
WALKING CITIES, LE CORBUSIER, UTOPIAS, LOST WORLDS, TATLIN, POLIPHILOS DREAM, THEORY OF THE DÉRIVE...
PLEASE TAKE MY CARD...
HEART
AT THE END OF THE NIGHT HER BUSINESS CARD HAD THE MOST UNUSUAL TEXTURE...
HASI
PARK
NARCHITEC

AAAAARGH!

WE BRIEFLY WORKED TOGETHER. I ADMIRED HER ASIAN VITALITY. SHE WAS ATTRACTED TO WESTERN IDEAS. WE THRIVED ON MUTUAL ORIENTALISM.

BUT IT COULDN'T LAST. SHE WAS ALREADY TOO WESTERN, TOO BRASH, TOO ROCK 'N ROLL...

...HASI WANTED TO REVIVE THE ABANDONED PROJECTS OF WESTERN AVANT GARDES. A NOBLE EFFORT...

LISTEN UP!

WE'RE BUILD- ING A PARTICLE ACCELERATOR!

CONSTRUCTIVISM, FUTURISM, SITUATIONISM, POST- MODERNISM... BRILLIANT PERFORMANCES ALL.

AN ATOM SMASHER!

BUT HER VITALITY ONLY FURTHER EXPOSED THE EXAUSTED WESTERN MODELS.

CLAP

CLAP

SMASH!

CLAP CLA

BACK TO WORK!

WOOP!

YE

WE COMPLETED ONE BUILDING TOGETHER. IN MOSCOW. SHE RUTHLESSLY DECONSTRUCTED MY CONTRIBUTION. MY NEXT PROJECT WAS IN JAKARTA. HERS WAS IN LONDON.

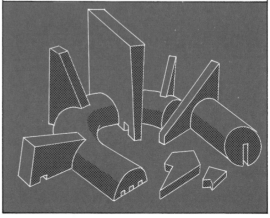

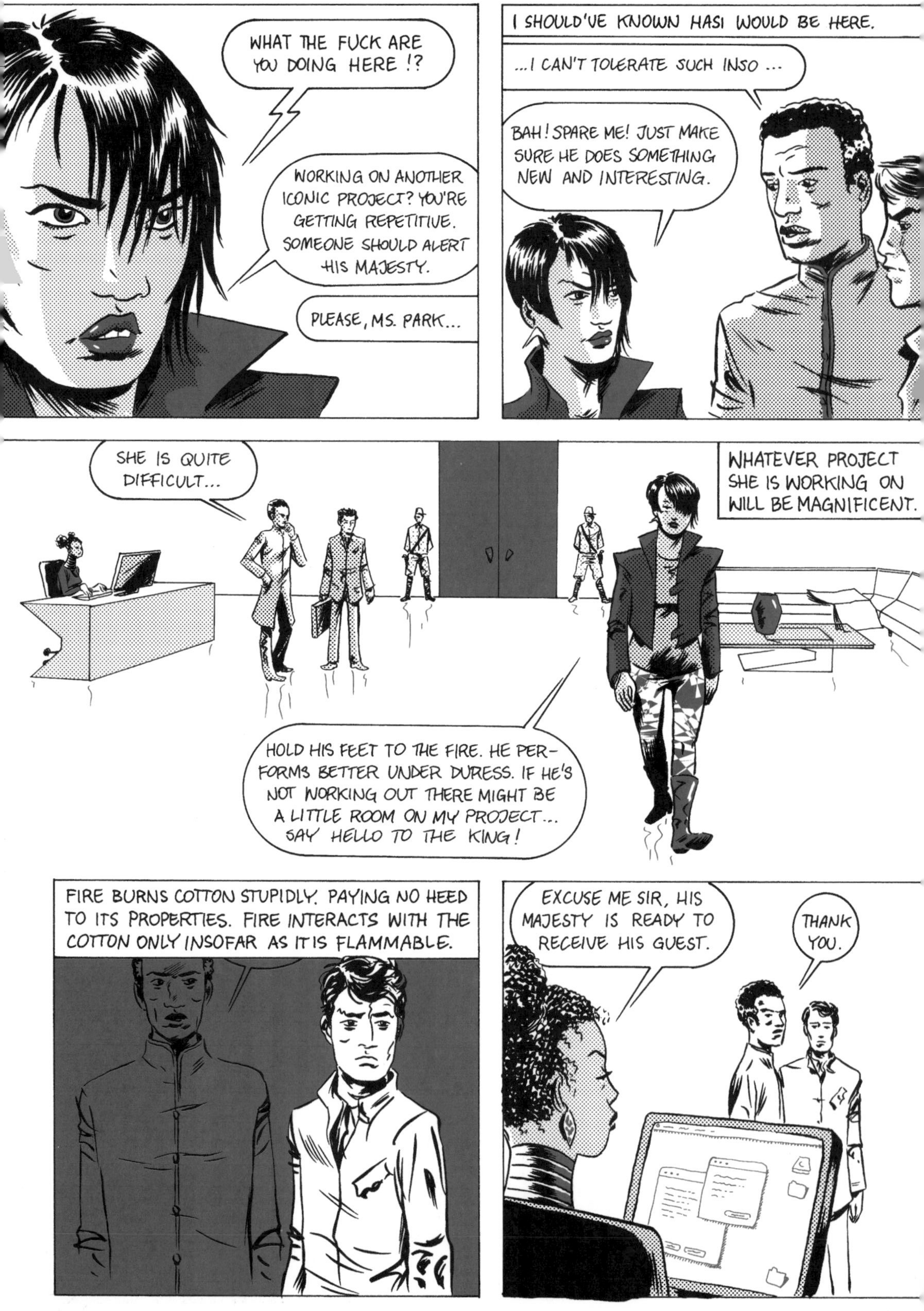
WHAT THE FUCK ARE YOU DOING HERE !?
WORKING ON ANOTHER ICONIC PROJECT? YOU'RE GETTING REPETITIVE. SOMEONE SHOULD ALERT HIS MAJESTY.
PLEASE, MS. PARK...
I SHOULD'VE KNOWN HASI WOULD BE HERE.
...I CAN'T TOLERATE SUCH INSO ...
BAH! SPARE ME! JUST MAKE SURE HE DOES SOMETHING NEW AND INTERESTING.
SHE IS QUITE DIFFICULT...
WHATEVER PROJECT SHE IS WORKING ON WILL BE MAGNIFICENT.
HOLD HIS FEET TO THE FIRE. HE PERFORMS BETTER UNDER DURESS. IF HE'S NOT WORKING OUT THERE MIGHT BE A LITTLE ROOM ON MY PROJECT... SAY HELLO TO THE KING!
FIRE BURNS COTTON STUPIDLY, PAYING NO HEED TO ITS PROPERTIES. FIRE INTERACTS WITH THE COTTON ONLY INSOFAR AS IT IS FLAMMABLE.
EXCUSE ME SIR, HIS MAJESTY IS READY TO RECEIVE HIS GUEST.
THANK YOU.

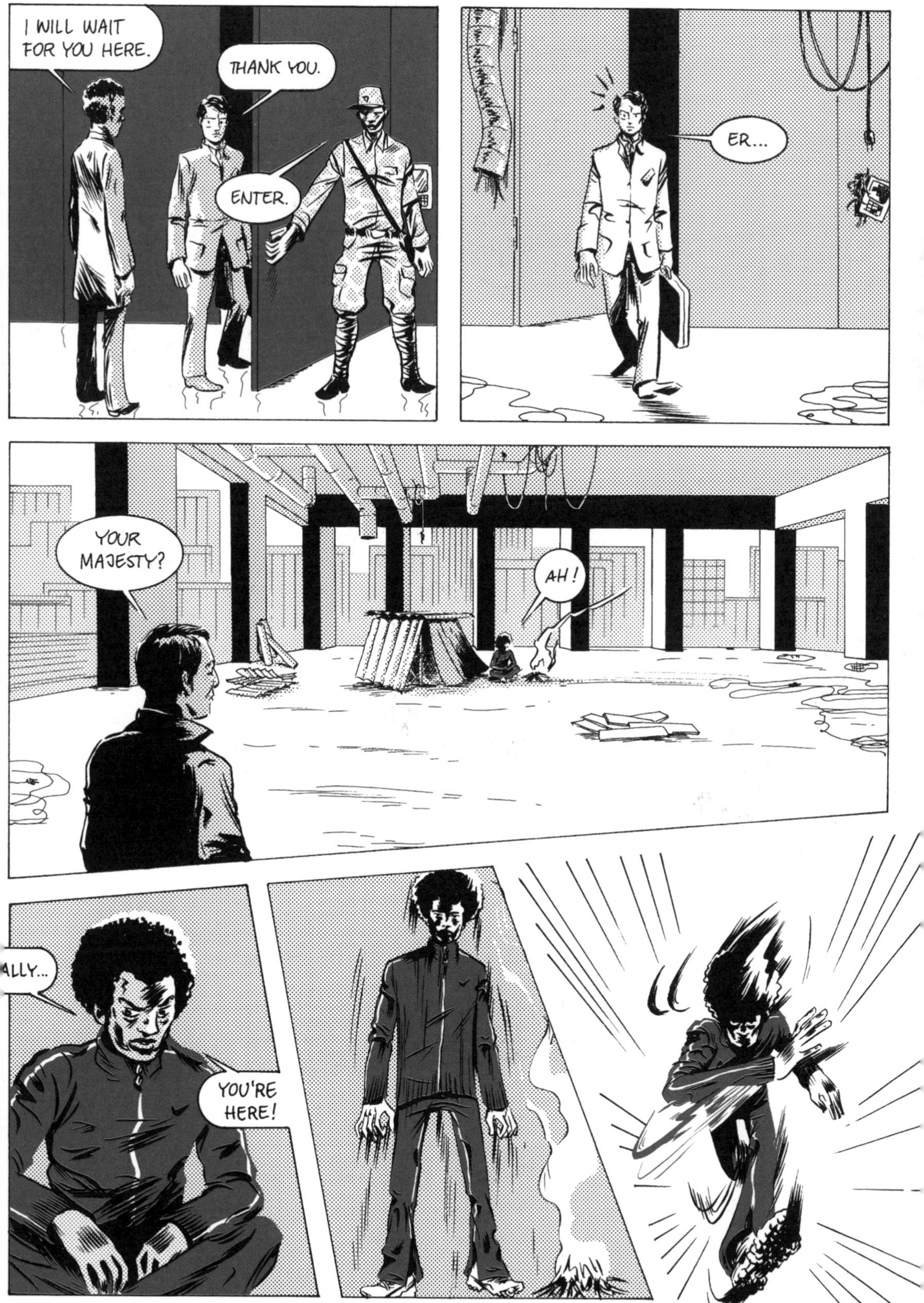
I WILL WAIT FOR YOU HERE.
THANK YOU.
ENTER.
ER...
YOUR MAJESTY?
AH!
ALLY...
YOU'RE HERE!

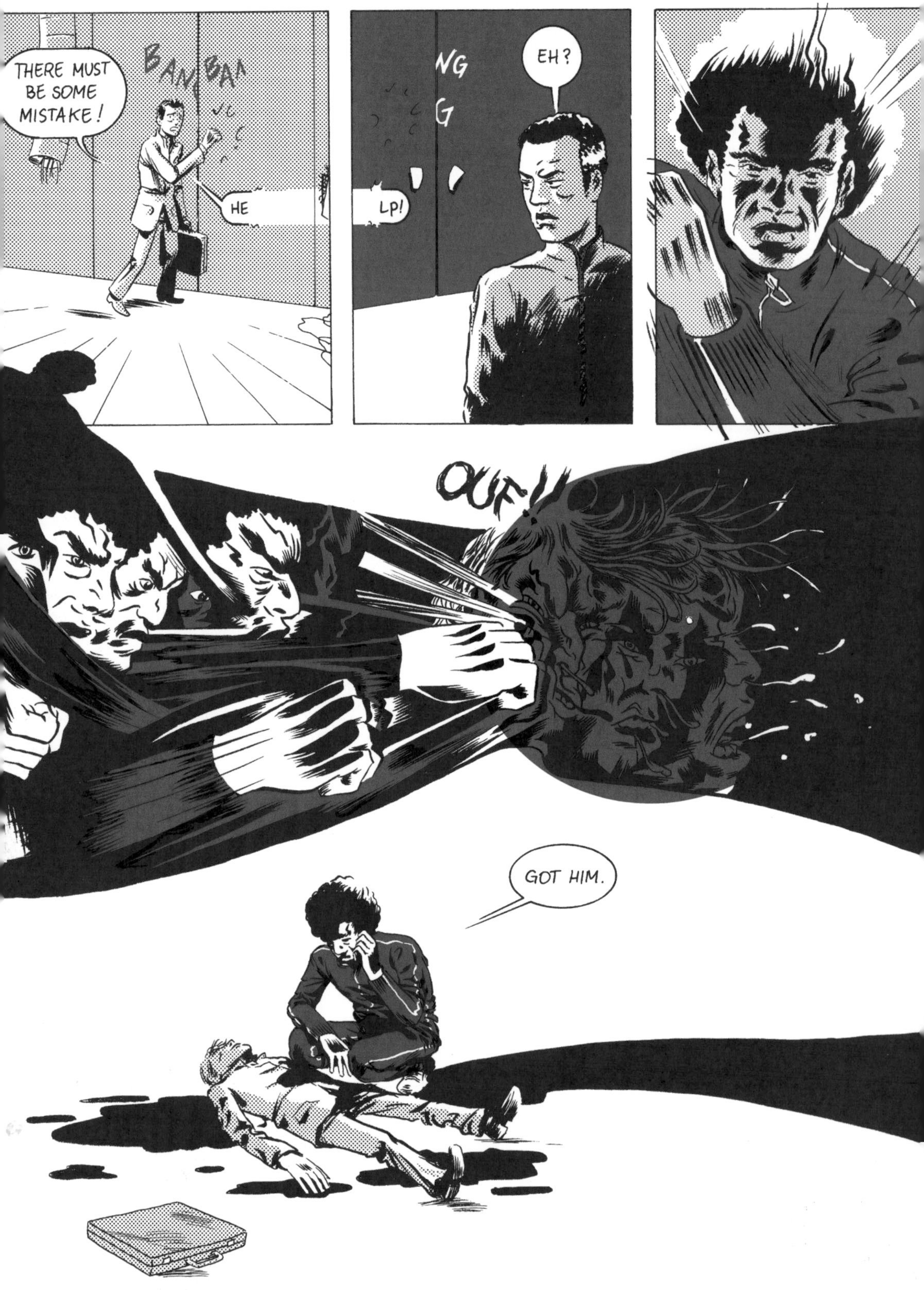
THERE MUST BE SOME MISTAKE!
BAN BA
HE
NG G
LP!
EH?
OUF!
GOT HIM.

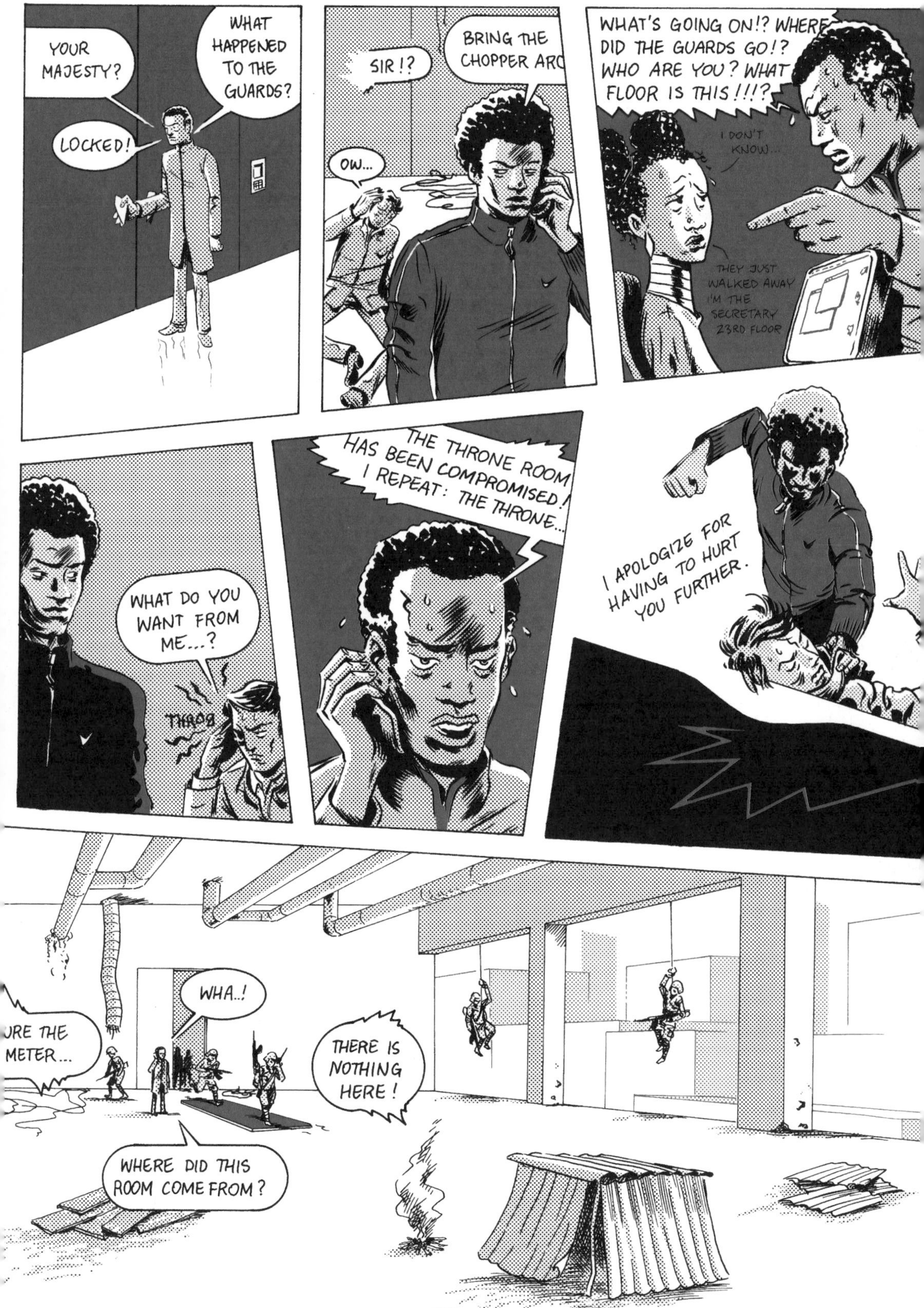
YOUR MAJESTY?
WHAT HAPPENED TO THE GUARDS?
LOCKED!
SIR!?
BRING THE CHOPPER ARO
OW...
WHAT'S GOING ON!? WHERE DID THE GUARDS GO!? WHO ARE YOU? WHAT FLOOR IS THIS!!!?
I DON'T KNOW...
THEY JUST WALKED AWAY I'M THE SECRETARY 23RD FLOOR
WHAT DO YOU WANT FROM ME...?
THROB
THE THRONE ROOM HAS BEEN COMPROMISED! I REPEAT: THE THRONE...
I APOLOGIZE FOR HAVING TO HURT YOU FURTHER.
URE THE METER...
WHA..!
WHERE DID THIS ROOM COME FROM?
THERE IS NOTHING HERE!

DO YOU REMEMBER
YOUR DREAMS?

I RARELY DO... UNLESS THEY CONTAIN *THE OBJECT*. ITS PRESENCE CRYSTALIZES PATTERNS AND CONNECTIONS...

OBLIQUE ONES...TO MEMORIES. NO... *THROUGH* MEMORIES.

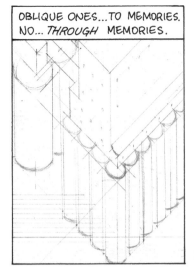

I WASN'T A GOOD STUDENT. ASSIGNMENTS ELUDED MY GRASP.

HUM...

YOU WILL NEVER BUILD ANYTHING...

HE WAS RIGHT...

ALL OF MY PROJECTS WERE HOLLOW... THERE WAS ALWAYS SOMETHING MISSING. THAT UNKNOWABLE, HIDDEN ESSENCE...

MERE TOYS!

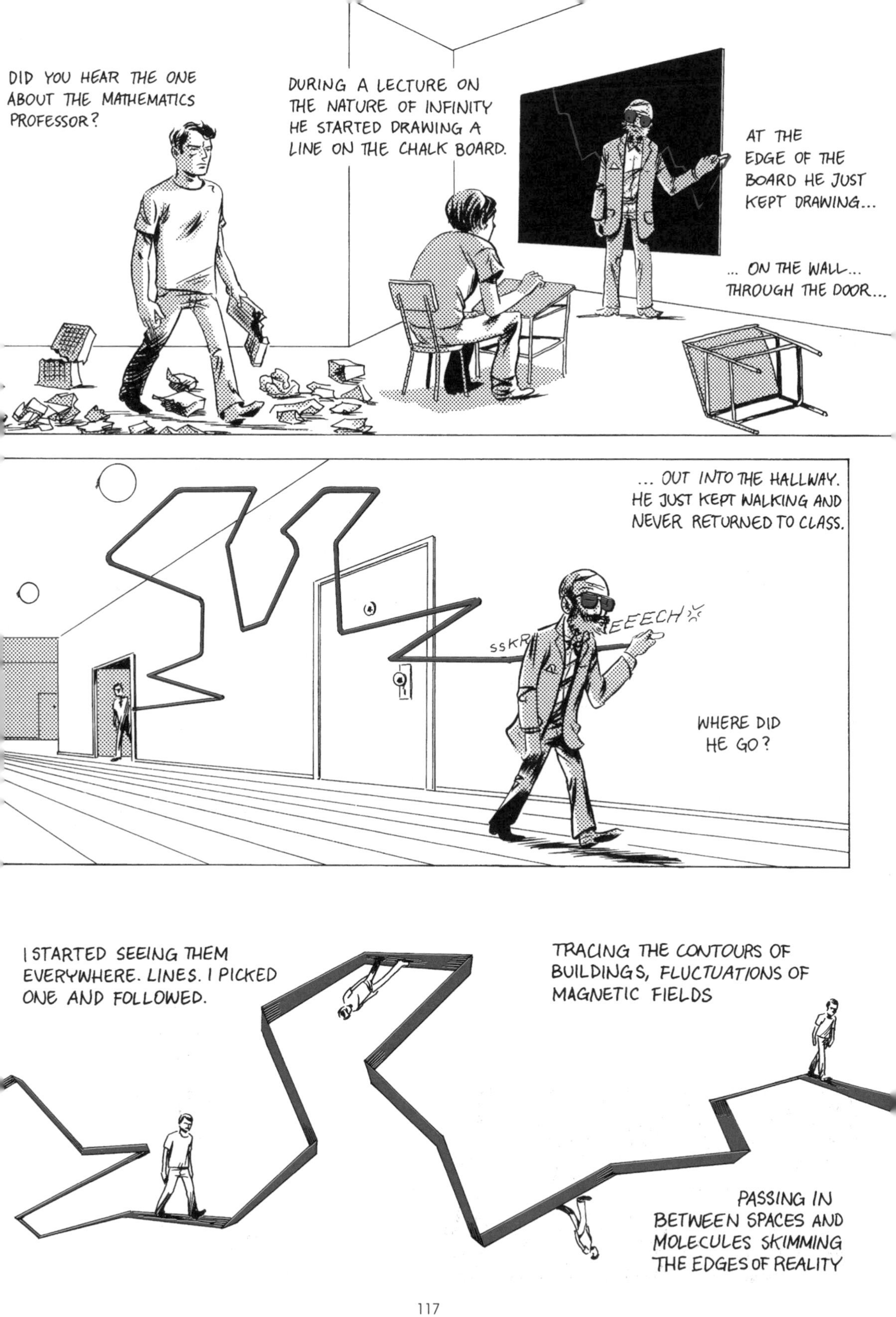
DID YOU HEAR THE ONE ABOUT THE MATHEMATICS PROFESSOR?
DURING A LECTURE ON THE NATURE OF INFINITY HE STARTED DRAWING A LINE ON THE CHALK BOARD.
AT THE EDGE OF THE BOARD HE JUST KEPT DRAWING...
... ON THE WALL... THROUGH THE DOOR...
... OUT INTO THE HALLWAY. HE JUST KEPT WALKING AND NEVER RETURNED TO CLASS.
SSKREEEECH
WHERE DID HE GO?
I STARTED SEEING THEM EVERYWHERE. LINES. I PICKED ONE AND FOLLOWED.
TRACING THE CONTOURS OF BUILDINGS, FLUCTUATIONS OF MAGNETIC FIELDS
PASSING IN BETWEEN SPACES AND MOLECULES SKIMMING THE EDGES OF REALITY

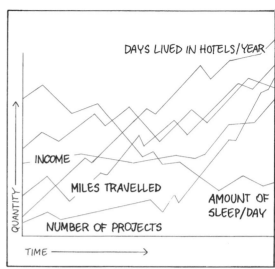

LINES. OUTLINES, TRAJECTORIES, VECTORS, TRENDS
QUANTITY
TIME
DAYS LIVED IN HOTELS/YEAR
INCOME
MILES TRAVELLED
AMOUNT OF SLEEP/DAY
NUMBER OF PROJECTS
QUANTITY
TIME
GDP, POPULATIONS, MURDERS, INTEREST RATES, GRAIN FUTURES, OIL RESERVES, GAS STATIONS, VEHICLES, DENSITY, ZONING PATTERNS...
STREETS SIDEWALKS INTERSECTIONS SQUARES
BOXES ENVELOPES NEIGHBORHOODS SLUMS DISTRICTS
CITIES. URUK.
MY PROJECT!

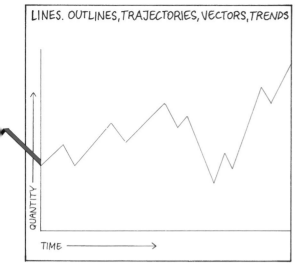

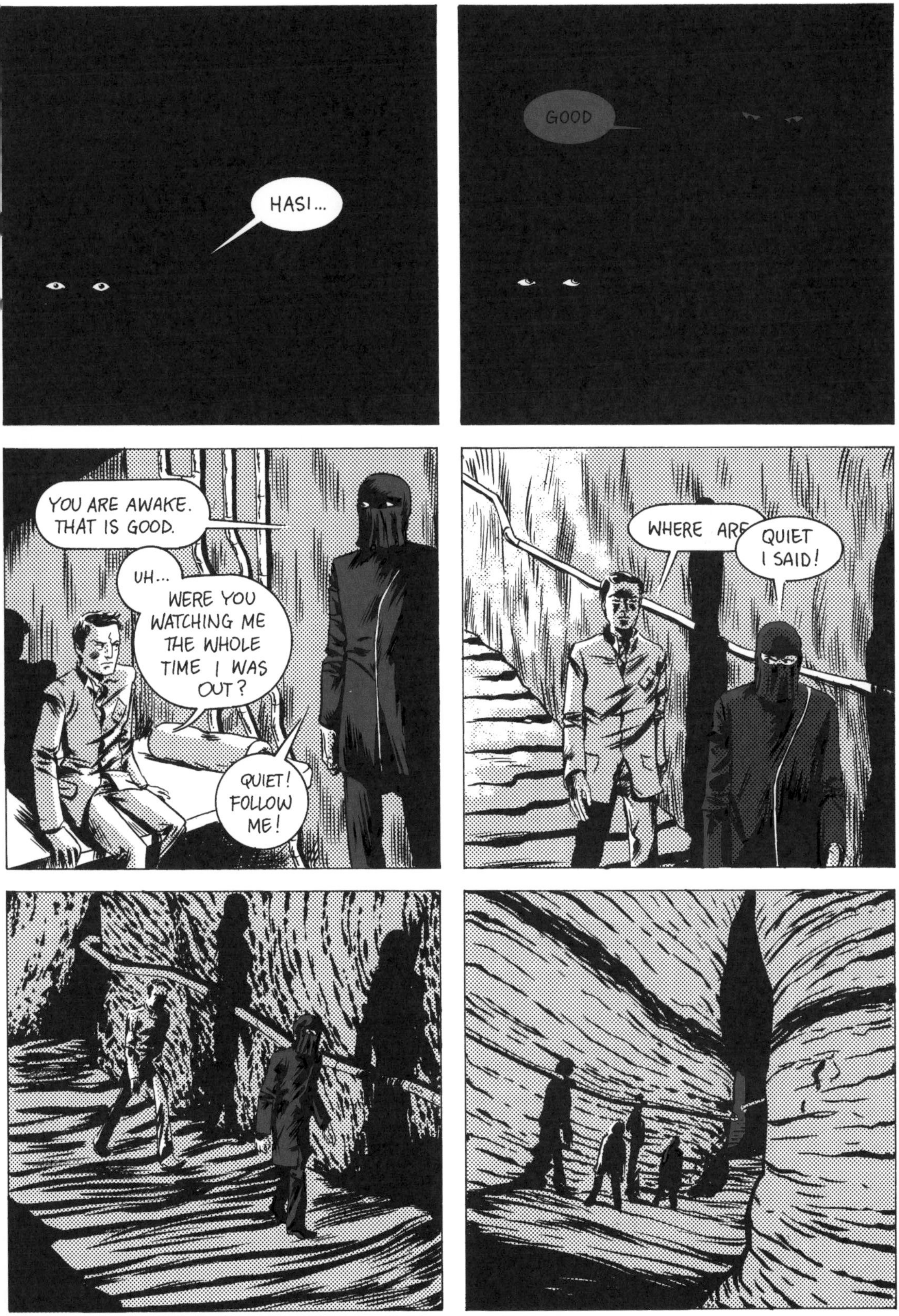
HASI...
GOOD
YOU ARE AWAKE. THAT IS GOOD.
UH...
WERE YOU WATCHING ME THE WHOLE TIME I WAS OUT?
QUIET! FOLLOW ME!
WHERE ARE
QUIET I SAID!

THE DOWNWARD MOMENTUM WAS IRRESISTABLE.
EVEN WHEN I WAS CLEARLY MOVING SIDEWAYS

OR UPWARDS...

I COULDN'T SHAKE THE FEELING OF CONTINUOUS DESCENT...

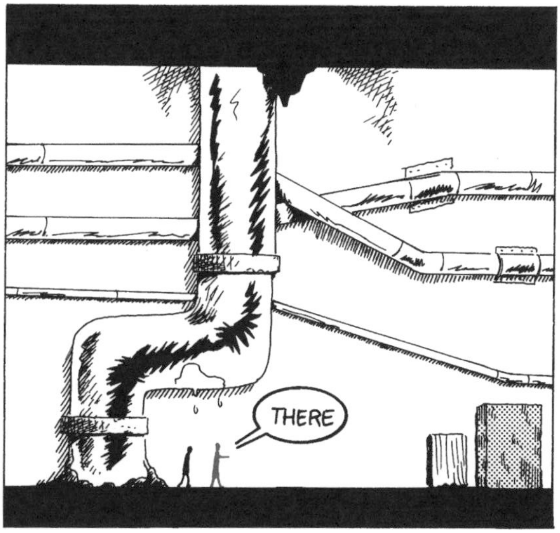
THERE

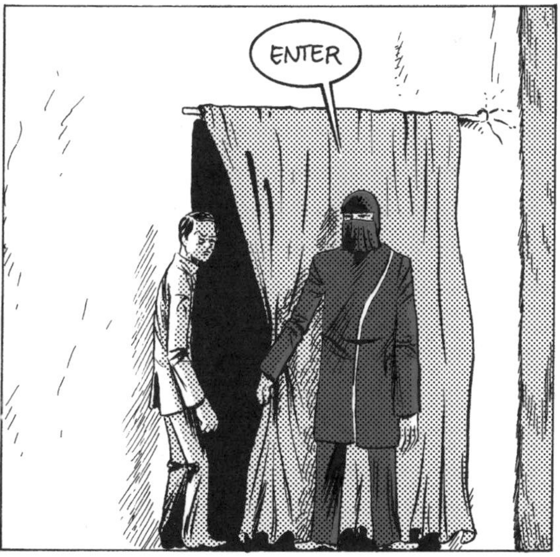
ENTER

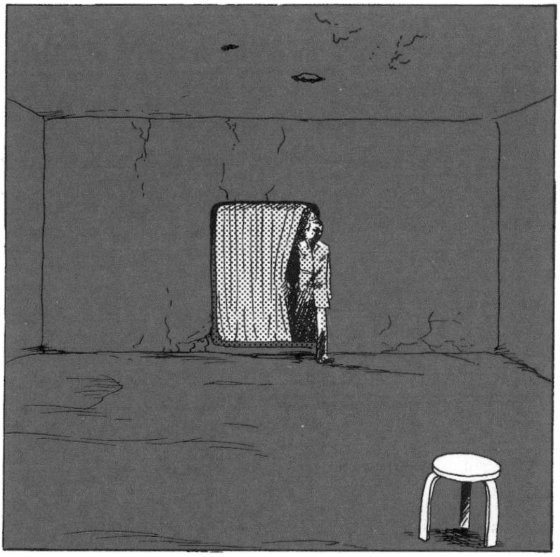

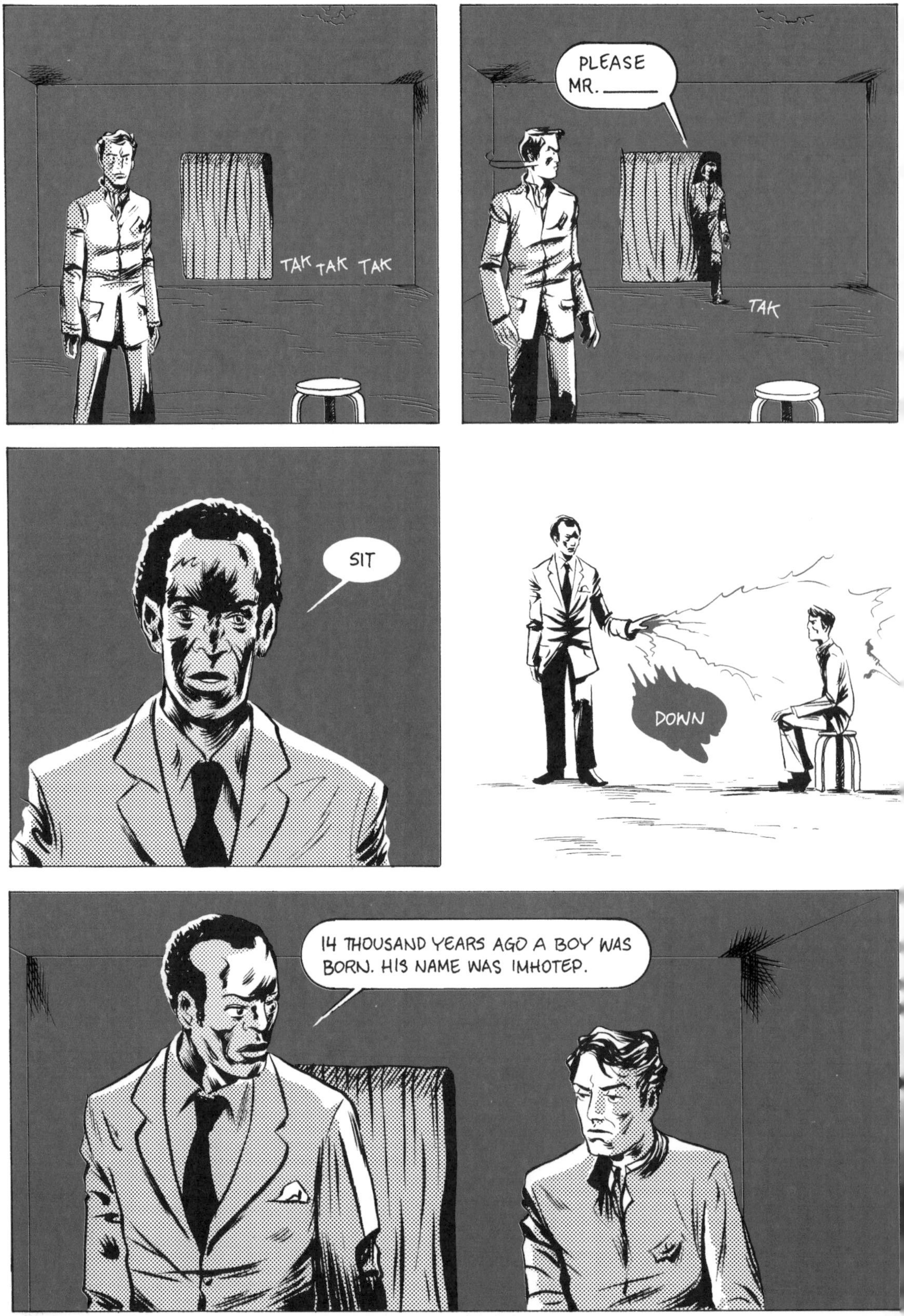
TAK TAK TAK
PLEASE MR. ______
TAK
SIT
DOWN
14 THOUSAND YEARS AGO A BOY WAS BORN. HIS NAME WAS IMHOTEP.

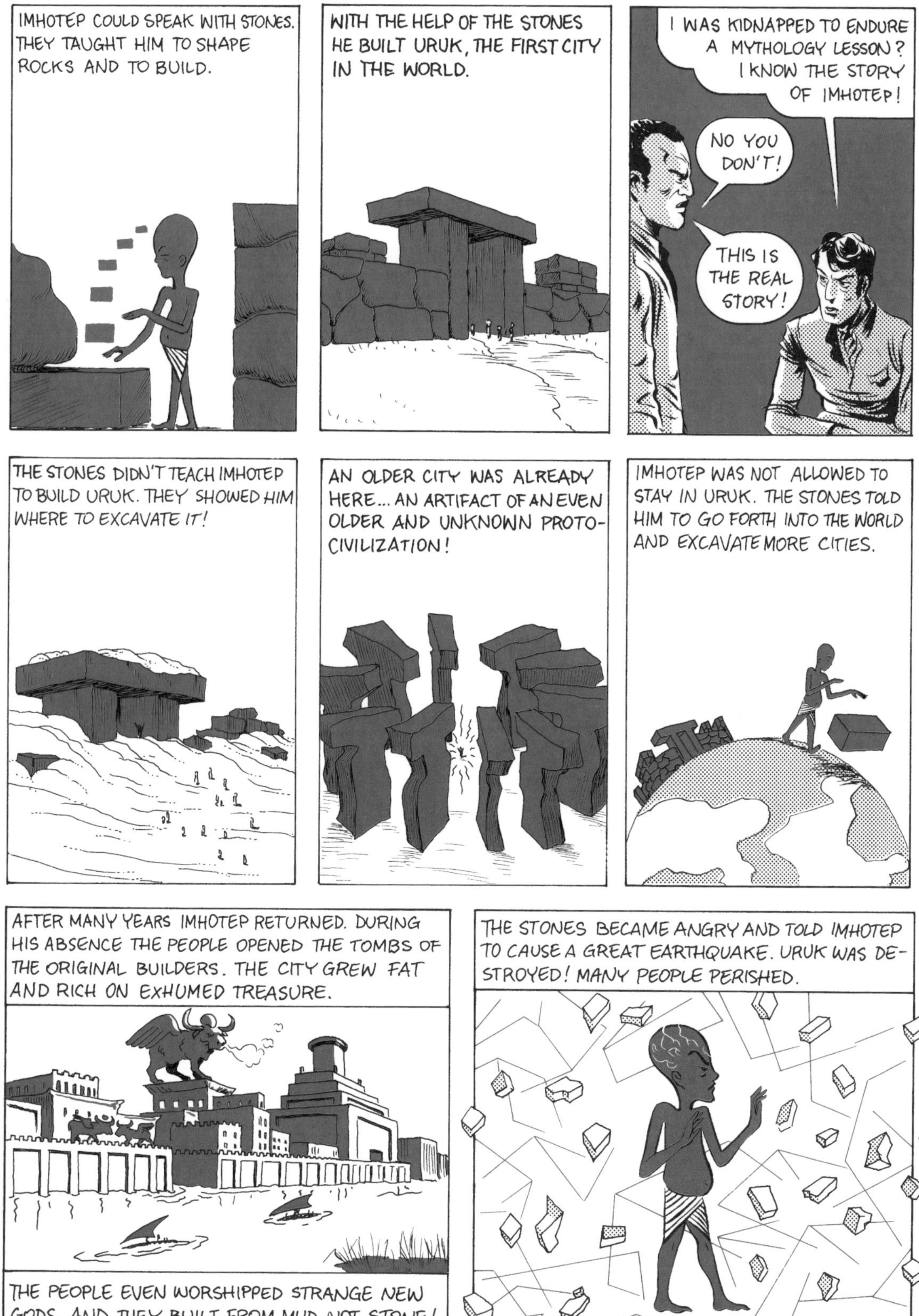
IMHOTEP COULD SPEAK WITH STONES. THEY TAUGHT HIM TO SHAPE ROCKS AND TO BUILD.
WITH THE HELP OF THE STONES HE BUILT URUK, THE FIRST CITY IN THE WORLD.
I WAS KIDNAPPED TO ENDURE A MYTHOLOGY LESSON? I KNOW THE STORY OF IMHOTEP!
NO YOU DON'T!
THIS IS THE REAL STORY!
THE STONES DIDN'T TEACH IMHOTEP TO BUILD URUK. THEY SHOWED HIM WHERE TO EXCAVATE IT!
AN OLDER CITY WAS ALREADY HERE... AN ARTIFACT OF AN EVEN OLDER AND UNKNOWN PROTO-CIVILIZATION!
IMHOTEP WAS NOT ALLOWED TO STAY IN URUK. THE STONES TOLD HIM TO GO FORTH INTO THE WORLD AND EXCAVATE MORE CITIES.
AFTER MANY YEARS IMHOTEP RETURNED. DURING HIS ABSENCE THE PEOPLE OPENED THE TOMBS OF THE ORIGINAL BUILDERS. THE CITY GREW FAT AND RICH ON EXHUMED TREASURE.
THE PEOPLE EVEN WORSHIPPED STRANGE NEW GODS. AND THEY BUILT FROM MUD NOT STONE!
THE STONES BECAME ANGRY AND TOLD IMHOTEP TO CAUSE A GREAT EARTHQUAKE. URUK WAS DESTROYED! MANY PEOPLE PERISHED.

THE EARTHQUAKE OPENED A GREAT CRACK AT THE CENTER OF URUK.

THE PEOPLE BEGGED IMHOTEP FOR HELP.

IMHOTEP CONSULTED THE STONES. THE STONES DEMANDED THE PEOPLE REPLENISH THE EMPTIED TOMBS.

AND THE STONES SAID: SLAUGHTER A THOUSAND SOULS YEARLY.

AND THE STONES SAID: MUMMIFY THE BODIES. AND RICHLY ADORN THEM.

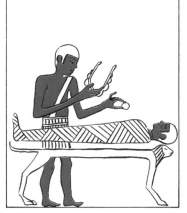

AND THE STONES SAID: ENTOMB THE MUMMIES UNDER THE CITY. IMHOTEP WEPT AT THIS. THIS IS NOT THE WAY HE SAID.

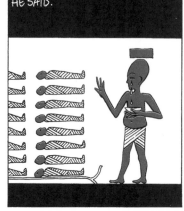

HE TOLD THE PEOPLE TO CARVE A CHAMBER IN THE GREAT CHASM. SEAL ME INSIDE HE SAID.

AND HE SAID: BURY THE CHASM AND BUILD A GREAT PENTAGONAL PYRAMID ON TOP.

AND HE SAID: I WILL REMAIN HERE FOR ALL ETERNITY AND SOOTHE THE STONES WITH MY TEARS.

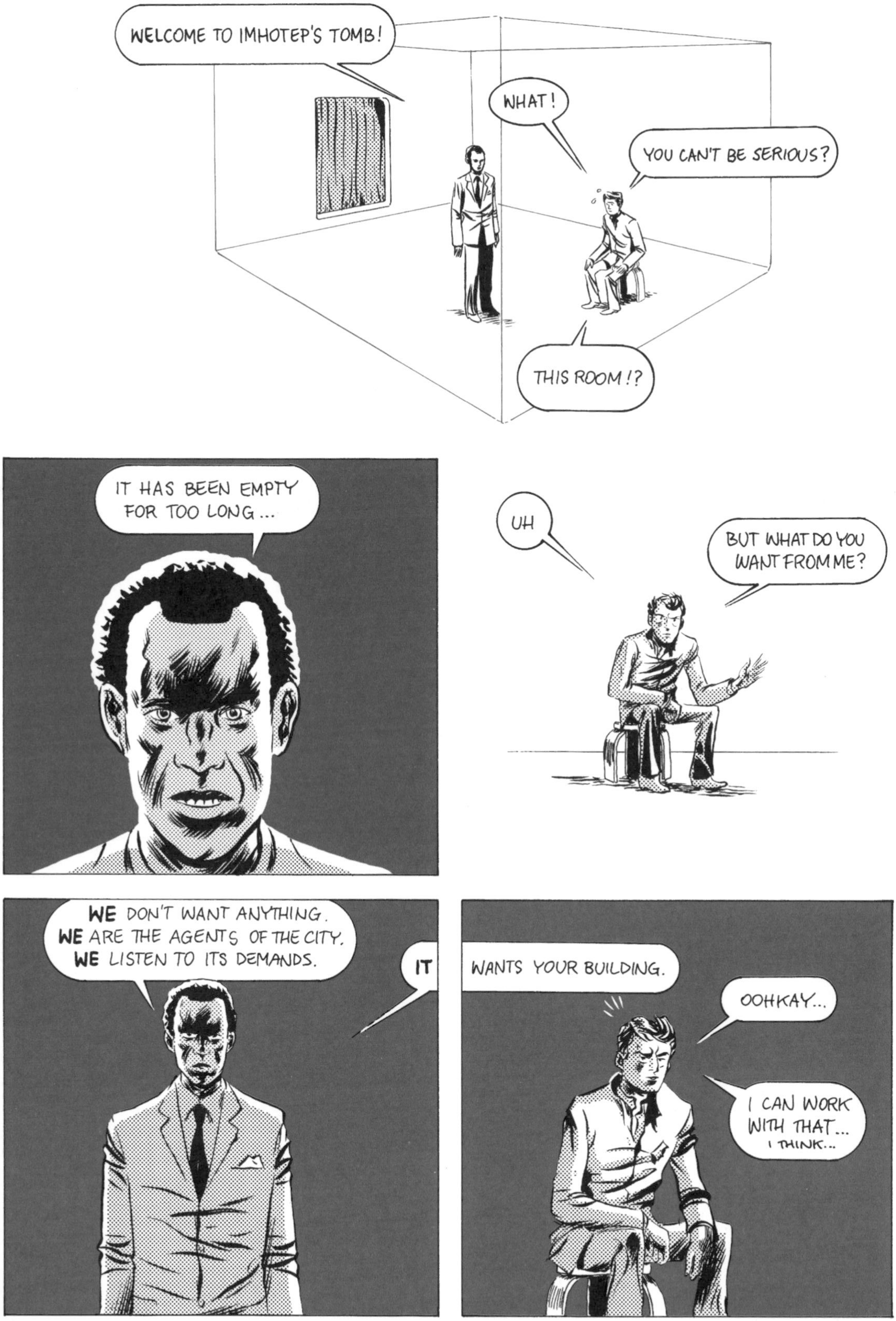
WELCOME TO IMHOTEP'S TOMB!
WHAT!
YOU CAN'T BE SERIOUS?
THIS ROOM!?
IT HAS BEEN EMPTY FOR TOO LONG...
UH
BUT WHAT DO YOU WANT FROM ME?
WE DON'T WANT ANYTHING. WE ARE THE AGENTS OF THE CITY. WE LISTEN TO ITS DEMANDS.
IT
WANTS YOUR BUILDING.
OOHKAY...
I CAN WORK WITH THAT... I THINK...

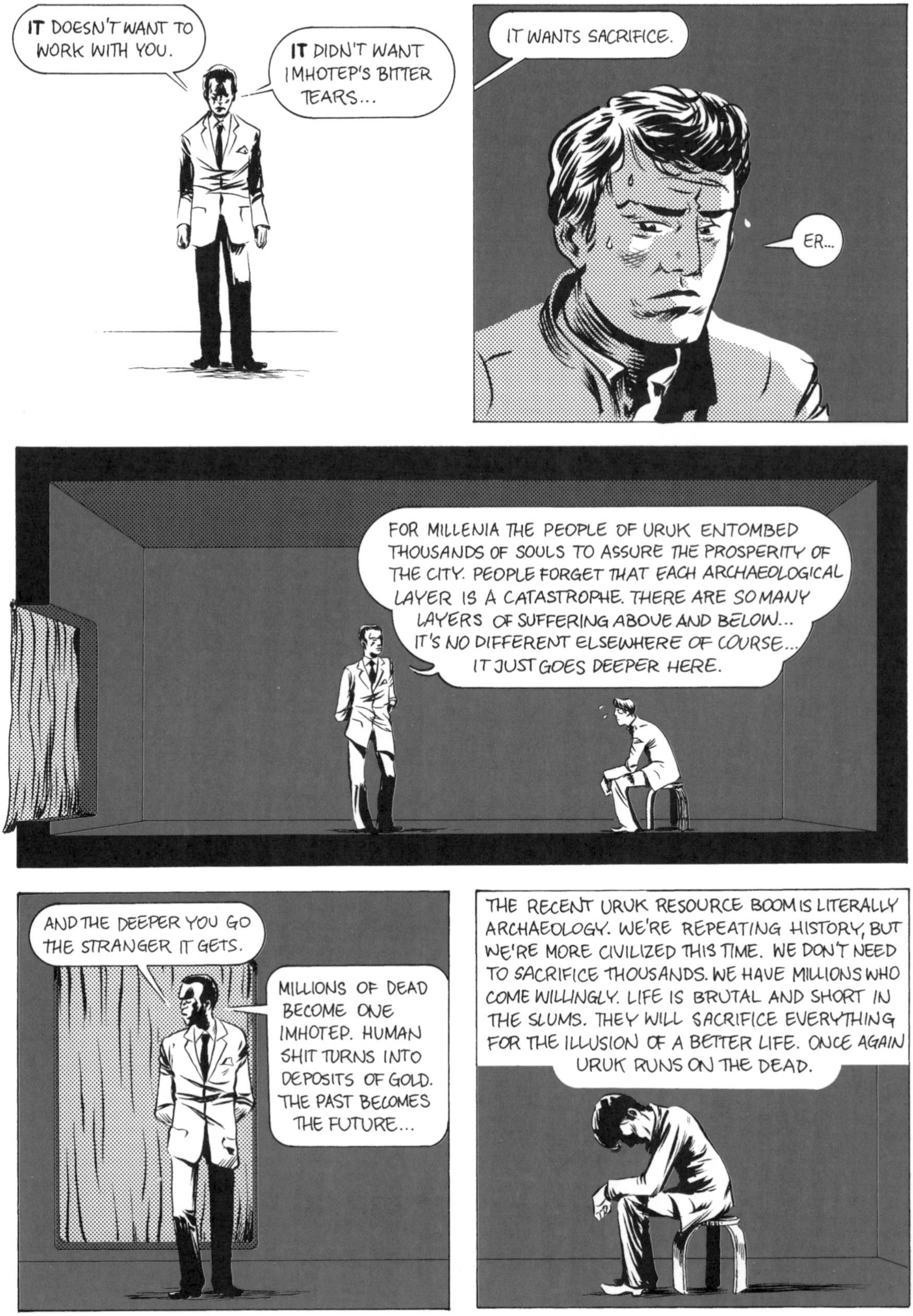

IT DOESN'T WANT TO WORK WITH YOU.
IT DIDN'T WANT IMHOTEP'S BITTER TEARS...
IT WANTS SACRIFICE.
ER...
FOR MILLENIA THE PEOPLE OF URUK ENTOMBED THOUSANDS OF SOULS TO ASSURE THE PROSPERITY OF THE CITY. PEOPLE FORGET THAT EACH ARCHAEOLOGICAL LAYER IS A CATASTROPHE. THERE ARE SO MANY LAYERS OF SUFFERING ABOVE AND BELOW... IT'S NO DIFFERENT ELSEWHERE OF COURSE... IT JUST GOES DEEPER HERE.
AND THE DEEPER YOU GO THE STRANGER IT GETS.
MILLIONS OF DEAD BECOME ONE IMHOTEP. HUMAN SHIT TURNS INTO DEPOSITS OF GOLD. THE PAST BECOMES THE FUTURE...
THE RECENT URUK RESOURCE BOOM IS LITERALLY ARCHAEOLOGY. WE'RE REPEATING HISTORY, BUT WE'RE MORE CIVILIZED THIS TIME. WE DON'T NEED TO SACRIFICE THOUSANDS. WE HAVE MILLIONS WHO COME WILLINGLY. LIFE IS BRUTAL AND SHORT IN THE SLUMS. THEY WILL SACRIFICE EVERYTHING FOR THE ILLUSION OF A BETTER LIFE. ONCE AGAIN URUK RUNS ON THE DEAD.

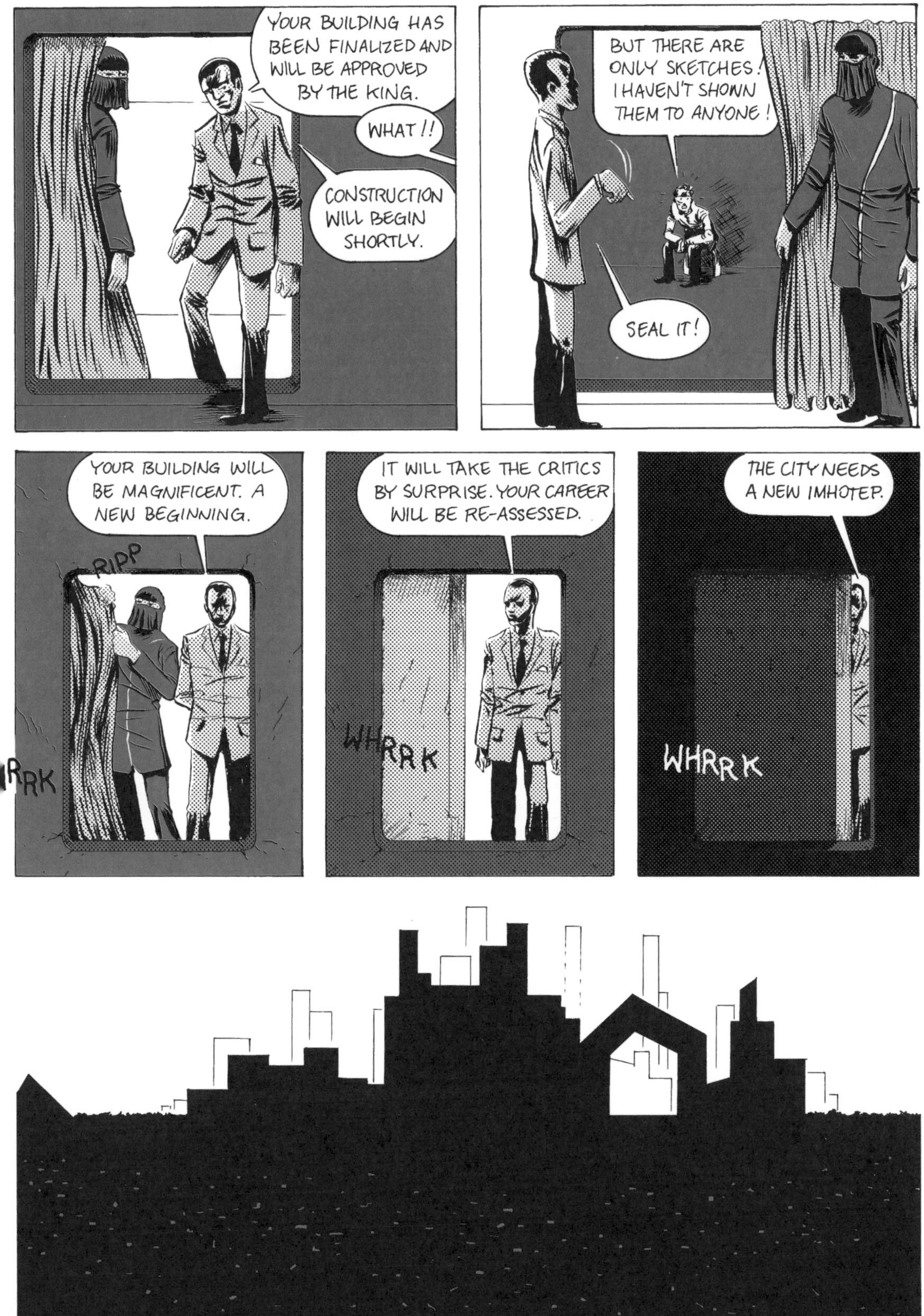
YOUR BUILDING HAS BEEN FINALIZED AND WILL BE APPROVED BY THE KING.
WHAT !!
CONSTRUCTION WILL BEGIN SHORTLY.
BUT THERE ARE ONLY SKETCHES ! I HAVEN'T SHOWN THEM TO ANYONE !
SEAL IT !
YOUR BUILDING WILL BE MAGNIFICENT. A NEW BEGINNING.
RIPP
RRK
IT WILL TAKE THE CRITICS BY SURPRISE. YOUR CAREER WILL BE RE-ASSESSED.
WHRRK
THE CITY NEEDS A NEW IMHOTEP.
WHRRK

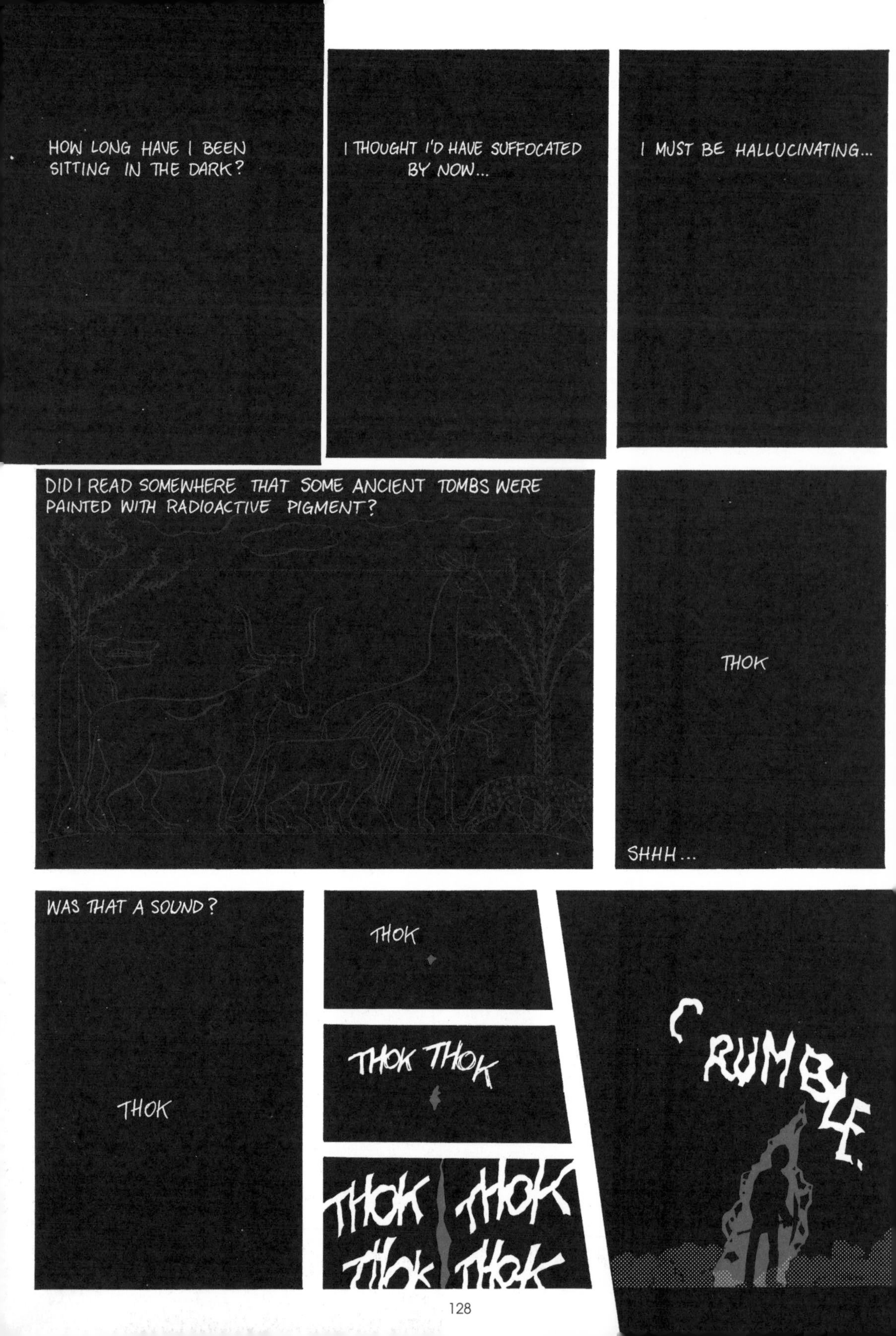
HOW LONG HAVE I BEEN SITTING IN THE DARK?
I THOUGHT I'D HAVE SUFFOCATED BY NOW...
I MUST BE HALLUCINATING...
DID I READ SOMEWHERE THAT SOME ANCIENT TOMBS WERE PAINTED WITH RADIOACTIVE PIGMENT?
THOK
SHHH...
WAS THAT A SOUND?
THOK
THOK
THOK THOK
THOK THOK
THOK THOK
CRUMBLE.

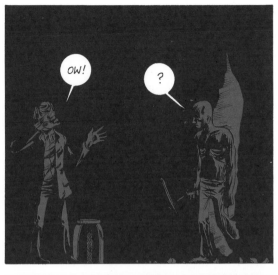

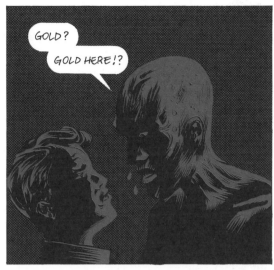

OW!
?
GOLD?
GOLD HERE!?
WAS HE IMHOTEP?
NO. THERE IS NOTHING HERE.
GRUNT
I LEFT THROUGH THE OPENING.
WEIRDLY, THE TUNNEL LED DOWNWARDS.
IT WAS LIT BY A STRANGE BIOLUMINESCENCE.

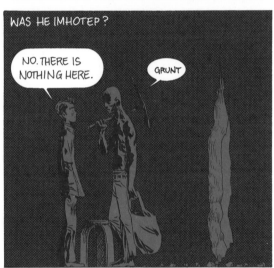

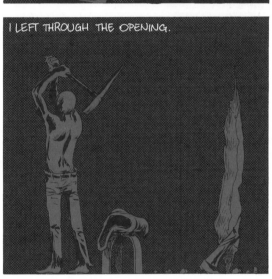

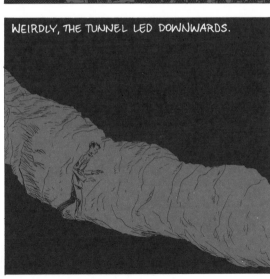

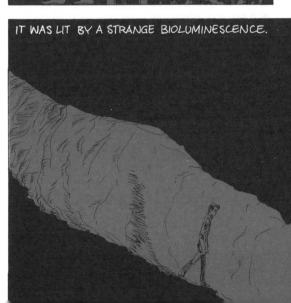

INDEX

ABOUT THE AUTHOR

Tom Kaczynski's comics have appeared in *The Drama, Punk Planet, Swindle Magazine, MOME, Best American Nonrequired Reading* and in countless mini-comics. *Trans Terra: Towards a Cartoon Philosophy*, his philosophical mutant memoir, has been translated into French and will appear in North America in 2013. As the publisher of Uncivilized Books he has worked with Gabrielle Bell, Jon Lewis, James Romberger and many others. He lives in Minneapolis, Minnesota with his partner Nikki.

THANK YOU!

Nikki Weispfenning, Jonathan Bennett, Gabrielle Bell, Jon Lewis, Karen Sneider, Michael Drivas, Zak Sally, Dan Wieken, Alex Holden, Vanessa Davis, Mike Dawson, Aaaron Renier, Dash Shaw, Frank Santoro, Eric Reynolds, Gary Groth, Annie Koyama, Kevin Huizenga, Jon Wright, Warren Park, Mehmet Bereket, Mach Arom (RIP), Joanna Kaczynski, Emilia Kaczynski, Damien Jay